NEW ANTHOLOGY

OF CONTEMPORARY AUSTRIAN

FOLK PLAYS

Edited by Richard H. Lawson

D1470847

ARIADNE PRESS
Riverside, California

Ariadne Press would like to express its appreciation to the Austrian Cultural Institute, New York and the Bundesministerium für Wissenschaft, Forschung und Kunst, Vienna for assistance in publishing this book.

Translated from the German:
Thomas Baum, *Kalte Hände*; Heinz R. Unger, *Zwölfeläuten*;
Friedrich Ch. Zauner, *Land*
©Österreichischer Bühnenverlag Kaiser & Co., Vienna
Performance rights: Österreichischer Bühnenverlag Kaiser & Co., Vienna
Elfriede Jelinek, *Präsident Abendwind*
©Elfriede Jelinek, Vienna
Peter Rosei, *Die Schuldlosen*
©Peter Rosei, Vienna
Performance rights: Thomas Sessler Verlag, Vienna & Munich

Library of Congress Cataloging-in-Publication Data

New anthology of contemporary Austrian folk plays / edited by Richard H. Lawson.
        p.   cm. -- (Studies in Austrian literature, culture, and thought)
        Contents: The bell tolls at twelve / Heinz R. Unger -- Cold hands / Thomas Baum -- A handful of earth / Friedrich Ch. Zauner -- President Evening Breeze / Elfriede Jelinek -- Blameless / Peter Rosei.
        ISBN 1-57241-020-5
        1. Folk drama, Austrian--Translations into English. 2. Austrian drama--20th century--Translations into English
        I. Lawson, Richard H. II. Series
        PT3826.D8N49   1996
        893.2'--dc20   95-53209
                                                            CIP

Cover design:
Art Director and Designer: George McGinnis

Copyright ©1996
by Ariadne Press
270 Goins Court
Riverside, CA 92507

Contents

Heinz R. Unger

The Bell Tolls at Twelve
A Styrian spoof in four acts

Translated by Michael Roloff

CHARACTERS

Inhabitants of Saint Kilian
GLASHÜTTNER, the old village priest
LINDMOSER, the inhabitant of a village hovel
SONNLEITNER, the village mayor
KATHI, his daughter
GRANDMA SONNLEITNER, his mother
FICHTELHUBER, a cuttingly athletic forester and head
    of the local chapter of the Nazi Party
BARBARA KOHNHAUSER, the feisty war widow
SCHWARZENEGGER, the fat innkeeper and butcher
SIMMERL, his plump son
JOGL, the village idiot

Partisans:
TONI LINDMOSER, the son of the owner of the hovel
FACUNDO, the blind Spaniard

Non-village Nazis:
The District Commander, a much-feared
    "Gold Pheasant";
SS-KROLL, the dangerous SS Sturmbann leader

*The action is set in a fictitious Styrian mountain hamlet in
late Winter and early Spring of 1945.*

ACT ONE

(Assembly of the militia of St. Kilian, the ringing of a church bell. From the distance the squeaky grinding music from an old organ. A cold winter morning, rigidly frozen snow. Jogl, wrapped in hand-knitted clothes and hand-me-downs that seem barely to keep out the cold, is sitting on a bench by the church wall. Next to him is his shovel.)

JOGL:Bim-bam! Bim-bam! Only an idiot will sit this way! A loser'd be inside the church with the others . . . *(He shivers from the frost)* The heat! The heat! Inside me. Like a fever. Got to cut up the freezing ground for that poor old Lindmoser woman. I feel all wet inside. . . . *(He takes a sip from a bottle of schnaps)* Moonshine, from Lindmoser: Right, Jogl, you'll do it! Then comes the big shot with his eyes like blackberries: Someone's got to do it, Jogl! And 'cause I ain't moving, the local Head Nazi says: They ain't that nice to their idiots everywhere that they let them run around free, unclean bad seed, what an inheritance that will produce . . . *(Jogl climbs onto the bench and screams across the chuch wall:)* Assholes, hypocrites! You's idiots much more than I am! Dumb, blind and deaf! The bells! Ain't you heard the bells? Who's supposed to have tolled the bells? Not me, the lordy guy it wasn' either and none of you either! But someone must have tolled them! So who then? *(The priest's voice becomes audible.)*

GLASHÜTTNER: Jogl! Jogl!

JOGL: Bim-bam! Bim-bam!

GLASHÜTTNER: *(The priest, usually a dignified old man, is coming awkwardly coordinated and with his cassock fluttering, around the corner of the church wall.)* You! Jogl! Right now, get it! The coffin.

JOGL: Finished preaching already?

GLASHÜTTNER: The coffin! The coffin! Pull yourself together! Let everything lie the way it is! The cart is already standing in front of the church door. Schwarzenegger will help load it up and then you drive the cart with the coffin to the grave. Slowly, lots of ceremony, but hurry, hurry up.

JOGL: Hard. Very hard. The frozen ground was already very hard when I was digging the grave! And now the coffin to boot.

GLASHÜTTNER: Jogl, I beg you, don't muck around like this, they're all waiting for you, think of the guys at the front, in the Russian winter, you're living like God in France here.

JOGL: God lives in France? Is he with the partisans?

GLASHÜTTNER: Jeez! Don't ask so many questions, child of God, do as you are told.

JOGL: (*Climbs down from the bench, picks up his shovel and stops mulishly.*) Why was the bell tower blocked off today, Father?

GLASHÜTTNER: None of your business! Get lost, for God's sake!

JOGL: (*Continuing to protract his departure.*) So who did toll the bell before?

GLASHÜTTNER: Off with you! You're supposed to go! Off to the grave!

JOGL: (*Departing*) Bim-bam, Bim-bam . . .

GLASHÜTTNER: (*Conversing with heaven*) Holy Bim-bam, soon I will be at the end of my rope! Not enough men to carry a coffin even! Father, who art in heaven, what a hell hole we managed to work ourselves into . . . (*meanwhile the forester is sneaking up, in his official garb, his gaze fastened onto an imaginary track on the floor of the stage. He is of course coming from the direction of the mountains.*)

FICHTELHUBER: Here you can still make it out but there it disappears in the trampled snow . . . too many feet!

GLASHÜTTNER: Fichtelhuber! Why aren't you at the burial?

FICHTELHUBER: All my commiseration, but this is more important, this is much more important, this is war business, Pastor!

GLASHÜTTNER: What is, for heaven's sake?

FICHTELHUBER: Partisans! And the tracks lead right into the village!

GLASHÜTTNER: (*is startled*) I have to get to the burial.

FICHTELHUBER: The district boss's got to come here! Tell him that something enormously important has happened, he must come at once!

GLASHÜTTNER: That's imposssible, he's at the burial.

FICHTELHUBER: Get him to sneak off.

GLASHÜTTNER: A forest ranger can sneak around but not a district boss.

FICHTELHUBER: For Christ's sake, Pastor! Partisans!

GLASHÜTTNER: Well, and so what? There's a war on! What do you expect from a war—tourists?

FICHTELHUBER: You, Your Honor, I'm Party Leader hereabouts, right? and I'm telling you that this is serious business for all of St. Kilian. Go into the church, read a mass and play the organ . . . but Sonnleitner's got to come here, secretly and at once!

GLASHÜTTNER: First of all, we put the old Lindmoser

woman into the earth, in orderly fashion, just like a Christian person ought to be put.

FICHTELHUBER: Don't play around with me! You've got no idea what I know! It's not just the partisans who are mucking about out there, the District Commander is on his way too, he'll be here any time now.

GLASHÜTTNER: Holy Mary!

FICHTELHUBER: All right then. You send me the mayor, if you please.

GLASHÜTTNER: How do you know all this, Fichtelhuber?

FICHTELHUBER: How? I'm supposed to go hunting with him.

GLASHÜTTNER: Hunting? But it's out of season.

FICHTELHUBER: It's war, nothing's out of season. (*The Priest runs off in the direction of the village. As though she had lain in wait for this moment, Barbara Kohnhauser comes out from behind the corner of the wall in mourning dress but happily excited.*)

BARBARA: Hubert!

FICHTELHUBER: Barbara, what are you doing here? You ought to be in church.

BARBARA: (*bursting with the urge to communicate*) I'm a widow, Hubert! It's official.

FICHTELHUBER: My congratulations, but can't you tell me that later on?

BARBARA: (*pulls a note out of his coat pocket*) A guy who was severely wounded saw him at the army hospital, he was the last one. He says it went real fast with Lois, a grenade, he didn't feel anything at all.

FICHTELHUBER: That guy got really lucky!

BARBARA: Anyhow, the Chief of Staff has recognized him

as having died a hero's death, not as an ordinary MIA.

FICHTELHUBER: Isn't that great! But now you're going back inside the church, Barbara! Looks terrible you standing around out here.

BARBARA: Aren't you happy, Hubert? Isn't that something, war widow! I mean, for three years you don't know what's up or down, and now this . . .

FICHTELHUBER: Get out of here! Sonnleitner is on his way!

BARBARA: I just wanted to tell you, so you'd know. (*She inspects him.*) But you can't take that gun with you to the graveside. And at least you should wear a black ribbon . . .

FICHTELHUBER: Get your ass out of here! (*Barbara goes off, encountering Sonnleitner on the way.*)

SONNLEITNER: Isn't that something! (*He looks after the disappearing woman.*)

FICHTELHUBER: Here, take a look! The tracks! That's how close the rabble are!

SONNLEITNER: (*Regarding the tracks*) Who knows who that was?

FICHTELHUBER: I saw them from far away. They came from the village and disappeared in the woods.

SONNLEITNER: Real partisans?

FICHTELHUBER: Guns and everything! What might they have been looking for in St. Kilian?

SONNLEITNER: Perhaps all they wanted was to steal a chicken.

FICHTELHUBER: You don't believe that yourself. So, what do we do?

SONNLEITNER: So, I'm going to the burial, I'm giving a graveside speech, brief and gripping.

FICHTELHUBER: As party chiefs we've got to do something.

SONNLEITNER: What?

FICHTELHUBER: Well, follow the tracks, hunt the bandits . . .

SONNLEITNER: If you hadn't seen it we'd know nothing about it. So we're going to act as if we hadn't seen anything. Forget it!

FICHTELHUBER: There was one other thing, Sonnleitner.

SONNLEITNER: Well what, Fichtelhuber?

FICHTELHUBER: The District Commander is on his way.

SONNLEITNER: Holy Mary!

FICHTELHUBER: I only know 'cause I'm supposed to go hunting with him. He'll be here any moment now.

SONNLEITNER: A person shouldn't even get up on a day like this.

FICHTELHUBER: Come on, get smart. It's good for us.

SONNLEITNER: How is that good for us?

FICHTELHUBER: 'Cause under the sharp eyes of the District Commander here on the home front we're earning perks by doing something for the Third Reich.

SONNLEITNER: Forester, you've lost it.

FICHTELHUBER: Instead of being a village that is under suspicion of harboring bandits, St. Kilian becomes known as the vanguard in the fight against the back-country bandits.

SONNLEITNER: How do you picture that?

FICHTELHUBER: We grab the bull by the horns!

SONNLEITNER: But how?

FICHTELHUBER: By being men.

SONNLEITNER: All right, which men?

FICHTELHUBER: All of them, Sonnleitner! We have to get a troop of country militia armed, the militia of St. Kilian. A matter of honor for the people of St.Kilian.

SONNLEITNER: You know what? I'll simply report it to the sheriff.

FICHTELHUBER: That would be inexcusably suspicious, Sonnleitner.

SONNLEITNER: You think?

FICHTELHUBER: Right now the tracks are fresh! Now you've got to hit them, the rabble! There's even a medal for fighting bandits, the hunter from Seeau got it . . .

SONNLEITNER: All right, after the burial we'll get them to come to the Brown Stag.

FICHTELHUBER: Every able-bodied man!

SONNLEITNER: That won't be many.

FICHTELHUBER: The bottom of the barrel.

SONNLEITNER: Aren't you coming to the burial?

FICHTELHUBER: With my gun?

SONNLEITNER: Shame on you, Forester.

FICHTELHUBER: Heil Hitler, my mayor!

(They walk off in opposite directions; Sonnleitner turns the corner of the churchyard wall, Fichtelhuber goes to the right, along the wall, in the direction of the village. The

murmurs of prayers are audible coming from inside the church. Two hands reach across the churchyard wall, a head becomes visible, heavily bandaged, only the lower part of the face is exposed: Facundo, the Spaniard. He cannot see but he senses.)

FACUNDO: Cuidado, Tonio! (*Watch out!*) (*Next to him there appears the wild woolly head of Toni Lindmoser.*)

TONI: It's all right, amigo.

FACUNDO: (*Quiet!*)

TONI: Don't shit in your pants, they're all at the graveside. Come on, Facundo! Over the wall. Adelante! (*Steps forward!*).

(*Facundo climbs the wall and then helps Toni, whose right leg is thickly bandaged and stiff. Both of them are wearing badly worn military coats, Toni is using his gun as a crutch. The villagers are at the graveside, which is why Facundo and Toni feel secure on this side of the wall. Facundo sits down on the bench, and Toni stands on the bench and looks across the wall.*)

TONI: Father has really shrunk! . . . But the old Sonnleitner is still alive in him . . . I know them all, the way they stand there. (*He looks to the side in the direction of the village.*) There's no smoke anywhere, except at the Brown Stag. That's where they are cooking the meal to honor the dead. It's a good place here, cause you can look down into the village. Everyone who's got a secret comes here, the couples and the schemers, the children and the partisans. . . . (*He takes another look at the burial scene.*) The priest hasn't changed at all . . . You can depend on old Glashüttner. He said if there's danger he's going to give the sign, he'll whistle three times. I hope he knows how to whistle . . . Now they're lowering the coffin . . . Bless you, Mama! (*suddenly startled*)

There's someone sneaking away from the grave . . . and someone else . . . They're coming here! Hurry! Get across the wall, alarma!

FACUNDO: (*helping Toni back across the wall, and climbing across himself*) Date prisa! (*Hurry up*) (*They take cover. Kathi Sonnleitner, in black mourning clothes, turns the corner of the wall, followed by the somewhat awkward and up-tight Simmerl Schwarzenegger*).

SIMMERL: And why not me? Tell me, Kathi! That's what I want to know.

KATHI: Let me be! Off with you. You disgust me.

SIMMERL: So why'd you sneak off like that? I thought you wanted to be alone with me.

KATHI: I want to be alone. Scram.

SIMMERL: Tell me. What is it, Kathi! Is it 'cause I'm not in the war like the others?

KATHI: Go, please, just go.

SIMMERL: You don't get it, do you! I'm the only young guy far and wide, and you . . . (*He turns away.*) You know, it hurts. You'll see, the day will come when I no longer have a liking for you, you beast! (*He looks back towards her.*) You saying anything? I don't hear nothin'. Come on, say somethin'.Who else is there? They're all in the war! Jogl, you want the Jogl? You like the village idiot more than you like me? (*He walks off. All we hear is his voice.*) You'll be beggin' me! Beggin'! But then it will be too late! . . .

(*Kathi takes a look around as though she had been expecting something in particular. She climbs the bench and looks in the direction of the cemetery and of the village. Toni appears from behind the wall.*)

TONI: Kathi! (*Kathi wants to scream, but he holds her mouth shut.*) Shut up! It's me! Your Toni. (*He lets go of her*) Lindmoser's Toni.

KATHI: What are you doing here?

TONI: I'm here for my mother's funeral.

KATHI: But aren't you off at war.

TONI: I'm in the war.

KATHI: But why are you here in that case?

TONI: Because the war is here.

KATHI: My God, the way you look! (*Facundo's bandaged head appears next to Toni's. Kathi is about to scream again, and Toni holds her mouth shut once again.*)

TONI: No screaming! He's a comrade of mine.

KATHI: Holy Ma . . .

TONI: He's a Spaniard.

KATHI: How a Spaniard?

TONI: From Spain. Ole Facundo is his name. We've had a lot of experiences together, until it got us, me   in Pernicia, him in Laaken . . .

KATHI: How so? What got you?

TONI: The SS! Me they got in the heel. And Facundo, he don't see any more.

KATHI: The SS? But how could the SS?

TONI: They were shootin' with incendiary ammo.

KATHI: Oh my God! But why was the SS shooting at you?

TONI: 'Cause they were chasing us, across the mountain. 'Cause we overran the guards at Soboth . . .

KATHI: What did you overrun?

TONI: The guardhouse at Soboth. Then they put in a cordon sanitaire, as they call it, and used a thousand guys to hunt us.

KATHI: But Toni, aren't you with the army?

TONI: Didn't the priest tell you?

KATHI: Only that I should sneak off and come here, it was supposed to be a surprise.

TONI: I'm with the partisans.

KATHI: My God, the things you do!

TONI: In the army hospital, when I was wounded, I got to know a corporal, he got an arm ripped out. He was from Leob'n. He already had contact with the partisans, 'cause he was having his troubles.

KATHI: That can't be true! You're with the bandits?

TONI: He got ordered away then, as an instructor for the People's Last Stand, 'cause you don't need two hands for that! Toni, he said to me, do you want to let them use you as cannon fodder at the front?

KATHI: If my father knew that, he'd stand you right up against the wall.

TONI: As an instructor he had a key to the weapons depot. Well, there we got ourselves a hoard of guns and munition and went into the mountains and joined the partisans.

KATHI: My father is Head of the Party here. And I'm the head of the Hitler girls' club in the village.

TONI: And I've been shot in the heel! And he is blind.

KATHI: And you are with the bandits, Bolsheviks is all they are.

TONI: But Kathi, you know who I am.

KATHI: A traitor, high treason is what you are.

TONI: Partisans are soldiers, too, except that they fight against Hitler instead of for him, like the Allies there.

KATHI: On my Hitler Youth honor dagger it says: The blade's for the foe, the handle for your friend.

TONI: Well then, you don't think that I'm your foe, do you.

KATHI: Crazy is what you are.

TONI: You've got to help us, Kathi. Pastor Glashüttner gave us a hiding place. But we gotta have something to eat.

KATHI: Toni, I can't just . . .

TONI: Simply bring the priest a basket with some food in it.

KATHI: All right, 'cause it's you.

GLASHÜTTNER: (*Returning excitedly from the village*) There's someone coming! There's someone on the way! I couldn't whistle with my lips being as dry as they are . . .

(*Toni and Facundo disappear, Kathi leaps down from the bench.*)

KATHI: I find myself speechless, Father.

GLASHÜTTNER: Thank God, Kathi, 'cause you shouldn't talk, not even in your sleep.

KATHI: I wouldn't have expected that from you, Father, not in my wildest dreams.

GLASHÜTTNER: Not I of myself either.

KATHI: You were always . . .

GLASHÜTTNER: What?

KATHI: For the cause.

(*Grandmother Sonnleitner, a sturdy old woman with a cane appears around the corner and encounters the priest as he is leaving.*)

GRANDMA: Adios!

GLASHÜTTNER: Damn cold today, isn't it.

GRANDMA: Deep into your bones it goes, Father. (*The priest disappears around the corner.*) Ah, there's the girl!

KATHI: I just wanted to ask the priest something.

GRANDMA: And I thought you were doing something on the sly with Simmerl. Your father says it's time to come home.

KATHI: I'll follow in a moment, you go ahead, Grandma.

GRANDMA: So what do you have left to do here?

KATHI: I want to do some thinking.

GRANDMA: That isn't healthy, my child. You father says its dangerous out here, there are even supposed to be some partisans about.

KATHI: But I'll come back here.

GRANDMA: What for?

KATHI: To feed the birds.

GRANDMA: At your age I had other things on my mind than feeding the birds.

(*While Kathi and the Grandmother walk off to the right, Josef Lindmoser appears from the left. He is a man who has been bent by sorrow, a man beaten by life, a weak crumpled old man. He looks around expectantly and, unsuccessfully, tries whistling, three times. Toni peers briefly across the wall, but Nazi Chapter Head and Mayor Sonnleitner has followed Lindmoser and grabs him.*)

SONNLEITNER: You can't just sneak off like that, Lindmoser! All my sympathy for your pain, but this happens to be a time when we've all got to be strong. After all, we all liked your Annie.

LINDMOSER: Now that Annie is underground, nothing matters any more.

SONNLEITNER: But we are an honorable community that supports something like this until you can stand on your own feet again! What you need is a job to put your mind on other things. And that is why I call to you in this difficult hour: Lindmoser! St. Kilian needs you.

LINDMOSER: The call of the homeland!

SONNLEITNER: Come with me to the Brown Stag, the others are there already . . . (*Sonnleitner tries dragging Lindmoser off with him, who however resists.*)

LINDMOSER: Go ahead, I've got to be alone for a while. . .

GLASHÜTTNER: (*Who has peered around the corner now comes to Lindmoser's assistance by dragging Sonnleitner off in the direction of the village*) Something important has come up, Sonnleitner. You know, I've got to talk to you about that, just the two of us. Lindmoser will follow us when he's good and ready.

SONNLEITNER: Can't it wait until later on?

GLASHÜTTNER: It's pretty sticky, Sonnleitner. The District Commander is on his way.

SONNLEITNER: So the church always knows everything.

GLASHÜTTNER: But do you know why he is coming?

SONNLEITNER: To go deer hunting.

GLASHÜTNER: To get our church bells. They want to take our church bells.

(*The two of them walk off, Lindmoser looks carefully around.*)

LINDMOSER: Toni.

TONI: (*Appears from behind the wall*) Father!

LINDMOSER: My boy! (*A touching moment, Lindmoser has to use his handkerchief*) So you were there, at Mama's burial?

TONI: Yes, father.

LINDMOSER: The priest told me. . . .

TONI: Facundo, help me. (*Facundo appears and helps Toni across the wall as he did before. He takes Toni on his back and lets him direct him toward Lindmoser. Lindmoser steps back.*) Stop, Facundo! That's a comrade, from Spain, he can't see anything . . .

LINDMOSER: (*touching his son*) What a shame, what a shame!

TONI: (*is moved*) But Papa! What is it?

LINDMOSER: (*embraces Toni and starts to bawl*) The shame! The shame. My son is a deserter! A bandit, who attacks his own people from behind.

TONI: Papa, are you mad?

LINDMOSER: My Annie, they just buried her, and my son is a bandit, and all that on one and the same day.

FACUNDO: Qué pasa? (*What's happening?*)

TONI: What happened, did you turn into a Nazi?

LINDMOSER: When I was a soldier there was a war on, too, but that wouldn't have been possible at that time! They would have put you up against the wall, that's what!

TONI: Papa, you know, they still do that today.

LINDMOSER: (*starts bawling again*) If your Mama knew that.

TONI: I believe Mama'd be happy that I was still alive.

LINDMOSER: (*blows into his handkerchief and starts to calm down*) But what if they find you, Toni?

TONI: The priest is hiding us right now.

LINDMOSER: Who would have thought that of old Glashüttner! For him they were always the devil incarnate, those trouble makers.

TONI: When a farmer went to him and asked him whether it wouldn't be better to turn us in when we spent the night in a barn, he told them no, that wouldn't be Christian. And when we were wounded and our people brought us to him at night, he was pretty frightened all right. Toni, he said to me and looked deep into my eyes, you didn't become a Bolshevik, did you?

LINDMOSER: And what did you say?

TONI: That I am fighting aginst the Fascists and for the liberation and against the exploitation and the war.

LINDMOSER: That's a good boy, Toni, just don't become a Commie.

TONI: That's what he said too.

LINDMOSER: But how is this going to go on?

TONI: Not much longer, then the war will be over. Then everything will be over, Papa.

LINDMOSER: And my Annie won't have lived to see it.

TONI: Not just a few, no, whole countries have died out, Papa. If you had seen what I have seen.

LINDMOSER: Most important thing is that you're alive! So what should I do, Toni?

TONI: The forester wants to form a militia. Don't let him pull a fast one on you, Dad. 'Cause our people, the ones who brought us here, they made a set of false tracks that lead into an ambush.

LINDMOSER: What times we live in!

TONI: You don't owe them anything, all they ever did was wipe their shoes on you. So don't agree to anything. The ambush is for the SS, but the forester wants to get them all riled up . . . (*The priest comes hurrying from the village.*)

GLASHÜTTNER: Get away from there. Get away. (*The priest helps the partisans across the wall. Lindmoser stands there, dumbfounded.*)

TONI: Watch out for them, Dad.

(*The stocky innkeeper and butcher Schwarzenegger and his splay-footed son Simmerl are on their way from the village. The priest and Lindmoser stay in the background by the church wall.*)

SIMMERL: They said that the son who inherits the farm doesn't have to join the army. All the young farmers, it's important that they stay home and work the farm 'cause of the war. And why are they changing it now?

SCHWARZENEGGER: Quiet now. And don't disgrace me, Simmerl, or I'll kill you.

(*The forester arrives from the village. He turns around impatiently and hollers towards the back.*)

FICHTELHUBER: What's taking you so long? Don't drag your feet like that.

(*Jogl arrives, carrying four guns in his arms. Then comes the mayor who has put a swastika armband around his left arm and is holding five more armbands at the ready.*)

SONNLEITNER: All right, are we all here? Lindmoser, too? Good. Then everyone will get a swastika armband, which you wear on the left. And the forester will hand out the carbines, those you put vertically across your shoulder, right?

GLASHÜTTNER: Is that the smart thing to do, Sonnleitner? Why don't you let the regular troops take care of it?

SONNLEITNER: The District Leader is already in the village. He's coming to inspect us. There's no turning back now, Father. Why don't you go read a mass or something.

LINDMOSER: I'd like to report sick, Sonnleitner. I don't feel so well.

SONNLEITNER: We can't do that, Lindmoser, you wearing mourning black over the swastika! Put the mournin' band on the other arm, so that they can see that you're mournin' but that your faith in the homeland is triumphant! All of us know how hard it is after the heavy blow that you just suffered, but think of our guys at the front! Think of your own boy, think of Toni! We on the homefront, we can't just go limp (*He turns to the others*) All right, stand up straight! Strike a posture, a military one. You're now the militia of St. Kilian at the Kraberg. Don't disgrace me.

(*Fichtelhuber, Schwarzenegger, Simmerl, Lindmoser and Jogl are now standing in semi-military posture in front of the church wall. Sonnleitner plays commander. The priest steps forth.*)

GLASHÜTTNER: People! Be sensible! This thing is going to be a bloody mess. What business is that of ours? Isn't it enough that you sent your sons off to war?

FICHTELHUBER: Priest, I've had it with you. You aren't preaching any more, you're undermining the fighting spirit of the people!

GLASHÜTTNER: You know who is undermining the fighting spirit? It's the war itself that's doing it! Twenty-nine sons is what we have lost from the village already.

SONNLEITNER: Stop it now. Or we're all going to get it! Or do you want St. Kilian to become known as a nest of bandits?

GLASHÜTTNER: At least don't be so eager and so military and in such a rush to run to your ruin!

(*The priest walks off to the left and around the corner of the church wall.*)

LINDMOSER: You know, Sonnleitner, I've got a twisted ankle!

SONNLEITNER: Now pull yourselves together! The District Commander is on the way! Look at yourselves the way you stand there!

LINDMOSER: And I don't see very good either!

SONNLEITNER: The forester will lead the way!

FICHTELHUBER: Yes, until we see the whites of that rabble's eyes.

LINDMOSER: But I was declared totally unfit. I can barely see my own hand when I stretch out my arm.

FICHTELHUBER: In hand-to-hand combat you'll be as

good a man as anyone, Lindmoser. The boys are all at the front, so there's no one left beside us.

JOGL: I had a dream today.

SCHWARZENEGGER: Back then he dreamed that Hitler'd be coming. Perhaps it's important.

SONNLEITNER: Not now, Jogl! You're supposed to stand straight now, not dream.

JOGL: The new Styrian flag!

SONNLEITNER: Bravo! A pretty symbol of our venture! What did it look like?

JOGL: Well—a swastika, in a white circle, not in the usual red but in a completely Styrian green field.

SONNLEITNER: That's all right, Jogl. We got completely different worries right now. Still, a nice idea, a flag like that embedded in a deep rich green of the eternal Styrian forests.

JOGL: Ah? So it comes from the trees? And I thought it came from the green bottles.

SONNLEITNER: Quiet now! Or "shut up," as the Germans say. I'm going to instruct you in strategy now, so that you know what the score is.

FICHTELHUBER: Men, this is what's up. I have discovered bandits, right at my front door.

SONNLEITNER: It's ME who's giving the instrucions! All right, the forester discovered them, and you've got to get them! The forester will be your leader, 'cause he can pick up a track like a bloodhound. And afterwards I'll be waiting for a mission accomplished report, if only 'cause the District Commander is in town.

FICHTELHUBER: All right, when the District Commander appears I will shout "Attention."

SONNLEITNER: I am the commander here!

FICHTELHUBER: All right, the mayor is the commander. Afterwards we're all going to stand 'stomach-pulled-in chest-facin'-out'. And then I'm going to report to the mayor: "Mr. Mayor! The Militia of St. Kilian stands at attention to receive your order!" And then the mayor will say "Thank you."

SONNLEITNER: Why do I say "Thank you"?

FICHTELHUBER: Because it's proper that way. Afterwards the mayor will stand at attention before the District Commander, he will give the Hitler salute, click his heels, all spit and polish, and he will say: "District Commander! Mayor Sonnleitner reports: The Militia of St. Kilian at the ready to hunt partisans."

SONNLEITNER: Just a moment there, not so fast. How does that go? "The Militia of St. Kilian stands at the ready to hunt partisans"? (*The vigorous District Commander, wearing a leather coat, comes marching from the village, followed by the dangerous figure of SS-Sturmbann Leader Kroll. Sonnleitner, facing the forester, hasn't noticed him yet.*)

COMMANDER: Heil Hitler! You may step back!

SONNLEITNER: (*Turns abruptly around*) Commander, Sir . . .

COMMANDER: Well, what is it? Step back!

SONNLEITNER: (*Takes an uncertain step to the side*) But Commander, I'm the . . .

SS-KROLL: (*Steps up and bellows*) Back in line, man! Line up and stand still! Snap to it. Where's your gun?

SONNLEITNER: (*Wounded*) But, I beg pardon, Commander, I don't need a gun . . .

COMMANDER: What's the matter with you, Mayor, you don't have a rifle? No matter. Sturmbann Leader Kroll will give you his, a special honor, as a loan. And now why don't you get into line?

(*Kroll gives his carbine to Sonnleitner who then reluctantly joins the formation.*)

SONNLEITNER: Beg pardon, Commander! I thought I was irreplaceable.

COMMANDER: Only the Führer is irreplaceable.

JOGL: What, Fichtelhuber is irreplaceable?

SS-KROLL: (*Abruptly turns around and eyes Jogl*) What did you say?

JOGL: If you please, Fichtelhuber, he's our Führer, because of the tracks . . .

SS-KROLL: (*Builds himself up in front of Jogl, who turns pathetically small*) What kind of bird do we have here?

JOGL: The Jogl-bird.

SONNLEITNER: Beg pardon, but his bird squeaks a little now and then. He is completely harmless but unfit for military duty.

SS-KROLL: The village idiot!

JOGL: I'm no idiot. I even made my own invention: the swastika fish-hook! You can catch four fish at once with that!

LINDMOSER: (*Raises his arm like a schoolboy*) And I twisted my ankle.

SS-KROLL: Twisted ankle?

SONNLEITNER: But he'll work out all right. Lindmoser will be our rear guard, doesn't have to be in the first line of fire.

JOGL: The front line is Fichtelhuber, 'cause he's our Führer.

SS-KROLL: Formation, quiet!

SCHWARZENEGGER: And I have asthma! Unfortunately . . .

SIMMERL: And I have flat feet!

SS-KROLL: What a pathetic bunch!

SONNLEITNER: Beg pardon obediently, all those of us who are fit are at the front. Now the only ones of us who are fit are the unfit.

COMMANDER: The man is right, Sturmbannführer. Look at it this way: the fighting people of the home-front, the last offering . . .

SS-KROLL: But this miserable human material!

COMMANDER: A few of them can still stand straight. For example, the innkeeper's son here.

SS-KROLL: (*Fixes his eyes on Simmerl*) Why aren't you at the front in the first place?

SIMMERL: Beg pardon, cause I'm the first born son of an inheritable estate, and as such I am absolved of military duty.

SS-KROLL: I thought you were the son of the innkeeper?

SCHWARZENEGGER: Beg pardon, I'm not only the innkeeper of the Brown Stag, I'm also a Brown Stag, that is, a member of the party, besides being the local butcher with a small store attached to it, and I'm also the owner of Lindmoser's farm, so that my how it happened that my Toni had to end up at the front, and his Simmerl is the inheriting son.

SIMMERL: And besides, I have flat feet.

COMMANDER: Anyway, they'll do for the local militia. The forester, too, still looks in pretty good shape. Why aren't you at the front?

FICHTELHUBER: The Reich Forestry Service put me in the category "Important to the War Effort."

COMMANDER: "Important to the War Effort?" A forester?

FICHTELHUBER: Yes, because of all that wood that is essential raw material for the war . . .

COMMANDER: We need steel! But why wood?

FICHTELHUBER: Well, 'cause of wood forms when you pour cement for the bunkers, right? . . .

SONNLEITNER: Besides, Fichtelhuber was the first party member in the region, a man of the first hour, at a time while it was still illegal. And he is the leader of the local party chapter.

JOGL: And then the Provincial Leader kept coming to go deer hunting . . .

COMMANDER: Well, well. And so the forester observed these bandits. How many of them are there if I may ask?

FICHTELHUBER: Reporting obediently, Sir. Exactly it was roughly a handful.

COMMANDER: What does that mean: roughly a handful! You call that exact? How many exactly?

FICHTELHUBER: At least three.

COMMANDER: What does that mean at least three? Do you call that a handful?, at least three? All right, precisely: how many?

FICHTELHUBER: Reporting obediently, Sir. Exactly it was roughly a handful.

COMMANDER: What does that mean: roughly a handful! You call that exact? How many exactly?

FICHTELHUBER: At least three.

COMMANDER: What does that mean at least three? Do you call that a handful?, at least three? All right, precisely: how many?

FICHTELHUBER: All right, precisely perhaps three, perhaps more. It might have been at least three.

COMMANDER: Exactly what did you see?

FICHTELHUBER: I saw them in my shooting light, except it was just a tad too far away for a shoulder shot, they stepped really nervously out of the woods and were sniffing to all sides.

COMMANDER: Are you talking about deer?

FICHTELHUBER: Well, about the Red Rabble, which we should exterminate.

COMMANDER: Fine, so you will walk ahead and lead the troop.

JOGL: You are our leader, Fichtelhuber! Just as I said.

COMMANDER: The others will follow in single file, no foolish heroics, now. Keep eye contact and be careful and ready for an engagement. It's absolutely possible that they have prepared an ambush for you.

FICHTELHUBER: That's why someone should walk ahead as an advance guard. 'Cause of the ambush.

JOGL: The leader always walks in front! Why else is he called Leader.

FICHTELHUBER: Think, you idiot! If he's the first one shot, he can't lead any more.

JOGL: But then the others know where he's led them.

SONNLEITNER: The leader leads, that's it! No discussions! This ain't no democracy.

COMMANDER: You're not to engage in any firefights, you're only supposed to stick to their heels. Sturmbann Leader Kroll will instantly put together a vigilante group of SS-men and field police and will come straight to you.

SS-KROLL: Right! I am also empowered to communicate to you that everyone who proves himself and also if he doesn't prove himself will be accepted into the People's Storm.

SIMMERL: You see, Dad, I told you! That was nothing but a fraud too, all this business about being the inheriting first born son.

FICHTELHUBER: And what about the medals?

COMMANDER: What medals?

FICHTELHUBER: Well, for acts of heroism at the homefront, that "Medal of Honor for Fighting Bandits," like the one that that hunter from Seeau got, 'cause he led the SS to the Bandit's winter bunker, near Tragoess.

COMMANDER: If you behave courageously, anything is possible.

FICHTELHUBER: Word of honor? 'Cause last time we came up empty-handed!

COMMANDER: How so? What do you mean by the last time?

FICHTELHUBER: The English pilot last year, the one who jumped out over the Krahberg with his parachute, and whom we cut to pieces! Our names didn't even appear in the papers!

COMMANDER: Ah that! Well, that really was no act of heroism, but an unbelievable act of stupdity.

FICHTELHUBER: Hey, look! We put up our man on the homefront, just the way we are ordered, and at the end we are the idiots?

COMMANDER: You were supposed to interrogate him, not beat him to death! That would have been important to the war effort.

FICHTELHUBER: But I don't know English . . .

JOGL: That ain't true! I understood every word that he said, that Tommy.

COMMANDER: Really? What did he say?

JOGL: Mama, Mama!

COMMANDER: (*Keeping his control by assuming a commanding tone of voice*) Stop the bullshit! Get under way! I am expecting a mission accomplished report!

SS-KROLL: Militia! Turn right! March off!

(*Although half the troop—Lindmoser, Simmerl and Jogl— first turned to the left, the troop manages a comparatively military departure to the left, that is, from the audience's point of view, in the direction of the mountain. The Commander and SS-Kroll look after the departing troop, but Toni's and Facundo's face, too, become briefly and carefully visible above the church wall, the priest peers around the corner of the wall; and Barbara, Kathi and Grandma Sonnleitner have gently intruded into the picture from the village side. All of them are gazing in the direction of the mountain.*)

COMMANDER: What more do you want? We sent the dogs to chase down the deer.

SS-KROLL: Lame dogs. The wrong dogs.

COMMANDER: Did you hear the bells a while ago? All the other villages have already taken down their bells to be transported off as their contribution to the war effort.

SS-KROLL: There's something rotten in this dump.

COMMANDER: What do you want? The Russians have entered Silesia.

(The scene freezes)

CURTAIN

ACT TWO

THE BELL OF ST. KILIAN DESERTS

It has become night. Moonlight. Priest Glashüttner, Grandma Sonnleitner and Barbara are waiting at the corner of the cemetery wall. They are carrying storm lanterns. Kathi is coming from the mountain.

KATHI: They're coming!

GRANDMA: Thank God!

GLASHÜTTNER: Sometimes praying really helps.

(*Jogl traipses exhausted onto center stage and stares at the waiting group.*)

BARBARA: So say something!

JOGL: What madness! What madness!

GLASHÜTTNER: Where are the others?

JOGL: Simmerl is carrying Lindmoser piggy-back.

GLASHÜTTNER: Did something happen?

JOGL: Nothing happened to us, 'cause Lindmoser luckily broke his ankle.

BARBARA: So tell us what it was like.

JOGL: It was cold.

GRANDMA: They've already made a rum toddy at the Brown Stag, a whole kettle full.

BARBARA: Where's the forester at?

JOGL: Our leader is way in back where he belongs.

(*Schwarzenegger drags himself heavily on stage and drops onto the bench with a groan.*)

SCHWARZENEGGER: No air . . . I'm not getting any air.

GLASHÜTTNER: So what happened?

SCHWARZENEGGER: I had to run like crazy.

BARBARA: Was there any shooting?

SCHWARZENEGGER: I haven't run like that for twenty years.

GLASHÜTTNER: So what happened?

SCHWARZENEGGER: Oh did we ever get lucky that Lindmoser broke his ankle.

(*Sonnleitner arrives and Kathi runs towards him.*)

KATHI: Father! What happened?

SONNLEITNER: It all passed passably, Kathily.

KATHI: What happened with the partisans?

SONNLEITNER: People! St. Kilian of Kralberg did its duty.

GLASHÜTTNER: So tell us, Sonnleitner!

SONNLEITNER: I'm telling you, I wouldn't be standing here if Lindmoser hadn't broke his ankle.

GLASHÜTTNER: Thank God that Lindmoser broke his ankle.

FICHTELHUBER: (*Stomping furiously on to the stage*) What lousy luck, what a damned shame that Lindmoser broke his ankle.

GLASHÜTTNER: But how so?

FICHTELHUBER: 'Cause we got to the front too late.

SCHWARZENEGGER: 'Cause we missed everything cause of Lindmoser's ankle.

BARBARA: The most important thing is you're back.

GLASHÜTTNER: Yes, and alive, too! That's what counts.

FICHTELHUBER: What use is that? We failed, we failed miserably.

SONNLEITNER: Beg your pardon, St. Kilian did the best it could, more you can't ask. Fearlessly we led them there, the fighters . . .

FICHTELHUBER: There's nothing we can do about it! We behaved in a totally warlike maner.

JOGL: How so? We didn't even get into a fight.

SONNLEITNER: Exactly! You recognize the experienced soldier by the fact that he doesn't run blind like a chicken into the fire.

FICHTELHUBER: I see, so that's what it's like now! Those who hold their head out for you at all the fronts, they are suddenly blind chickens!

JOGL: Blind as hens, ha ha ha. Blind as hens.

SCHWARZENEGGER:You couldn't really say blind, they looked pretty stupid when the shooting started all of a sudden.

JOGL: They passed us like rabbits, up there in the mountain.

FICHTELHUBER: You can't say that!

JOGL: So what do you say?

FICHTELHUBER: They straightened out the front line.

(Simmerl trudges on stage, breathing heavily, carrying Lindmoser piggy-back. He sets him down carefully.)

SCHWARZENEGGER: Ah, there you are!

LINDMOSER: Dear God, Simmerl. That was a close call.

GLASHÜTTNER: What was close?

LINDMOSER: A close call past a hero's death into which our house painter of a leader nearly chased us.

FICHTELHUBER: You shut your mouth now, Lindmoser! It's all because of you we didn't get to launch our attack.

GLASHÜTTNER: Thank God!

LINDMOSER: Yes, you can thank me for that.

FICHTELHUBER: I think you're even glad that it happened?!

LINDMOSER: Of course!

FICHTELHUBER: You coward! You're a cowardly dog.

LINDMOSER: Better than being an inscription on a hero's monument any day.

FICHTELHUBER: Cowardice in the face of the enemy is what that's called.

LINDMOSER: And so what?

FICHTELHUBER: You belong in front of a court martial, that's what.

LINDMOSER: Are you nuts?

GLASHÜTTNER: You can't be serious, Fichtelhuber!

FICHTELHUBER: The German people are engaged in a murderous defense of their homeland and you, you want to sneak off?

LINDMOSER: Exactly!

FICHTELHUBER: Well, not me. My honor is semper fidelis! The Commie is standing in Hungary. Silesia and Prussia are encircled. They're bombing Graz!

SIMMERL: (*Suddenly notices that Lindmoser is walking about normally*) You, Lindmoser! How come you can walk like a normal person all of a sudden?

LINDMOSER: My, so I'm doing better suddenly.

FICHTELHUBER: Ha! A saboteur is what you are, a shabby saboteur!

SIMMERL: Tell me, you got any idea how heavy you are? You call that being a comrade?

FICHTELHUBER: High treason is what that is!

SIMMERL: Is that supposed to mean that I dragged you the whole long way across the mountain, and you can walk?

(*The angry forester's gun is pointed at Lindmoser.*)

FICHTELHUBER: I'm going to tell the Commander about that, you scab on the back of the people! Someone like you belongs in front of a firing squad.

LINDMOSER: (Remembers that he, too, is carrying a gun, and points it at the forester) Watch out, forester! Don't be crazy! I've got a gun, too!

FICHTELHUBER: You wouldn't dare!?

LINDMOSER: You yourself are daring it!

FICHTELHUBER: You'll die! And what a difference that is.

LINDMOSER: What kind of difference?

FICHTELHUBER: A murderous difference: I dare to pull the trigger 'cause I'm a hunter.

LINDMOSER: (threatening) And nothing makes no difference to me! (*The two men stand facing each other threateningly.*)

GLASHÜTTNER: Come on, someone step in between.

BARBARA: Come on, stop fighting! Like two little boys! Wherever you go, you play at soldiers.

SONNLEITNER: Don't be foolish. Main thing is that all of us came back healthy.

JOGL: But only 'cause Lindmoser broke his ankle!

(*The situation begins to relax.*)

SCHWARZENEGGER: Yes, health is the most important thing.

SONNLEITNER: All right men, the fatherland thanks you. St. Kilian doesn't need to be ashamed of us.

JOGL: There's a hunter's tea abrewing at the Stag.

FICHTELHUBER: Well, the Commander is really going to thank you, Sonnleitner, that nothing happened.

SONNLEITNER: What do you want? We can't do more than do.

GLASHÜTTNER: (*steppping forward*) Children, unfortunately there's somethin' else we have to do today.

SONNLEITNER: What?

GLASHÜTTNER: In one word, it concerns our bell.

SONNLEITNER: Let's talk about it tomorrow.

GLASHÜTTNER: Tomorrow is the day they're going to come pick it up and melt it down.

SONNLEITNER: Yes, and what's the matter with that?

GLASHÜTTNER: We don't want that.

SONNLEITNER: Who doesn't want it?

GLASHÜTTNER: Most folks in the village don't.

GRANDMA: *(stepping forward)* We don't want to give it up.

SONNLEITNER: Well, are you a nut? What do you mean give it up? We gotta give it up, it's an order.

FICHTELHUBER: Yes, what was this just now. A revolt? My cup runneth over! They're dying at the front for us, and we can't even give up the bell, to melt it down for a V-2 rocket?!

SCHWARZENEGGER: There, you're gonna go down and never get up again! That can't be! They're gonna put us in a concentration camp for that!

SONNLEITNER: I mean: am I dreaming this? Don't you have any other worries, you folks?

GLASHÜTTNER: That's what I said, too. Really think about it, is what I said. It's madness. I, myself, is what I said, and I am your pastor, I don't need the bell, I'd give it to you. A bell isn't the most important part of a church. I can whistle you to church with a dog whistle, is what I said. I have other worries, by God, than whether I can toll the bell at 12 o'clock. But they're such mule-headed critters, all of them together, and they got it into their skulls to make the bell disappear.

SONNLEITNER: That they do what?

GLASHÜTTNER: Disappear.

GRANDMA: Just imagine, it disappeared overnight.

SONNLEITNER: The bell disappears overnight?

JOGL: (*too forward*) At Easter it flies off to Rome, too.

SONNLEITNER: Well, have all your screws suddenly come unloosed, as the Germans say.

SCHWARZENEGGER: What nonsense. Where's it gonna disappear to overnight.

GRANDMA: Somewhere: on the mountain, to the meadows, into the foxhole.

FICHTELHUBER: What? Into the foxhole?

GRANDMA: Anyhow, it'll have disappeared the next day, and no one would know where to. At some point the point is reached and the cup runneth over.

SONNLEITNER: I don't believe this! Knock that nonsense out of your heads, people. Mama! Have you gone mad?

GRANDMA: Sylvester! Come here a second! (*Sonnleitner steps obediently in front of his mother*) Bend down! (*Sonnleitner bends forward and gets a smack in the face from her.*) Your father was still someone who hunted out of season, and he couldn't look any forester straight in the eye! And you, you made it as far as mayor, that's all! But at least this one thing you should be able to do.

SONNLEITNER: But Mama, you don't know what you're asking! We have a war on, and that means that martial law is in effect! And an order is an order. And refusing an order, well they don't mess around for long before they act: noggin off, as the Germans say, and that's it.

GRANDMA: What can they do to us if the bell suddenly disappears? Isn't long anyway until the war is over. No one will know who it was and how.

SONNLEITNER: They wiped out whole villages. They hanged mayors from the trees.

SCHWARZENEGGER: And how come no one knows anything about it? All of us know.

GRANDMA: 'Cause no one is going to say anything.

FICHTELHUBER: And why won't anyone say anything?

GLASHÜTTNER: 'Cause all of us gotta stick together.

SONNLEITNER: Don't be so naive! Stick together! What do you know about the Gestapo!

FICHTELHUBER: Really, can this be happening! St. Kilian, which has always been a mainstay of the movement suddenly stabs the Führer in the back!, and this right in the middle of the decisive battle for the German Reich.

GRANDMA: It's only a bell.

SONNLEITNER: Only a bell, only a bell.

FICHTELHUBER: I wouldn't have thought you could do something like that, Mrs. Sonnleitner, though I was a little surprised when I heard that you were from Judenburg.

SONNLEITNER: Let the old woman be, Fichtelhuber.

FICHTELHUBER: Well, you look great standing there, Sonnleitner, first the mess with the militia and now your own mother is a traitor.

SONNLEITNER: You're gonna stop right now, forester! She's an old woman, she doesn't know what she is saying.

GRANDMA: The others are all for it, too, the old and the young.

SIMMERL: I as a first-class member of the Hitler Youth, not me. I am not for this. Heil Hitler! I already dragged Lindmoser across the hill, I don't want to have to drag a bell too.

KATHI: And I'm with the Hitler Girls and I am FOR the bell, Simmerl. And I'm telling you one thing: if you ever want to even look at me again, you better be for the bell too.

GRANDMA: A bell is important for a village like ours. It tolled when you came into the world and when you got married and when your people died! And it should go on ringing when I die and when Kathi gets married.

BARBARA: And also when I get married.

GLASHÜTTNER: Yes, that's exactly what I told them too. But it's like talking to a wall. You stupid sheep, is what I said, what do you want? Back then when your men and sons went off to war, you waved after them with the flags. And "Sieg Heil Sieg Heil" you screamed, and it's still ringing in my ears. And there was no talk about one of them suddenly disappearing overnight, say onto the meadow, or into the foxhole. Twenty-nine from the village have croaked in foreign lands, where they had no business in the first place. And now you're coming at me with this crazy bell, I said to them. What kind of people are you? But they're just mules and not a ray of light enters their skulls, Lord have mercy. But that's what they're like, you can't just close your eyes to it. If they refuse to let us talk them out of that bell business, it's just as important that afterwards we can all depend on each other.

BARBARA: Now I'm going to tell you something: I didn't know my husband Lois for even half a year and they drafted him. When he died it was like some stranger died, a distant relative, someone you once met a long time ago. And all the things we planned to do during that half year! Children, the house, we were going to slave so we would make something of ourselves. And what happened? War. It was over. And now I have had it. The list is too long: A Hero's death for Führer and Reich. I'd like to have something of my life, you understand! And the bell is supposed to disappear by early tomorrow morning, until we can let it toll again, the end of war.

SONNLEITNER: After the war we will build a nice big war memorial in St. Kilian, I promise you! Each and every name will be inscribed on it in gold letters. But please forget about the bell, please.

GRANDMA: But the community has already decided!

SONNLEITNER: Has decided what?

GRANDMA: The community.

SONNLEITNER: I crap on the community! I am the mayor here!

FICHTELHUBER: Right on, Sonnleitner! That's speaking clearly!

LINDMOSER: Well, if you ask me, I don't think anything of this community business either, if only 'cause a body can't trust nobody around here.

GLASHÜTTNER: What are you talking about, Lindmoser?

SCHWARZENEGGER: You can't say something like that, Lindmoser. We're a community thick as blood in St. Kilian. We've always been able to depend on each other.

LINDMOSER: Don't make me laugh out loud!

SCHWARZENEGGER: Do you remember, Lindmoser? In the year thirty-four, when you hid the two guys from Leoben in your shed, the two Reds, that the cops were looking for. We knew all about it, that you were keeping them hid, and no one tattled on you. Fine, we cut you a little bit, but only in business matters.

LINDMOSER: Cut me a little! You ruined me!

SCHWARZENEGGER: What, didn't I help you back then? You see, that's St. Kilian!

LINDMOSER: Yes, you Schwarzenegger, you're the exception, you're a decent person.

SCHWARZENEGGER: You still got your farm, except that it doesn't belong to you anymore.

LINDMOSER: Yes, I'll never forget it, Schwarzenegger! Where would I be without you today?! But you know, it really got to me that when Annie lay a dying, in her fever, and the doctor wouldn't, just wouldn't come 'cause he had to take care of the animals in your sheds.

SCHWARZENEGGER: You're bitter, Lindmoser, I can understand that. My Simmerl was the one who got the doctor, and he wouldn't even have come if he hadn't known that he gets a side of bacon from Schwarzenegger, and eggs. What can you do? Most of the doctors are off to war too. And where your huts are it's a little too far outside town, and it was snowing too, and he did get there at some point didn't he? But what would have happened, Lindmoser, without my bacon? Ha? Nothing would have happened, Lindmoser, nothing at all would have happened. Don't forget that.

LINDMOSER: (*moved*) You are right, Schwarzenegger, you're right in your way! I can see that. You're a soul of a human being. You have convinced me! How could I have been talking such nonsense!? The community of St. Kilian, yes, you can depend on it, they all support each other, it's like a tree with many branches! All right, then, let's get a hold of it, the bell.

SCHWARZENEGGER: How so the bell? Who said anything about the bell?

FICHTELHUBER: Are you by any chance for the bell, too, Schwarzenegger?!

SCHWARZENEGGER: What are you talking about? I didn't say anything at all. We were talking about something entirely different.

LINDMOSER: We were talking about the community being as thick as blood.

SCHWARZENEGGER: Right.

LINDMOSER: And it is—for the bell.

GLASHÜTTNER: Yes, they won't let anyone talk them out of the bell anymore.

FICHTELHUBER: The community as thick as blood is now going to sneak on home into their hovels, and at once! Otherwise all hell will break loose! Have you understood what I said, all of you? The mayor says no, and no it is! This is an order.

SONNLEITNER: Come on, get some sense, people.

(Barbara steps up to Fichtelhuber.)

BARBARA: Tell me, Hubert, what do you need a radio for out in the woods with you?

FICHTELHUBER: What are you talking about?

BARBARA: What do you need a radio for. 'Cause you're listening to an English station?

FICHTELHUBER: You're out of your mind.

BARBARA: But they talk in German.

FICHTELHUBER: How so?

BARBARA: 'Cause I caught you listening.

FICHTELHUBER: Ain't true.

BARBARA: I swear it is.

FICHTELHUBER: Barbara! What's this supposed to mean.

BARBARA: Do you know the penalty for listening to an enemy station.

FICHTELHUBER: That's a lie.

BARBARA: Prison and you'd get lucky, you Nazi Chapter Head you.

FICHTELHUBER: A dirty made-up smelly lie is what that is.

LINDMOSER: But it sure is funny that you need a radio out in the woods.

FICHTELHUBER: 'Cause of the weather report!

LINDMOSER: Oh come off it, weather report! my ass! Who's going to believe that?

GRANDMA: She's on to something when Barbara says something like that.

LINDMOSER: That's almost like a spy, listening to an enemy station.

BARBARA: Don't need to be so afeerd, Hubert, if it ain't anything.

GLASHÜTTNER: If we stick together, no one will give you away.

LINDMOSER: Well, the community is as thick as blood.

SONNLEITNER: All right, my patience has snapped, this is too much for me! What do you think you are doing? Denouncing an honest party member, a man of the first hour! That's like a Commie conspiracy! I don't want to hear any more of it!

GRANDMA: (*walking up to the mayor*) And you, my boy, I'm going to tell you something now. It's hard for me to do it, 'cause it's an admission, like a confession, that intimate. I never told anyone else about it, but now is the right moment, father he's dead already, and I'm an old woman, and what people say: I couldn't give a hoot.

SONNLEITNER: Mother, I beg of you, what are you planning?

GRANDMA: Your father was not your father!

SONNLEITNER: What? Mama! In front of all the people! What is this? And who would be my rightful father?

GRANDMA: A Jewish panhandler, that's who!

SONNLEITNER: Mother!

GRANDMA: I would have liked to have taken the secret with me, to my grave, but now it's out, now the whole village knows. Sorry, Sylvester, I would have liked to have spared you.

SONNLEITNER: But Mother, how?

GRANDMA: Something like that doesn't take long.

KATHI: Holy Mary! Grandma! That means I'm not of pure blood.

GRANDMA: Ignatius was his name!

FICHTELHUBER: Well, if that isn't a story!

SONNLEITNER: You be very quiet there, you secret spy, you.

FICHTELHUBER: I don't let a half-Jew tell me anything at all.

SCHWARZENEGGER: Well, what's gotten into you all. Have you all gone mad?

FICHTELHUBER: And you shut your mouth, too, you black marketeer.

SCHWARZENEGGER: You take that back, Fichtelhuber!

FICHTELHUBER: A black butcher is what you are! A scab on the body of the people! (*The three men are standing aggressively opposite each other.*)

GRANDMA: All right, then, let's get to the bell. The pulley is already up in the belfry, all we have to do is lower it and get it up the mountain. (*The men look at each other with increasing astonishment.*)

SIMMERL: Up on the mountain? But it's far too heavy, the bell! How're we gonna get it up the mountain?

SCHWARZENEGGER: That weighs tons, we're never going to make it.

GLASHÜTTNER: A little more trust in God, please. We're going to let someone help us.

FICHTELHUBER: Who's going to help us? The SS?

GLASHÜTTNER: We made a connection there with a group, fine people, and they said they'd help us.

FICHTELHUBER: What kind of people?

GLASHÜTTNER: Solid guys who know how to grab ahold.

(*He whistles three times. Toni Lindmoser and Facundo come around the cemetery wall. They confront the villagers. Frozen scene. The gnashing of Fichtelhuber's teeth can be heard.*)

CURTAIN

ACT THREE
A VILLAGE IS INTERROGATED

(Two, three weeks later, after the thaw. A rooster is crowing: it's early morning. Jogl has set up his card table in front of the bench, now he is spreading a table cloth over it. Sonnleitner places a swastika flag on the table, nervously opens his ledger and gets his writing material in order.)

SONNLEITNER: You shouldn't always be askin' so many questions, Jogl. I'm telling you, this is the only proper place for an interrogation like this. The Commander is having breakfast at the Stag, Schwarzenegger made him a huge ham omelet and a real cup of coffee. So we have maybe half an hour for us to clean up our gutter. I thought the story would fall asleep, but no, suddenly it pops up again and creates a whole bunch of fuss. Now hurry up, so that it looks all nice and clear; there already are some pre-investigation records here. *(He writes)* Protocol of the Interrogation. What day is it today? Better leave the date out. Perhaps we can pre-date it later on. In the matter of: The Bell that Disappeared. What's keeping all of them?

SCHWARZENEGGER: *(Coming from the village)* He's still at his grub.

SONNLEITNER: Where are the others? Go Jogl, you whip 'em along, we don't have that much time. *(Jogl goes off in the directon of the village.)* And now let's get to you, Schwarzenegger. *(He writes:)* First interrogation of Party Member Leopold Schwarzenegger, innkeeper in St. Kilian. All right then, Schwarzenegger, what do you have to say about the case of the disappeared bell?

SCHWARZENEGGER: What am I supposed to say?

SONNLEITNER: Well, ain't you suprised that it's gone?

SCHWARZENEGGER: How so?

SONNLEITNER: Well, a bell like that in a belfry can't just disappear overnight.

SCHWARZENEGGER: Oh yes it can.

SONNLEITNER: How so, it being so heavy and all that?

SCHWARZENEGGER: I got a backache even now.

SONNLEITNER: Schwarzenegger, I beg you, watch what you say. I can't put that in the protocol.

SCHWARZENEGGER: So what am I supposed to say?

SONNLEITNER: Look, you've got the inn in town, the community center so to speak, someone might have dropped an incriminating comment there which you picked up. You remember anythin'?

SCHWARZENEGGER: All right, when the priest came and said the bell's disappeared! someone at the inn, I don't remember who, said: Gosh, such a heavy bell?

SONNLEITNER: Fine, we'll formulate that like this (*he writes*): The witness presumes that the bell was of such a heavy weight that at least a dozen strong men would have been required to drag it away. St. Kilian, however, at most has half a dozen strong men at its command.

SCHWARZENEGGER: Not even.

SONNLEITNER: Exactly. And how do you explain it to yourself?

SCHWARZENEGGER: It's a puzzle to me.

SONNLEITNER: Well, someone must have done it!

SCHWARZENEGGER: Perhaps the partisans took it.

SONNLEITNER: (*writing*) He thinks it was the partisans. And didn't you notice anything special that day?

SCHWARZENEGGER: Nothing.

SONNLEITNER: And at night, they stole it at night.

SCHWARZENEGGER: Of course, at night. When else?!

SONNLEITNER: And you didn't notice anything that night?

SCHWARZENEGGER: How should I have been able to notice anything? You could barely see your hand before your eyes. First I stumbled over a rotten cedar tree, and a branch hit my fingers so that I heard all the angels in heaven sing.

SONNLEITNER: Hold it together, Schwarzenegger! You keep that up and you'll talk yourself into a rope round your neck! (*he writes*): The witness claims he noticed nothing unusual at all that night.

SCHWARZENEGGER: But that doesn't sound very advantageous: claims not to have noticed. I ain't CLAIMING nothing, it WAS like that, I didn't notice anything 'cause there was nothing to notice. Write: The Party Member with the best of his good will and to his own regret noticed nothing! (*The priest is coming around the corner of the cemetery wall.*)

SONNLEITNER: A good thing that you've come, Father. I've got to take a protocol from you. What do you have to say about the bell?

GLASHÜTTNER: I don't know what to say.

SONNLEITNER: (*writing*) The priest is left speechless. Again not a single clue. The case is becoming more and more mysterious.

GLASHÜTTNER: What a cross it is to bear. They always want everything proved and logical.

SONNLEITNER: I can't write that, but I've got to write something! All right: what explanation do you come up with, Pastor?

GLASHÜTTNER: I don't need any explanations. I'm a believing Christian.

SCHWARZENEGGER: You got it easy!

SONNLEITNER: And how do you think it happened?

GLASHÜTTNER: Listen, Sonnleitner, what is this bullshit? You know how it happened as well as anyone. Do you want me to start lying in my old age?

SONNLEITNER: Well, I really beg of you, most heartily, that you do, Father. Lie for Heaven's sake, lie for the sake of mercy, 'cause the truth would be dreadful. The People's Court, a concentration camp with electric barbed wire all around, a guillotine that would be the truth.

GLASHÜTTNER: Well listen to that! Suddenly I hear the mayor tell the truth.

SONNLEITNER: The truth is everyone wants to get by somehow the best they can.

GLASHÜTTNER: What do you mean by somehow?

SONNLEITNER: For great God's sake! No one stays clean who goes down into a mine shaft! And all of us are going to go to confession, after the war is over! And anyway, I don't remember hearing any objections from you when the Nazis got here, back then. Go with God, you said, instead of Heil Hitler. And instead of one arm you raised both your arms, like during a blessin'. That was all.

GLASHÜTTNER: And my sermon about David and Goliath? Was that nothing? (*Sonnleitner regards him with a sigh*) We of course slithered into this condition innocently, not that that makes it forgivable, into this mess.

SONNLEITNER: Well, you really did knit your brow the day the Nazis picked up old Anzinger.

GLASHÜTTNER: Yes, and you made a fist, in your pants pocket. Now it's all over with our innocence, now we've become guilty of no end of things. All right then, write that I didn't see anything. I really didn't see anything.

SONNLEITNER: It's just a protocol, so folks can see that St. Kilian doesn't take this bell business lightly. (*writes in the ledger*)

SCHWARZENEGGER: What times these are! Nazis are already interrogating Nazis! But what does that mean, Nazi? National, right, that isn't something terrible. And German? We speak a kind of German, right? Of course the socialist made me a bit suspicious at first. You never know. But all that was was tactics, and besides, we were always social, that is Christian Social, right? We didn't think anything of it. Words! Words and stamps and party booklets. And the Jews? Well, I never found them very kosher . . . (*Sonnleitner regards Schwarzenegger darkly*) 'Scuse me, Sonnleitner, I totally forgot that you're of impure blood in the first degree, which of course I don't know officially at all.

SONNLEITNER: Just so that no one makes any slipups with his tongue. (*Lindmoser is on his way from the village, he's already shouting from afar.*)

LINDMOSER: Under my name you can write, Lindmoser Josef didn't see anything, hear anything, smell anything or do anything!

SCHWARZENEGGER: Lindmoser's hopping about again like a young goat since Toni came back . . . (*all of*

*them regard him sharply, and he stops in his
tracks.*) . . . which of couse I have no idea of officially.

SONNLEITNER: Let's not talk nonsense.

SCHWARZENEGGER: I'm as silent as a war hero's grave!

LINDMOSER: Now that the war is almost over, it'd be stupid if they still crucified us.

SCHWARZENEGGER: At night they heard . . . it sounded
like distant thunder, coming from Hungary.

SONNLEITNER: The Russkie has reached Lake Platten.
And in the north he's by the River Oder, that's only
a hop skip and jump to Berlin. And the Americans
are at the Rhine.

LINDMOSER: The partisans blew up the traintracks near
Leoben.

SCHWARZENEGGER: Yes, yes yes, the days are upon us,
you can count 'em.

GLASHÜTTNER: After the war the church will need a new
roof, and new glass windows. And the gold is flaking
off from the Mother of God . . .

LINDMOSER: Of course, that will be the most important
thing! (*Barbara is coming from the village.*)

BARBARA: I made it a point to bring him a raisin cake. But
who knows if he likes it. His SS guy is walking
around the village, asking questions.

SONNLEITNER: I've got to get cooking, all I've got are
three testimonials in my protocol. That's far too few,
and besides, none of it is very intelligent.

LINDMOSER: Don't shit in your pants. What can happen?
The war is nearly over, don't you think the Nazis
know what's going on? They are not going to dare
act up any more.

SONNLEITNER: The Commander will. He still believes in the miracle weapon. (*Grandmother Sonnleitner arrives from the village, supported by Kathi.*)

GRANDMA: I brought him a can of milk, but he doesn't like the fat on top, which is the best part of it.

KATHI: Father, what's going to happen?

SONNLEITNER: You don't know anything! Play stupid! You are the dumb little country girl picking your nose with your finger.

KATHI: And what if they find Toni?

SONNLEITNER: This name won't even cross your lips! You've never heard of him, and if you did you've long since forgotten! He doesn't even exist in your life.

KATHI: 'Cause he wants to marry me!

SONNLEITNER: (*is perplexed*) Well, you ask yourself, is that possible? We are trembling for our lives, and you've got nothing else in your head but that!

GRANDMA: Calm down, they've got to marry!

SONNLEITNER: How so? Why must?

GRANDMA: 'Cause I caught them, "in flagrante."

SONNLEITNER: There's an Italian involved too?

GRANDMA: There's got to be order! What do you say to that, Lindmoser?

LINDMOSER: Well yes, now that the war is nearly over—

SONNLEITNER: And there I thought he was wounded.

KATHI: But only his foot.

SIMMERL: (arriving from the village) He's already by the café.

SONNLEITNER: Holy Mary! He's already by the café! (*He*

writes hurriedly into the ledger:) Lindmoser Josef, didn't see anything or hear anything. Barbara Kohnhauser didn't notice anything suspicious. Kathi Sonnleitner was busy elsewhere . . .

SS-KROLL: (*comes marching from the village. He sees the people, turns around and hollers into the wings.*) Over here! You were right, Commander! This is where the rabble are! (*makes himself monumental on center stage*) Everybody up against the wall, march, march! One next to the other! (*The villagers line up next to each other against the cemetery wall.*) What a fine group of folks we have here! A dandy nest of bandits, eh!

SONNLEITNER: Beg your pardon, sir. St. Kilian was always a movement town, a jewel box of the East . . .

SS-KROLL: You only speak when asked! Understand? So, I am asking you: where is the bell? (*No reply. The Commander arrives from the village and regards the scene, brooding ominously.*) Where's the bell is what I want to know! (*Kroll points at Sonnleitner.*) Speak! I advise you, do so for your own good!

SONNLEITNER: Please, the investigations so far, which I started at once, unfortunately show not a single useful clue . . .

COMMANDER: Nice conditions here in St. Kilian.

SS-KROLL: I don't trust a one of these beet-eaters.

COMMANDER: Listen all of you. I have been empowered to inform you that the Gestapo has offered a reward of 10,000 Reichsmark, which will be given to anyone who delivers up a bandit, dead or alive, or who contributes to his arrest! (*Jogl has arrived from the village and now stands there in a state of confusion.*)

COMMANDER: Did you all get that? 10,000 Reichsmark!

So, and now once more and very kindly. Sturm-bannführer, ask your questions.

SS-KROLL: Firstly: where is the bell? Secondly: who in the village noticed anything suspicious?

SONNLEITNER: First of all: it disappeared, secondly, no one knows how, 'cause no one noticed anything.

JOGL: Oh yes, I noticed something suspicious all right! (*the villagers freeze.*)

COMMANDER: What? Speak up man!

JOGL: The bell didn't toll, there I knew at once that something had tolled, namely something suspicious.

SONNLEITNER: Well it wasn't able to toll, you nerd! 'Cause we had dismounted it!

JOGL: Oh, so WE did that?

SONNLEITNER: It was prepared to be taken away! Suddenly it was gone.

COMMANDER: What is that supposed to mean suddenly it was gone? Who was supposed to have carried it off? (*no reply*)

SS-KROLL: Answer!

SONNLEITNER: How am I supposed to know that?

LINDMOSER: Perhaps the partisans.

COMMANDER: I see. The partisans! Very clever! In your opinion the partisans have nothing better to do but to go around stealing church bells?

LINDMOSER: They've done a lot of other things too.

COMMANDER: (*ready to pounce*) What for example?

LINDMOSER: Well, for example, they blew up the railroad tracks in Leoben.

COMMANDER: Hey Kroll! Did you hear that?! The guy just revealed who he is! That's a top state secret! That wasn't in the paper and wasn't broadcast on the radio. He should not have known that.

SONNLEITNER: Beg your pardon, Sir. Lindmoser is only telling what every child in the village knows.

SS-KROLL: So that means that the whole village is collaborating.

SCHWARZENEGGER: But no, the mailman told it to us at the inn, and he heard it from a railway worker in Leoben.

SS-KROLL: I can feel it in my kidneys that there's something wrong about this village.

COMMANDER: Where's the village party leader? Why isn't he here?

JOGL: Beg your pardon, sir. I went looking for Fichtelhuber everywhere, even the chicken pen, but he's nowhere to be found.

COMMANDER: (*pulls out a letter*) Very odd! Because he wrote me that he had an important message for me, which he was going to give me here today.

SS-KROLL: Very odd!

JOGL: Perhaps he's gone hunting, Fichtelhuber.

SONNLEITNER: He's usually a dependable person. Perhaps he's sick.

COMMANDER: Sturmbannführer, you search the entire village, every nook and cranny! We've got to find the forester (*Kroll walks off in the direction of the village.*) We're going to make this St. Kilian shape up! And if our least suspicion is confirmed . . .

SONNLEITNER: Beg pardon, St. Kilian was always completely clean of Jews and of Commies, since ever!

JOGL: At least since they took away old Anzinger it was.

COMMANDER: Was anyone here from the village arrested?

SONNLEITNER: Old Anzinger, three years ago.

COMMANDER: Hey, look at me. And what was the matter with Anzinger? A saboteur? A secret Communist perhaps?

JOGL: No, it was just his sense of humor was too good.

SONNLEITNER: 'Cause, old fool that he was, he told a joke.

JOGL: Yes, the one about the Führer and the eggs.

COMMANDER: I see. What kind of joke?

SONNLEITNER: A silly joke.

JOGL: Why the Führer always keeps his hands crossed in front the way you do, Commander Sir.

COMMANDER: (*who is holding his hands Führer-fashion in front of his fly, abruptly alters his stance. Foxily:*) Very interesting! And what else?

JOGL: Nothing else!

COMMANDER: Where's the point?

JOGL: I don't know where it is.

COMMANDER: But what kind of joke is it where the point is missing?

JOGL: Better than you're missin' your head.

COMMANDER: And what's that supposed to mean?

JOGL: I ain't saying anything else.

COMMANDER: I order you to tell the end of the joke, at once.

JOGL: I ain't that much of an idiot.

BARBARA: Old Anzinger, they beheaded him, in Graz, that's the point.

LINDMOSER: Are we going to put old Anzinger on our hero's monument after the war?

(*SS-Kroll returns hurriedly from the village, he takes the Commander aside and whispers something to him. The Commander is visibly struck.*)

COMMANDER: Party Chapter Leader Fichtelhuber was found a moment ago.

SONNLEITNER: Thank God, I was starting to get worried.

BARBARA: Where is he keeping himself?

SS-KROLL: He's hanging in the belfry!

COMMANDER: He is dead.

SONNLEITNER: That's not possible! Tell me it ain't true.

LINDMOSER: What? He hanged himself?

SCHWARZENEGGER: Well I'll be damned, hangs himself for a bell in the belfry.

JOGL: Except that he don't toll at twelve.

BARBARA: Hubert is supposed to have killed himself?

GLASHÜTTNER: Dear God, accept him in your Reich and let him hunt the forests of your blissedness, amen.

COMMANDER: This isn't some ordinary crime, this is high treason!

SONNLEITNER: Beg pardon, if he hangs hisself he don't betray anything, he sort of deserts, that's all.

COMMANDER: It all fits together. The Chapter Leader

has something urgent to communicate to me,
shortly afterwards he is dead.

SONNLEITNER: But perhaps it was only a confession,
and he didn't have the guts . . .

COMMANDER: What kind of confession?

SONNLEITNER: How do I know! Perhaps 'cause of the
bell! If he stole the bell, he might have got scared,
and hung himself in his despair . . .

SCHWARZENEGGER: And in the belfry he did it! That
gives us an insight.

LINDMOSER: He was a little odd the last few weeks.

COMMANDER: This is a case for the Gestapo! I herewith
declare the village and the entire vicinity off limits!
The sheriff's department is going to go through everything with a fine-tooth comb. Everyone is under
suspicion, the whole village! We'll find these lice!

SS-KROLL: I had a funny feeling from the very beginning.
I smelled something all along. What a bunch of
tricky bastards.

JOGL: (*leaping up from the bench and up on the cemetery
wall, he shakes his fists in the direction of the village
church and screams:*) Fichtelhuber! You foolish stag
in heat! What did you do to us with your idiotic act!
Now we're a whole village suspected of murder and
are going to be put in a concentration camp just
'cause of you.

SS-KROLL: Gone mad has he!

JOGL: But St. Kilian won't let this black spot besmudge its
reputation, Fichtelhuber! We will revenge you! Why
do we have our militia! (*He leaps from the wall down
into the cemetery and reappears with five rifles.*) A
good thing I had the carbines hid right behind the

angel of peace! We need to reach out towards each other, brothers! St. Kilian must be cleansed. He hands the rifles to the villagers and climbs back across the wall. The men are handling the weapons awkwardly. (*Kroll and the Commander retreat out of earshot of the villagers.*)

COMMANDER: Kroll! What do you say to this? This is an obvious rebellion.

SS-KROLL: Watch out! They're in the majority!

COMMANDER: Kroll, the impudence of it! It gives me food for thought. Perhaps the village is full of partisans.

SS-KROLL: Let's proceed tactically, Commander! We've got to somehow work our way out of the spot we are in! Most important: don't let them notice us panicking.

SONNLEITNER: (*approaching the twosome*) Commander! Mayor Sonnleitner reporting: The St. Kilian Militia at the ready to hunt for the murderer.

COMMANDER: Thank you, Mayor. But this is a matter for the police, you don't need to trouble yourselves over it.

SS-KROLL: The sheriff's department and the police will take care of that. Hand over your weapons and go home.

SONNLEITNER: No, we can't do that! Our Germanic pride won't let us! This is and will remain our business.

(*The Commander and Kroll walk aside and converse.*)

COMMANDER: Kroll, what do you suggest?

SS-KROLL: I suggest we leave while the wind blows favorably, Commander. And then we'll sick the cops on them.

COMMANDER: Won't that give the appearance of flight?

SS-KROLL: Not at all. We withdraw carefully and quietly.

COMMANDER: I wouldn't have thought something like this possible.

SS-KROLL: Keep it cool! The Russians are in West Prussia!

COMMANDER: (*approaching Sonnleitner*) All right, Mayor! You are in charge here. Investigate the incident. Unfortunately we have business elsewhere and have to leave now. Heil Hitler! (*They turn on their heels and depart.*)

VILLAGERS: Heil Hitler! Heil Hitler!

BARBARA: Who would have thought Hubert could do a thing like that?

SONNLEITNER: Irresponsible! Hangs himself and lets us dangle.

SIMMERL: Daddy, do you think the war will be over before the cops come?

SONNLEITNER: I have to start a new protocol at once.

JOGL: And I've got to dig another grave.

(*Frozen scene*)

CURTAIN

ACT FOUR
FREEDOM IN ST. KILIAN

(*A few weeks later. A light green, very early spring day, golden light, the first buds. Toni Lindmoser is sitting on the bench and Facundo whose eye is still bandaged is preparing to shave him. Facundo is humming Los cuatro generales . . . , binds a cloth around Toni's neck, beats lather in a bowl and starts to soap Toni's face.*)

FACUNDO: Lean back, Tonio! Be very calm! Ralación, amigo! The war is over, get used to it!

TONI: Facundo, old man, it will take me a long time to get used to that.

FACUNDO: You know, Toni. Human beings are quick to habit.

(*Jogl comes from the village, pushing his pushcart which is filled with Nazi left-overs.*)

JOGL: Here, Jogl, please be so kind, is what they said to me. Now I have all this metal on my hands: fourteen copies of *Mein Kampf*, swastikas galore, and at least a pound's worth of party insignia. (*He holds up a picture of Hitler.*) Who would have thought of that? And now I'm even going to bury the Führer.

TONI: Do you have to burn all of that, Jogl?

JOGL: Don't burn it, is what they said. Bury it, Jogl, who knows, perhaps you'll be able to use it one day! (*Jogl regards the scene on the bench.*) But Toni! Are you getting a shave?

TONI: You know, Facundo is actually a barber by profession. He had a little barber shop in Barcelona.

JOGL: But he can't see anything!

TONI: He does that by feel only. He's a real master.

FACUNDO: (*sharpening his knife at the strop*) Salón de peluquería! is what it said on my glass door, in brass letters, and under that was my name, but my real name, not Facundo.

TONI: 'Cause with the partisans he always had to be called something else, 'cause of betrayal, you know?

JOGL: But he speaks German.

TONI: That guy knows a lot of languages, he was in the International Brigade, back then. . . . (*Facundo is shaving.*) There were a lot of Austrians in Spain back then, and now he's here with us.

JOGL: Perhaps he'll stay with us, we need a barber here in town.

TONI: We never used to need one before.

JOGL: But now we do. We want to be a little cleaner.

TONI: Hey, Jogl, tell me, is it possible that you only played chameleon during the war, and that in reality you're a real sly fox?

JOGL: (*startled*) No, no. I'm a real idiot in some ways! Word of honor. You only think I'm sly 'cause I grasped a few things about life, a secret.

TONI: What secret?

JOGL: (*mysteriously*) No one is worth shit, and God shits on everyone.

(*Facundo has finished shaving one half of Toni's face and interrupts his activity and listens: they can hear the singsong of women's voices coming from the mountain. Grandma Sonnleitner, Barbara and Kathi have gathered firewood and are carrying baskets full of it into the village. They are happy, confident and cheerful.*)

BARBARA: You look like a bridegroom, the way you've been freshened.

KATHI: Don't you cut him now, Barber!

GRANDMA: That would by the day, had enough blood already.

JOGL: He does that just by the feel of it, 'cause he's an international master.

KATHI: Father thought he'd send you a white shirt so that you'd look like something.

BARBARA: Yes, and wear something beside your square business suit, 'cause the bride will be in her holiday best.

GRANDMA: With a genuine doily blouse! It will be a really festive feast! We just got the wood to bake the cake! And what a fire we're going to build. Spring chicken and rabbit! And we'll have some singing too. (*The women put down their baskets with the wood in them and form a choir.*)

The Song of the Women Who Gather the Wood:

> The girl sneaks into the forest,
> steals wood like a thief.
> Without wood there's no fire,
> without fire no love.
> Holi-reu, holi-ho, fetch the wood.
> And the girl got very calm,
> and the farmer he laughed.
> Yes, in daytime the wood keeps growing
> and at night there grows love.
> Holi-reu, holi-ho, fetch the wood.

FACUNDO: Pretty, I like singing, I always used to sing too when I was cutting hair. (*He starts to shave the other side of Toni's face, humming a Spanish melody in accompaniment.*) There were always four or five people in the store, one in front of the big mirror, the others all waiting and smoking and reading papers. Don Hernando, a haircut? Only a shave and a little pomade! Don Andreo, you want your part a little lower? If it's still possible, amigo! And then they talk about God and the world, the generals are rebelling against the republic, Los cuatro generales, and all that craziness. A good barber doesn't quarrel with his customers. But Don Manuel, for example, he was a fascist, I shave him, I put the knife to his throat, and I say: too bad that isn't General Franco sittin' there! From that day on I was suddenly a political barber.

TONI: And what would you have done with Franco?

FACUNDO: (*laughing*) Dictators shave their own faces! (*Facundo has completed shaving Toni and takes off his barber's cloth.*) All done, Sir, and smooth as a baby's ass! Bueno?

TONI: Feels as though I had a future after all.

BARBARA: (*fetches a bunch of pussy willows, takes them to Facundo and presses them into his hand*) There! Pussy willows! You can caress them.

(*The sounds of a bass tuba can be heard coming from the village. Schwarzenegger and Simmerl, who carries the tuba, appear. They see the group and stop briefly.*)

SCHWARZENEGGER: All right then, let's go, Simmerl! Let's get it over with. Kathi is there too, the one the partisans snapped away from you. What matters now is to save face, my boy, don't let it all hang out.

SIMMERL: It makes no difference to me, Daddy. Yesterday I went serenading.

SCHWARZENEGGER: Really? Where at?

SIMMERL: At Barbara's.

SCHWARZENEGGER: And? What happened?

SIMMERL: She wasn't home. (*Schwarzenegger and Simmerl join the group.*)

SCHWARZENEGGER: There they are, bride and bridegroom.

SIMMERL: All right, I just wanted to say, right, that I don't carry no grudges, for no one, and a lot of luck too, to you Kathi, and you, and I make you a gift of my Styrian hat!

TONI: Thank you, Simmerl.

SCHWARZENEGGER: And my wedding gift is your farm. Toni. Yes, you are hearing right, you can have it back, Toni, that's only fair and square.

SIMMERL: Well, it's not square.

SCHWARZENEGGER: Shut up, Simmerl!

TONI: Thanks a lot, Schwarzenegger. You're a soul of a fellow.

SIMMERL: Toni, just imagine, if the war were still on, you'd be the inheriting first-born!

SCHWARZENEGGER: Well, I'm sure glad that your father is the new mayor. Someone who's clean all the way.

SIMMERL: My father, you know, right after we finish celebrating he's got to go down to get denazified.

SCHWARZENEGGER: Yes, that's going to be hard. But the commander of your partisans, a man of real character let me say, I was completely suprised, he felt that at least I had something going for me with that story about the bell, right. And you've got your farm back, too.

KATHI: That's what my father says too: If we didn't have the bell, but we have it.

(*The Priest, with Lindmoser and Sonnleitner at his side, arrives from the village.*)

GLASHÜTTNER: And so the best man will carry the bridegroom into the church?

LINDMOSER: Piggy-back.

SONNLEITNER: Yes, and from the belfry we will unfurl the new flag.

LINDMOSER: You and all your flags.

BARBARA: There they are, the three village saints!

SONNLEITNER: What kind of assembly is this here now?

GLASHÜTTNER: Children, don't waste your time, the church isn't spic and span yet.

SONNLEITNER: And you, Mama, you still have to sow a white stripe over my swastika flag.

GRANDMA: Flags, I think, are the most important thing in your life.

GLASHÜTTNER: And you all still have to change.

BARBARA: Suddenly it can't go fast enough for you!

SONNLEITNER: And when I as the father-in-law have to go to be denazified! The commander of the partisans should wait until the ceremony is over, if only because it's also been declared a feast of liberation.

GLASHÜTTNER: You have to celebrate the feasts as they come your way.

BARBARA: All we did was pick some wood.

GRANDMA: And now we're going to light it up. And then we celebrate. And then we look to how we get the livestock through the spring and do the sowing.

(*Kathi, Grandma and Barbara take their baskets full of wood and walk off in the direction of he village.*)

JOGL: And I only went collecting, and now I'm going burying. (*He pushes his cart around the cemetery wall.*)

TONI: And all I did was go to the barber. (*Facundo carries Toni piggy-back in the direction of the village. The three village saints, Glashüttner in the middle, sitdown on the bench.*)

GLASHÜTTNER: Everything will be all right, everything will be all right.

SONNLEITNER: (*shyly*) A difficult time, but a beautiful day!

LINDMOSER: Yes, the weather! If it weren't for that . . .

GLASHÜTTNER: Really, do you have to talk about the weather at this moment, something so historical?

SONNLEITNER: That we're going to get our children, Lindmoser, that is certainly a great good fortune. Toni is really a capable boy, and courageous.

LINDMOSER: It isn't very long ago that you called them bandit rabble.

GLASHÜTTNER: No quarreling, no quarreling.

SONNLEITNER: That was only German office talk! If you become mayor now, you'll notice that there's no escaping official German.

GLASHÜTTNER: What a lucky place we are after all, for each and every situation we have the right man. St. Kilian can look forward to wonderful days.

LINDMOSER: And back on a brown past!

SONNLEITNER: Looking back, looking back, it's easy to be a smart-aleck.

GLASHÜTTNER: They're not going to give you all that

much heat, the way they are cooking, the denazifiers.

SONNLEITNER: I believe the story with the bell will bring a lot of credit to me!

GLASHÜTTNER: Yes, the bell, if we didn't have that!

LINDMOSER: But the story with old Anzinger?

SONNLEITNER: But how? No one could have imagined that they'd cut off his head right away for something like that.

LINDMOSER: But someone must have turned him in.

GLASHÜTTNER: Yes, one of my sheep must have been a swine.

SONNLEITNER: Must have been Fichtelhuber, that guy was such a fanatic.

LINDMOSER: You think so? And what about Lois Kohnhauser?

SONNLEITNER: What do you mean? He fell at the front.

GLASHÜTTNER: Yes, in the penal battalion.

LINDMOSER: But how did he get the into the penal battalion?

SONNLEITNER: He always was a stubborn s.o.b.

LINDMOSER: But someone must have turned him in.

GLASHÜTTNER: Don't suspect anyone unless you have proof.

LINDMOSER: What do you think—Fichtelhuber?

SONNLEITNER: A very plausible idea.

LINDMOSER: But they will have asked if anyone would vouch for him, they would have checked with you as the mayor.

GLASHÜTTNER: Please, I beg you, stop these accusations, only accusations!

SONNLEITNER: You still have to learn that, Lindmoser. A mayor always has to go by the constitution, no matter whose constitution it is.

LINDMOSER: What did you think, who murdered Fichtelhuber?

SONNLEITNER: The forester? He hanged himself.

LINDMOSER: Are you sure?

SONNLEITNER: Look, the old Nazi saw the war is lost, his thousand- year Reich fell apart, his world is caving in, and he didn't pack up and leave, he said goodbye for good.

LINDMOSER: But Sonnleitner! He wrote the Commander a letter.

SONNLEITNER: Yes, perhaps in his first emotional upheaval! The faith of the Nibelungen, as the Germans say. But then he realized that he was the Judas of St. Kilian. And he decided it was better to do away with himself.

LINDMOSER: Looked at this way, actually wonderful of him.

SONNLEITNER: Yes, this faith to the homeland! A clean sweep as it were.

LINDMOSER: But how are you going to explain that we hunted partisans as the Militia of St. Kilian?

SONNLEITNER: Hunting is saying too much. We led the SS into an ambush.

LINDMOSER: And the English pilot who was beaten to death, who came down with his parachute on the Krahberg?

SONNLEITNER: Look, during the confusion of war, right?! The people were funny in the head with all that Goebbels' propaganda. And Fichtelhuber was their instigator.

GLASHÜTTNER: Sonnleitner, perhaps you'll work your way through the interrogations with your crap like that, but purgatory is waiting for you even now.

SONNLEITNER: My God, Pastor, isn't there anything but revenge, revenge?

LINDMOSER: Tell me, Sonnleitner, have you ever eaten a human being?

SONNLEITNER: What do you mean?

LINDMOSER: 'Cause that would be something that hasn't happened in St. Kilian yet.

SONNLEITNER: (reflectively) The palms of the hands aren't supposed to taste all that bad, allegedly.

GLASHÜTTNER: The devil be with you! Will you finally stop with these horror stories! Instead of discussing how we are to go on . . .

SONNLEITNER: Do you think it will take a long time, this denazifying?

LINDMOSER: The place is going to boom, you'll see.

SONNLEITNER: You think so? Why?

LINDMOSER: Tourists! They haven't been on summer vacation during the whole war, and no winter vacation either.

SONNLEITNER: There's one thing I would hate: Siberia.

GLASHÜTTNER: Don't you think people will have other things to worry about now?

LINDMOSER: Sure, they're going to come with their other

worries first. Where else can they get a side of bacon these days?

GLASHÜTTNER: But no one will have any money.

LINDMOSER: But they will have rugs, gold jewelry, pianos . . .

SONNLEITNER: Perhaps they'll only make me pay a penalty.

GLASHÜTTNER: But what do we do with all that junk?

LINDMOSER: We'll decorate our hotels with it!

GLASHÜTTNER: What hotels? (*noise, screams and shots from the direction of the village*). They're shooting!

LINDMOSER: It's in the village. Who could that be?

SONNLEITNER: There are still gangs of SS fleeing. They don't want to be captured by the Russians; they're moving across the hill to the Americans.

GLASHÜTTNER: God in heaven, will the war never end?

LINDMOSER: What are we going to do?

SONNLEITNER: What CAN we do?

(*SS-Kroll is coming from the village, dead drunk he is balancing on the churchyard wall, a revolver in one hand. The three saints go into hiding behind the bench. Kroll fires into the air.*)

SS-KROLL: To the wesht! Whatch way to the whesht?! The Amis! hatsch still at least people, the Amis. Whitsh, big and blond and rish! I want to know je way to je wesht!

(*The three saints point mutely in the direction of the mountain. Kroll leaps down from the wall and careens left towards the mountains. The three men gradually straighten up. Jogl peers across the church wall.*)

JOGL: Miserable human material.

LINDMOSER: What does he expect the Americans to do for him?

SONNLEITNER: (*very drily*) A piece of chocolate. (*Simmerl comes running from the village.*)

SIMMERL: He killed him! He killed him. The SS killed the blind barber! (*Barbara arrives*)

BARBARA: He's dead! He's lying in front of the church! Covered with blood.

KATHI: (*arriving*) He couldn't see anything! He ran directly into him.

GRANDMA: (*following Kathi*) What an injustice! It screams to high heaven.

SCHWARZENEGGER: (*huffs and puffs his way there*) The Spaniard got it! The others all went into hiding, why risk anything now! He was the only one, he couldn't see him coming.

(*Toni Lindmoser limps up to the corner of the church wall, raises his rifle and shoots in the direction of the mountain.*)

SIMMERL: Did you hit him?

TONI: He's stumbling!

SIMMERL: 'Cause he's drunk.

TONI: Die, you beast!

SIMMERL: I can't see him any more.

GLASHÜTTNER: Stop it! You're not going to bring a single corpse back to life with that! Not the Spaniard either. What are we going to do with him now? We don't even know his rightful name! What name should we inscribe on his grave?

JOGL: (*who has climbed on top of the wall*) Facundo! Barber from Barcelona. International master.

GLASHÜTTNER: Amen!

TONI: And what do we do now?

GLASHÜTTNER: What we have to do!

LINDMOSER: A freedom celebration, a wedding and a burial at the same time! (*All of them go off in the direction of the village, except for Jogl, who sits down on the wall, dangling his feet.*)

JOGL: What madness! What a mad madness! (*The bell begins to toll*) Bim-bam, bim-bam, bim-bam . . .

CURTAIN

Thomas Baum

Cold Hands

Translated by
David Ritchie and Gertraud Ingeborg
in Collaboration with
Udo Borgert

CHARACTERS

SILVIA
HEINZ LEHNER, Silvia's father
DANIELA, Silvia's mother
SCHOOL DOCTOR (female)
TEACHER (female)
PRIEST
SCHOOL PRINCIPAL

Scene 1

(Living room: one door leads into the bathroom, another into the kitchen.)

HEINZ: *(shaving)*
My timing is good
Quick quick ladies and gentlemen
yesterday the egg was too soft
At least four and a half
four and a half minutes
Shaving takes
somewhat longer
with a brush
People are
irresponsible
You have to be ashamed
for humanity
on the whole
But I
I don't spray any holes
in the ozone layer
(leaves the bathroom and goes to a living room window)
Have you looked outside yet
You should see it
The fog
makes me feel dull
and sluggish
The fog befogs me
This viscous milk
brings me to my knees
Fight against it
with all your willpower
or else you sag
else you go under
Poor old me

I've got to go out
into this pea-soup
Can you bring me
the beige shirt

DANIELA: (*from the kitchen*)
The beige one is dirty
It needs washing

HEINZ: But darling
I'm lost
without the beige one
In that
I feel
most confident
The beige one
is like a shield
One should not
underestimate
the influence
of clothing
on one's self-confidence
Above all
it makes me look slim
Or doesn't it
Or does it not
make me look slim
Darling
am I
too fat
(*Pause*)
Am I too fat
for you

DANIELA: Yes

HEINZ: What

DANIELA: Much too fat

HEINZ: (*stepping onto the scales*)
           A hundred and seventy pounds
           Not an ounce more
           I'm too fat for her
           at a hundred and seventy
           Did you hear
           only a hundred and seventy
           All right
           I could
           A hundred and sixty-five
           A hundred and sixty-five would be
           my ideal weight
           You're right
           I am fat

DANIELA: Ever since I've known you
           You've been developing a paunch
           Always five pounds too much
           You'll always be like that
           Just like my idea of straight hair
           I go on struggling
           with my curls
           and you
           with your body
           And so we always lug
           a minor disease
           around with us
           as part of our baggage
           and so we can always
           tease and torment each other
           Twenty shirts
           freshly ironed
           in your wardrobe
           Last week
           we bought you a striped one

wickedly expensive

HEINZ: You don't know the regional inspector
            He is an arch-conservative
            The striped one is a
            boutique shirt
            If he sees that
            he'll think
            I am
            an anarchist
            No no
            Not too snappy
            not too casual
            That is precisely what distinguishes
            the beige one
            that it's respectable
            and smart at the same time
            It radiates
            a mischievous
            simplicity
            Absolutely ideal as an inspection-
                day shirt
            After all I do want him to write an
                excellent report

DANIELA: Beige for the inspector
            Gray for choir practice
            At parish council meetings white
            For the Community Action Group colored
            You change your clothes
            your colors your face
            You always want
            to be someone else
            Put on the light blue one
            Big collar
            Long out of fashion
            That will warm the cockles

of your inspector's heart

HEINZ: It seems
              you can't get on
              in life
              without compromises
              Perhaps in the future
              you could bear in mind
              that on stressful days
              I'd rather disguise
              myself in the beige one

DANIELA: The coffee machine
              Doesn't work
              it hardly drips
              It badly needs
              decalcifying
              Breakfast
              is ready

HEINZ: (*sits down at the table*)
              Aren't you
              a loving
              wife

DANIELA: What do you want

HEINZ: Salt

DANIELA: (*gets salt*)
              Too much salt
              is bad for the kidneys
              and leads to
              fluid retention
              Five past seven

HEINZ: Wake her up
              (*checks his bag*)

Medium-term preparation
Long-term preparation
Yearly-weekly-and-daily preparation
All there All perfect
God's musician
Te Deum
Stocky
a wretched man
Greatest difficulties
with women
(*aloud*)
The egg
is perfect
(*to himself*)
Wagner definitely
valued Bruckner
And Bruckner Wagner most highly
I even
dug up
a set of slides
The stations of his life
They've been told
and know
how to answer
each question
Who what when
I have arranged it all
Faultless
Open
Free
Educational
An illusion
For the sake of the inspectorial
   conscience

DANIELA: She's wet the bed
              again

HEINZ: Again

DANIELA: It makes you despair
              It can't go on like this
              How should I react
              We can't let her
              go on like this

HEINZ: She hasn't been allowed to watch
                  television
              for a week now
              Hard enough
              for a child
              of her age
              Punishment is useless
              it's only a sign
              of helplessness

DANIELA: At breakfast
              a little educational wisdom
              for the stupid retarded housewife
              Go upstairs change the bed
              open the windows
              so the mattress gets aired
              load the washing machine
              plug in the iron
              and then sit down
              cross your legs
              bow your head towards Mecca
              and talk
              to ordinary people
              about punishment
              I'll take her to the doctor
              I'll have her examined
              He's got to prescribe something
                  for her

HEINZ: It is psychosomatic
             Psychosomatic
             How often
             how often
             do I have to
             explain this to you
             She is going
             through puberty

DANIELA: Her sphincters
             They don't function any more

HEINZ: Because she lets herself go
             I agree with you
             You have to control yourself
             Even in times
             of psychological transformation
             radical physical change
             You have to be firm with yourself
             She's got to come and have breakfast

DANIELA: She is ashamed of herself
             It's making her suffer
             She's sitting in her room crying

HEINZ: Why is she crying
             That's not what I want
             That's not necessary
             That's just hysteria
             (*aloud*)
             Breakfast Silvia
             Right now Though
             where is my shirt
             Quarter past seven
             and I am still half naked
             I've got a hell of a day ahead of me
             I have to be outstanding for

<pre>
                my inspection
                And at breakfast I actually
                have to talk about pissing the bed
                Whereas I should be doing nothing
                but concentrating on Anton Bruckner
                You show no regard for who I am

DANIELA: Three times a week
                you scream for
                excessive
                consideration
                because some problem or other
                is knocking at the door
                Is there ever a day
                when you don't have
                to concentrate on something
                    earth-shattering

HEINZ: Perhaps you think
                I always have
                Anton Bruckner
                at my beck and call
                This is a head on my shoulders
                not a computer
                But intellectual work
                is in no way respected
                in this house
                You have an intellectual for
                    a husband
                A laborer prepares his tools
                hammer chisel what do I know
                eats his toast in peace and quiet
                leaves the house
                does his work
                and that's it
                The tool of a teacher however
                is among other things and anyway
</pre>

> his head his brain his intellect
> and last but not least his imagination
> (*to Silvia, who enters*)
> Again Why
> Do you have to
> Is it absolutely necessary
> to pee in your bed
> at the age of twelve

SILVIA: I'm sorry

DANIELA: I would appreciate it
            if you didn't always
            say sorry
            That doesn't help
            You wet the bed and that's that
            We have to live with it

HEINZ: Don't be so aggressive

DANIELA: She should go to the toilet
            if she's got to go

SILVIA: I do go to the toilet

DANIELA: Not often enough

SILVIA: Twice mummy
            In the evening
            and during the night
            It still happens to me

DANIELA: Then you are sick

HEINZ: Really
            you have to be
            as stubborn as you are

Two minutes ago
two minutes ago
here
at this table
I told you

DANIELA: It is psychosomatic
I know

HEINZ: Well then

DANIELA: But it's not normal

HEINZ: It is not appropriate to her age
Whether it is normal
that's a quite
different question
Normal my dear
is I hope what none of us are

DANIELA: Thus spoke the Guru
of normality
and of bed-wetting
I beg you
spare me
your lectures
at least in the morning
At this age
you don't pee
all over yourself any more
Nobody
nobody's going to tell me that

HEINZ: Silvia
go and wash yourself

DANIELA: But thoroughly

                    Silvia
                    thoroughly

SILVIA: (*goes to wash herself*)

DANIELA: It started
                    I think it was
                    three years ago
                    At that time
                    we smiled about it
                    At first only
                    from time to time
                    Irregularly
                    Little by little though
                    more and more often
                    We neither hit her
                    nor shouted at her
                    On the contrary
                    We talked to her
                    spoke to her kindly
                    cheered her up
                    and gave her positive reinforcement
                    In the meantime
                    I have to wash her sheets
                    every second, third day
                    And soon
                    she'll do it
                    daily
                    Doesn't it strike you
                    that in general
                    she is sort of obstinate confused
                    To me she seems withdrawn
                    Distant tied up in knots mixed up
                    She's got problems
                    He's simply not listening to me
                    Is God knows where with
                        his thoughts

>
> while I struggle
> to understand our child
> And someone like that whose ears
>   are plugged
> when it comes to the education
> of his own daughter
> calls himself a teacher
> The great pedagogue
> mouths wise sayings
> that's just about all he's capable of

HEINZ: Bon appetit

DANIELA: Bon appetit

HEINZ: Why always me
Everything
is always loaded onto me
Please for once
make a decision
by yourself
Without me
Speak to her
Have a serious talk
An educational discussion
Between mother and daughter
What do I know what about
But please
just for once
leave me out of it

DANIELA: That's not right
You distort things
You just see them from your own
narrow point of view
You make it much
much too easy on yourself

At best she meets her father
at breakfast

HEINZ: Tonight I'll be home
            for instance

DANIELA: Forced to more or less

HEINZ: I have a job
            Please don't forget that

DANIELA: And a thousand other
            voluntary obligations
            which are more important to you
            than your own family

HEINZ: My freedoms
            my modest
            little freedoms
            I won't let anyone
            take them away from me

DANIELA: And what freedoms
            do I have

HEINZ: Only those
            which you
            take for yourself

DANIELA: With you
            none at all
            With you
            I've got
            no room
            to move

HEINZ: A stupid idiot with a vacant grin

who studies the sports pages
smug in his family's lap
no doubt you'd prefer someone like that
Please
Don't kid yourself
Don't fool yourself
If anyone it's me
who's being neglected
But I don't complain
I don't get upset
You keep me short
so short
Have you heard me
moan about it once recently
I gave up
reproaching you
for that
long ago

DANIELA: With which once again
we're onto our old subject
There where everything begins
and everything ends
Every argument
leads to your obsession
with bedroom frustration

HEINZ: Not even once in weeks

DANIELA: Once a month
we have a sermon
on sex on the agenda

HEINZ: I am a man
A man with
normal needs
But nothing

Nothing at all
I gave up daring to dream
about you taking the initiative
long ago
Silly old me
always starting another
laughable attempt
And yet again
I stumble
fall flat on my face
Because she either squeezes
her legs together
or she says
she is tired
What should I do
I ask myself
Cry
or throw up

DANIELA: Really
you are
pitiful

HEINZ: I don't want to hear any more
               about it
           As I said I don't complain
           I've come to terms with it
           and I won't let myself be drawn into
           any more discussions

DANIELA: Try to remember
           Focus your mind
           Which evening
           last week
           were you
           at home

HEINZ: Here we go
Always the same
One can't
talk to you
Impossible
A factual discussion
you aren't capable of that
You digress immediately
You change the subject
as it suits you

DANIELA: Precisely that
Heinz
precisely that
is the subject

HEINZ: No

DANIELA: Precisely that

SILVIA: (*enters from the bathroom, sits at the table*)
We've got dictation today

DANIELA: Die is spelled

SILVIA: d-i-e

DANIELA: and past tense

SILVIA: d-i-e-d

DANIELA: to dye red

SILVIA: d-y-e

DANIELA: and past tense

SILVIA: d-y-e-d
            If I get
            an A today then perhaps
            I'll get a B
            on my report card
            I didn't wet my bed
            on purpose
            Daddy
            honestly

HEINZ: Please may I now
            think through my music lesson
            just for a few seconds
            would that be possible
            please
            I can't put on a run-of-the-mill lesson
            for the inspector
            I must present something special
            Above average
            Not a watered-down
            hackneyed
            bloodless
            Anton Bruckner
            I want
            to elicit
            special facets
            of this romantic
            monster-composer
            I don't like him
            but I have to act
            as if I am
            devoted
            only to him
            and to his music
            Awakening the pupils' interest
            and keeping it alive
            Things like that

were once
my professional ethic
Unfortunately today
they are so uninterested
Today your father
is going to be assessed
and wants to distinguish himself

SILVIA: Really Daddy
it is not
my fault

HEINZ: It's all done with
All forgotten
As long as it doesn't
happen again
Tonight
I'll be at home
No tea
no water
no juice
No fluids for you
after five
I'm going to
make sure of it

SILVIA: (*to Daniela*)
Won't you
be here tonight
at all

DANIELA: Even your daughter
is amazed
when I set aside
an evening
for myself

SILVIA: But I can't

do my math
And tomorrow
there's a geography test

DANIELA: This time
like it or not
your father
will have to help you

HEINZ: Of course of course
we can manage
We two Silvia
Daddy and you
we'll have a nice
evening together

SILVIA: No mummy
please stay here
stay with me

DANIELA: Well we'll see

HEINZ: No we won't
We won't
see
anything
First you complain about
your lack of space
now you've got it
and you're dithering already
Otherwise your mother
will be grumpy
Right
Lets go now

DANIELA: Silvia quick
Schoolbag lunch

	Daddy is in a hurry
SILVIA:	I'd rather go alone I'm meeting my girlfriend
HEINZ:	Out of the question Hanging around with these louts in the park and pawing each other I know all about it
DANIELA:	(*to Heinz*) Go now
HEINZ:	Yes yes
SILVIA:	Bye bye mummy
DANIELA:	Be good Bye bye
HEINZ:	This kissing and cuddling you shouldn't even be thinking about that Bye bye

Scene 2

HEINZ:	(*sits at a desk over a pile of exercise books.* *Talks to a full glass of wine*) What do you say? There is nothing more annoying than scribbling away in someone else's exercise book

with a red pen
This one here lacks any imagination
but who can collect all their thoughts
in a mere fifty minutes
Above all this girl
despite the greatest effort couldn't
    guess
what would be acceptable and please
her dear teacher
at five in the afternoon
Perhaps two hours ago
grandmothers and horses
would still have interested me
Now unfortunately
I find it very difficult
to get excited
about such banalities
They don't get me going at all
so to speak
Or this one here
he's told me
yesterday's soap opera
He couldn't give a shit about the topic
Main thing is
to get rid of his TV rubbish
And I am called upon
to put the fateful mark
under this tediousness
(*to the wine*)
Friend
give me
some advice
An A or an F
A C or a D
You say B
In all earnestness you say B
That puts me

in an awkward position
But wait
we'll straighten it out
In vino veritas
Let's not ignore
that
(*pause*)
Once there was a feeling between us
of being in love
That has subsided
as time led to habit
Two people worn in
We fit together
like the shells of an oyster
As one half opens
so does the other
And the closing too
takes place
at the same time
well almost
(*pause*)
Idealism
means nothing to me
Life is
a rubbish heap
and if you find
something usable
then that is good
After all
you get a broader perspective
over the years
One matures
from soldier
to strategist
Behind us
spontaneity
before us

only
the intellect
One becomes reasonable
instead of now and again
getting thoroughly mad
for once
The only sloppiness
on my desk
is a glass of red wine
The paper is neatly stacked
and the fountain pen is to the right
on its own immaculate sheet
That's how it is
That's what one becomes
(*to the wine*)
Everything under control
except the future
Where it will draw me
Where it will lead me
One should not
hope for
too much
Will one
be asked
to pay
Will one
be held
accountable
The question of responsibility
God after all
Judgment day
I say my conscience
must decide
I alone
Whether I may
Whether it should be so
Whether I do the right thing

We all have a skeleton
A skeleton in the cupboard
Should anyone come forward
unstained
untarnished
then I would be the first
to put the stone
into his fist
I admit nothing
No confession
no court
no authority
I'm not up
for discussion
Addle your brains
about something else
Terrorism
for example
Ecology
The world economy
The Third World
Something really
stinks there
I on the other hand
am clean
HE is my witness
Nevertheless
for the broad masses
The stake would be
my only rightful place
Tie me to it and light the fire
And the sober citizens
warm themselves and applaud
Good fine if that's what you want
Lets fold our hands
across our stomachs
Discipline gentlemen

Tied down pigeon-holed
penned-in what the hell what
   the hell
Hey you don't you spread your legs
since that is frowned upon
Don't go to all that bother
with your charms
I don't even want to get in
because I am tamed
like all the others
Don't you know lovely lady
we prefer
the illusion
of the screen
to the reality
of our dreams
Our desire seeks
a fulfillment
at the movies
There we fantasize
what could be possible
what must
be possible
must
(*to the wine*)
Yes yes
you and I
we know
we would gladly
wear beards long ones
like the hippies
and hats like artists
and braces
and buckled shoes
conceal nothing anymore
hide nothing anymore
certainly not

various depravities
I love my daughter
What is so bad
about that sentence
I love her
and I need her
like the bread I eat
(*pause*)
I know full well
I should be
more adult
We accept
the atrophy of the libido
One has to cope with
sexual impoverishment
I don't teach biology
for nothing
Sex education
Vagina
for example
Everything in great detail
How one does it
How it functions
They carve cunt
into the wood
of their desks
while I
in all openness
reveal the processes
of fertilization to them
One has to proceed
cautiously in this
Anything but harm
the child
in its childishness
That would be awful
We would regret that

bitterly later on
Far too many wounds
are irreparable for life
The ignorance
of those involved in the bringing
    up of children
is a
never-ending problem
And yet
childish naiveté
exerts
a deep
fascination
on the adult mind
There is
a wisdom
hidden there
which we
cannot outdo
She is
so far ahead of me
I would like to look
behind her eyes
and guess
what goes on in her
and grows
and takes shape
If she senses anything
She scares me
She will inform on me
confront me
hate me
To say nothing of
her mother
Above all no traces
no clues
no indication

We must stay above suspicion
Not even the shadow of a doubt
I fear chance
Chance
is a dangerous
insidious swine of a thing
Especially the child
One single mistake
I don't
want to think
about such a disaster
For my wife
the greatest betrayal
She would never
be able
to grasp it
I could
lose everything
It must not
come to light
(*occupies himself with an exercise
    book*)
A catastrophe
That's detective inspector
and not detective inspecter
(*counts the mistakes*)
One two three three and a half
four five six seven
eight nine ten
Spelling, barely passing
Content well
let's say a C
Expression
(*closes the book, reads the name*)
Mühlberger
(*laughs*)
Mühlberger What

should I give you
Well today the inspector
wrote me an outstanding report
therefore in honor of the occasion
let's just scribble satisfactory
under Mr. Mühlberger

SILVIA: (*coming home*)
            Hi daddy

HEINZ: Nearly half past five
            my girl
            It's almost dark
            outside

SILVIA: Youth Fellowship
            every Wednesday
            From four to five

HEINZ: Did you come home
            alone

SILVIA: A few kids came
            some of the way with me

HEINZ: And were there boys

SILVIA: No

HEINZ: Of course there were boys
            what else

SILVIA: No daddy
            definitely not

HEINZ: You don't tell
            your father

          barefaced lies
          like that
          After all
          we do worry
          and you hang around
          with shady characters

SILVIA: But we only chat to each other
          Surely one is allowed to do that
          We don't do anything
          Nothing bad anyway
          We only fool around

HEINZ: You what

SILVIA: Fool around

HEINZ: Nothing but dirty thoughts
          in the heads
          of these youths
          You are too precious to me
          for that
          It's got absolutely nothing to do
          with being too strict
          There probably isn't a father
          more tolerant than I am
          I mean well toward you
          There is no more delicate stage
          in a person's life
          than the awakening of the body
          Stirrings timid and strange
          a bewildering phase
          Hm you
          us two
          daddy
          and you
          So now

                    quick march
                    into the bathroom
                    Take off all
                    those things
                    and wash away
                    the dirt

SILVIA: What dirt
                    I have to wash
                    my hands
                    nothing else
                    that's enough
                    And then I've got
                    to do my homework
                    English German Geography

HEINZ: And Math yes yes
                    that comes later later
                    It's unhygienic
                    absolutely unhygienic
                    to spend the evening
                    with the dirt
                    of a whole day on you
                    So now hop into the bath

SILVIA: Always the same
                    When mum is out
                    I have to bathe
                    Always Just because of you
                    I always
                    have to smell good for you
                    and be beautiful
                    and clean
                    I'll bathe
                    before I go to bed

HEINZ: Clean yourself

and right now
do you hear

SILVIA: Do I have to
Do I
really have to
(*goes into the bathroom*)

HEINZ: And your things
stay in the bathroom

SILVIA: Why

HEINZ: This answering back
all the time
Because they are dirty
obviously

SILVIA: They are not dirty

HEINZ: And this snapping back
Always this answering back
and this snapping back
I say those things are dirty
And I say they are staying in the
bathroom
You will undress down to the skin
Down to the skin Naked
That's exactly what I want

SILVIA: (*scurries naked out of the bathroom.
Makes for her room*)

HEINZ: Stop

SILVIA: Daddy no
I'm cold

HEINZ: Beautiful child
             stay there
             come to me

SILVIA: No
             (*runs into her room. Slams the door*)

HEINZ: (*after her. Flings the door open*)
             This is
             an open home
             We do not hide from each other
             Besides you don't slam the door
             in your own father's face
             People
             lock themselves up
             fence themselves in
             and then they get
             lonely and ill
             I bought you something
             I've got a present for you
             (*gives her a pair of black, lace panties*)
             Exquisite and expensive
             Made of the finest
             the finest of all materials
             Hear how it whispers
             My lady
             come
             make yourself beautiful
             for your lover
             Put them on and no argument
             (*closes the door. Goes into the bathroom.*
             Examines Silvia's clothes. Looks at her
             panties. Holds them up against the light)
             You'll be sorry
             if I find
             one
             spot of

strange sperm
(*smells them*)
No
nothing
(*looks at the clothes*)
Were you
in the woods

SILVIA: Hide-and-seek

HEINZ: Well well
Hide-and-seek
at dusk
One doesn't need
much imagination
to work out
what actually goes on
Catholic Youth Fellowship
don't make me laugh
They lie
on top of each other
in the fields
Touching each other
Groping each other
Carrying on with their love-play
Insatiable mouths
Hungry lips
And the feel
of nakedness and skin
They drive themselves
crazy
Over-hasty and eager
One has to rein them in
stop them
drag them back to earth
We mothers and fathers

> we mustn't
> lose track of things
> Where is she then
> I am ready
> I am ready
> beautiful child

Scene 3

(The living-room. Ambience of dusk. Silvia, wearing the black panties, which are too big, and a vest. Heinz with a rifle.)

HEINZ: *(touches Silvia's bottom with a pointed finger)*
            There
            Exactly
            That is
            the spot
            Not to miss
            that is
            the first rule
            I would
            hunt with a passion
            with a passion
            (aims the rifle)
            Through the heart

SILVIA: Geography test daddy
            I have to study
            like mad
            At least fifteen pages
            And I can't
            make any sense
            of it

HEINZ: A rifle

is a
dangerous weapon
My forefinger
Sensitive
like a speedometer needle
Between the eyes
a hole
Your head
breaks apart
Silvia an
immense force
The top of the skull
in a thousand pieces
awesome
Not for a roebuck
and certainly not for a stag
On no account
damaging the skull
We are after
the trophy
But humans
don't even have
the tiniest antlers
Next to the skull
of a deer
the human head seems
ridiculous
Colorless
pale
Practically
featureless
We don't
even have
little antlers
Don't go

SILVIA: I am
terribly cold
It's boring too
I'm going to get dressed
You've got to help me
you promised mummy
you would

HEINZ: (*puts a red light-bulb into the desk lamp*)
In a moment Silvia
in a moment you'll feel warm
(*turns the light onto her*)
What do you say now
Don't turn away
I want to see you
(*turns all the other lights off*)

SILVIA: Turn it off daddy
Please stop it
Where are you
Where are you

HEINZ: Here we go
here we go
Your vest
come take it off

SILVIA: I'll catch
cold

HEINZ: Off with it

SILVIA: (*takes the vest off*)

HEINZ: Silvia
our sex show

we'll put on
our own sex show

SILVIA: But I don't want
to put on a sex show

HEINZ: Mouth open
your tongue
stick it out

SILVIA: Why

HEINZ: Quiet Stop it
I give you presents
reward you
Slip you pocket money
And you
you get
impudent
My expensive
little lover
take care
don't go too far
Don't play with fire
I am not going
to be let down
It is strictly forbidden
to disappoint me
most strictly
most strictly forbidden
Now then
mouth open

SILVIA: (*opens her mouth*)

HEINZ: Tongue

SILVIA: (*sticks out her tongue*)

HEINZ: Move it

SILVIA: (*moves her tongue*)

HEINZ: Your hand
               in your panties

SILVIA: (*puts one hand into her panties*)

HEINZ: Come on
               Touch yourself

SILVIA: (*moves her hand*)

HEINZ: And
               Is that good
               Does that excite you

SILVIA: Don't know

HEINZ: Between your fingers
               Do you feel anything

SILVIA: Only my hand

HEINZ: Excite
               It has to
               excite you
               Arouse
               You have to
               arouse yourself
               arouse
               Come Go on

SILVIA: Yes daddy yes

HEINZ: (*opens his trousers*)
            Your tongue
            must rotate
            properly
            And wet
            you have to be wet
            my love
            Kneel down

SILVIA: No daddy no
            I'm not going to do that
            Not again
            I won't take him
            in my mouth

HEINZ: Strictly forbidden
            I said
            No disappointment
            Of course we'll take
            him in our mouth
            Look here
            Look at that
            How he's already waiting
            for your lips
            for your teeth

SILVIA: I feel sick
            I'll throw up

HEINZ: Kneel down

SILVIA: I won't take him
            I just won't
            take him
            in my mouth

HEINZ: It's quite easy

and tastes lovely
Silvia lovely

SILVIA: Please leave me alone
You always do things
like that to me
Things I don't want
things I don't like

HEINZ: Stay there

SILVIA: Your dick
I don't want it anymore
Never again never again
Your dick it smells
And you you smell too
You smell of shit
of shit and piss
Go away
Go away from me
right now
(*runs into her room. Slams the door*)

HEINZ: Good then
No problem
Fine
Just stay in there
Such a narrow-minded
squeamish prude
We'll just leave it then
Your mother
In one hour
Pity
You've brought it
upon yourself
I'll have to tell her unfortunately
When she finds out

what her precocious little hussy
has been up to and how she's
       carried on
and that with her own father
My dear that won't be
much fun for you
She'll probably
throw you out
Your own choice
what can I do
The decision
is entirely up to you

SILVIA: (*comes slowly out of her room*)

HEINZ: Luckily we humans
are equipped with something
generally described as
common sense
You won't get away
from me
Hiding
is useless
I'll
get
you
Silvia
Anywhere
anywhere

Scene 4

(*Corridor in Silvia's school. Daniela sits on a chair in front of a door. Smokes*)

HEINZ: (*just arriving*)

What's the matter
What's this all about

DANIELA: About Silvia
That's all I know

HEINZ: You call me out of class
just for that
During a lesson
That's too much

DANIELA: I'm sure your pupils
will be able to cope
I'm not going to face
disturbing news
about our child
on my own

HEINZ: What did she say

DANIELA: That it is urgent
and important and serious
That she has to talk
to you and to me

HEINZ: I'll have to make up
the lesson
I can't walk out
just like that
Anyway what can it be
Something trivial
You alone
that would have been enough

DANIELA: Official phone calls
drive me
half crazy

I need
your support
I'm nervous
I'm worried

HEINZ: Now now
What can it be anyway
That she wets the bed probably
        so what
We found out about that
a long time before
this doctor
On account of
a trifle
a colleague has to
step in for me

DANIELA: You will be kind enough
to go in with me
I need you
It is about our daughter
not just about mine
Let's hope
that it's nothing serious
Let's hope
that I really did call you away
from your lesson
for nothing

HEINZ: We'll deal with it
don't worry
I'm only saying
it was a bit awkward
I love you
We'll see
in a minute or two
Something harmless

certainly nothing more
School doctors are in general
pretty frustrated people
They just like to make themselves
important

DANIELA: I'm not certain of that
It calms me down
when you are with me
Nobody can know
what lies in wait for us

HEINZ: I know about these things
They only examine
superficially
Mouth open–Aaahhh
Size weight
Maybe she hasn't
grown enough
Or too thin
Or too fat
But darling
we're not going to let
something like that
upset us
Are we supposed to wait for her here

DANIELA: She is in there

HEINZ: Should I knock

DANIELA: I don't know Knock

HEINZ: Good I'll knock
(*knocks*)

DOCTOR: (*opens the door*)

Ah yes good morning
You are Mr. and Mrs. Lehner
I have been
waiting for you
Please sit down

DANIELA:　My husband
I got hold of him
straight–away

DOCTOR:　What it's about
to put it bluntly
and without
beating about the bush
I have
examined Silvia
A matter of routine
I had already
seen her several times
Straight–away I thought
something is not right here
a woman's instinct
if you like
that is I am certain
well your daughter
that is she is
well she is pregnant

HEINZ:　She is pregnant

DOCTOR:　Everything points to it
I asked her
she's stopped menstruating

DANIELA:　Of course
You are right
The periods

DOCTOR: Consequently I examined her
           rather more thoroughly
           Her vagina
           I have to tell you
           that inside
           really
           she indicates considerable abuse
           She is far too young

DANIELA: The periods
           Now that you
           say it
           My child
           What
           We must
           A mistake

DOCTOR: I take it that
           that your daughter
           that an adult
           With some brutality
           Otherwise
           it would not be possible

HEINZ: That's crazy
           absolutely crazy
           To have this
           thrust in my face
           All of a sudden

DANIELA: Not a word
           Not a single
           word

HEINZ: This is madness
           This is madness
           This is sheer madness

DANIELA: She trusts me
Why didn't she say anything
Out of the blue
We don't know a thing

DOCTOR: But there must have been
a change
in her behavior
recently

DANIELA: A change in her behavior
She locks herself in when she showers
She is modest very modest
Somewhat obstinate that certainly
Withdrawn But then that's normal

DOCTOR: You can't always be there
watching over your child
Have her constantly under control
There are changes of course
She is reaching puberty

DANIELA: Such a thought would never
occur to you
You'd never imagine such a thing
It's in the papers every day
But not your own child

DOCTOR: You have nothing
to reproach yourself for
Think about it
Perhaps you noticed
something

HEINZ: We have nothing
to do with the matter
Not to blame No Not to blame

You must understand
I am an educator A teacher myself
We have always brought up our child
quite freely
but also
not without
a certain strictness
Why me
Why me
Why should this mad thing
happen to me

DANIELA: Someone who
molests children
Warped perverted
through and through
An animal

DOCTOR: The police
they must be informed
immediately

DANIELA: The pig

HEINZ: Just a moment Stop
Let's not rush things
Let's not do even
more damage
Doctor you are setting
such a pace
You'll run
over the child
I say
Take care Slow down

DOCTOR: Your daughter
someone has to talk to her

I wasn't in the position to do so
Besides it would really be better
if you undertook it yourselves

HEINZ: I'll be
            the first
            who talks to her
            Me
            (*to his wife*)
            You would
            break down
            One has to keep one's wits
            about one

DANIELA: The child
            carries a child
            around
            in her

HEINZ: No reports nothing
            First of all a talk
            Between her and me

DANIELA: An abortion
            We must make
            a decision

HEINZ: As always
            you are too hasty
            much too hasty
            One thing at a time
            I have always been
            a vehement opponent of it
            The unborn child
            No one has the right
            and so on and so on
            At a stroke

My position
has changed
Now I am
personally affected
As a father
so to speak

DOCTOR: With the best will in the world one
               can't say
            what is easier to cope with
            for a twelve-year-old girl
            An abortion is no child's play

DANIELA: And she doesn't even know it yet
            Her childish mind
            She won't be able to grasp it
            Such a pig
            Such a disgusting
            filthy pig

HEINZ: Daniela

DANIELA: Such a disgusting
            and rotten
            Such a perverse
            filthy pig

HEINZ: A homeless person
            a derelict
            perhaps

DANIELA: Or someone
            whom we meet daily
            whom we greet kindly
            It could also have been
            someone like that

DOCTOR: As far as I
            am able to judge

he has had repeated intercourse
with her

DANIELA: Then she must know him

HEINZ: Not at all
Not at all
she doesn't have to know him
Please let's not
get carried away
with totally obscure
assertions
On every corner
In every doorway
Strange faces
Dark figures
Open the newspaper
Not a day
without one serious crime
No one is safe
from things like that
By our very nature
evil
lies dormant in all of us
So it could have been
anyone
really anyone
He lies in wait for her
pounces
and disappears
as if in that moment
he hadn't ruined
the life of a child
That's
how complicated
how difficult

how confused it is

DANIELA: A criminal

HEINZ: A criminal yes
             Or a person
             who happens to commit a crime
             who sort of
             stumbles into a crime

DOCTOR: We're not going to have
             any sympathy for him
             that's for sure
             The principal's office
             I'm going to
             inform them

HEINZ: Out of the question
             You will
             inform nobody
             You are bound
             to observe confidentiality

DOCTOR: Also bound to report it
             If I think it is
             in the best interests of the child

HEINZ: In the best interests of the child
             One punishment one punishment
                 on top of another
             Another smack on the head
             It will get blown up and built up
             Get out of our hands Make headlines
             and get sensational above all
                 sensational
             They'll swoop like vultures
             on this story
             A sexual assault

You could talk for hours
about something like that
arouse suspicion make assumptions
Malicious
nasty gossip
Running the gauntlet

DOCTOR: I must report it

DANIELA: He must
be given
no peace
The principal's office obviously
The police as well obviously
He will stand before me
and I will look him
in the eye
I will look this brute
in the eye
I want to know
I must know

HEINZ: Where is she

DOCTOR: In class

HEINZ: You are right
of course
absolutely right
Right now
I can hardly
think clearly
Let me
see to everything
Me
Me of course
I must keep

track of things
Above all with Silvia
I must
talk to her

DOCTOR: If you need anyone
I'd gladly offer my service
And take your daughter to a
    gynecologist as soon as possible

DANIELA: I have tried
to imagine it
I'm sweating
all over
I feel sick

Scene 5

TEACHER: (*entering a class*)
All rise
Well what a lazy bunch
we have today
Good morning Sit down So then
Where is the register Good thank you
We'll take it later
Leave your exercise books closed
    for the time being
To begin with we have to have
a talk about a matter
which concerns the girls above all
You see something has happened
While I am speaking I want
complete silence
Well then on TV and in the papers
we hear again and again more's
the pity

of so-called sexual assaults
and of so-called sex-offenders
We are dealing here with men
Sick men
who make approaches to women
and also to girls
sexually molest and even attack them
and this can lead to so-called rape
These men have a deficiency
physically as well as psychologically
in short they are not normal
and that's exactly why they
are dangerous
You are still young and in
    every respect
at the beginning of your development
You need time to discover yourselves
Sexuality is an important part
of our lives and deserves
to be treated with circumspection
I know that and it is to be hoped
    that you do too
but there are people
who do not respect this
They cannot control
their urges
Cannot satisfy them in the usual
normal way
This is pitiful and terrible at the
    same time
For example he places himself in
    front of you
and hangs out his equipment
Takes pleasure
in masturbating in front of your eyes
or wants you to touch him
Or they ask you to come for an

ice-cream
you think nothing of it and get in
    the car
suddenly you find yourself alone
    with him
on a secluded road
you have to strip naked
so that he can interfere with you
so to speak
Stand up at once Are you stupid
    or what
What is there to laugh about
It really is most stupid to laugh
about such a delicate and difficult
    matter
The last row doesn't seem to do you
    any good
What a clod Did I say you could
    sit down
You are not in kindergarten
any more my friend
I'm breaking a promise for you
I shouldn't utter a word a syllable
I'm only doing this because the
    matter is so serious
and children anything but funny
It directly concerns
a girl from this school
This should put all of us all of us
on the alert
No not from your class Fortunately
I am not allowed to give the
    name away
A tragic and terrible story
But please you don't know a thing
You must give me your word on that
Good then Once more Suppose

a strange man approaches you
Don't take any presents Don't let
   him paw you
Don't get in a car Call for help
   at once
And no miniskirts
No tight pants
When this man's been caught
you can indulge your vanity again
Good Then I'll stop on that note
And you can sit down again
Take out your exercise books
Turn to page forty-seven
in the text book

Scene 6

(*at confession*)

PRIEST: Oedipus stands as an example
      when dealing with the excesses of
         childhood fantasy
      Psychology offers several
         explanations
      My child you've dreamt all this
      It does happen that dreams
      in their vividness and intensity
      attain the character of reality
      But please Let's keep our feet firmly
         on the ground
      It should not and could not have
         been like this
      Mind you seldom as exaggeratedly
      as in your case

SILVIA: But it's true

I am not lying to you
There's no one I can talk to
I am not allowed to say anything
But you can't
hide it from God

PRIEST: I am sure that our dear Lord
values your father just as I do
as a thoroughly decent man
Committed and full of integrity
Charismatic in his dealings
    with people
So be careful my girl with your
    accusations
We all know that much grief has
    befallen you
But think it over compose yourself
At your age without exception every
    man is a father
Your father stands for a man as such
Despite your inner distress one must
    not be tempted
to bear false witness

SILVIA: He did
get into
bed with me
He did put on
sex shows
with me

PRIEST: There are things
which are
better not addressed
They are not meant
for the ears of strangers
it is better to

keep them to oneself
He has got into bed with you then
And Was that all

SILVIA: No

PRIEST: What else

SILVIA: He stroked me

PRIEST: Where

SILVIA: Everywhere

PRIEST: Where everywhere

SILVIA: Everywhere

PRIEST: Down there too

SILVIA: Yes down there too

PRIEST: You were dressed

SILVIA: No mostly not

PRIEST: Naked

SILVIA: Yes

PRIEST: Completely
Completely naked

SILVIA: Yes

PRIEST: And what else

SILVIA: He stuck it
inside me

PRIEST: You mean that he
            actually
            You and he in fact

SILVIA: He stuck it
            inside me
            Often
            Sometimes even
            two three times a day
            but only
            when mummy
            wasn't there

PRIEST: Now stop this fantasizing
            That's enough It is almost
                unbelievable
            what can get into children's heads
            You surely don't want to plunge your
                father into the deepest misfortune

SILVIA: No Father

PRIEST: Then keep quiet

SILVIA: But I have to
            tell the truth
            He who lies at confession
            commits a great sin

PRIEST: There is truth and there is truth
            Let's just hope that the Lord our God
            forgives you your unclean thoughts
            Really slowly I am getting very angry
            Who do you think you are my girl
            To do the most wicked harm to your
                father
            The fourth commandment you walk

all over it
No You're not going to lead me onto
    thin ice
with your stupid depraved ideas
How can I give you
my blessing
wilfully ignorant thing

SILVIA: I had to put on
                special underwear
                black with lace
                I am his lover
                you see
                We two
                daddy
                and I
                we are
                real
                lovers

PRIEST: He may be it is quite possible
                going through a personal crisis
                Midlife crisis He's too young for that
                but he's heading that way
                Some earlier some later
                In women my child it's called
                      menopause
                where by and large
                only the body changes somewhat
                while the man finds his whole
                      existence
                looming up in front of him
                He questions the meaning of life
                Has one wasted squandered one's
                      talents
                Taken up one's chances
                What else may one

expect from life
A deep-reaching
existential crisis
Don't provoke him
Keep out of his way
Avoid the opportunity
And don't get yourself lost
in untruthful false stories
Do you hereby repent your sins
now and evermore
before the Lord our God

SILVIA: I repent

PRIEST: Three Our Father
One Hail Mary
But don't simply rattle them off
my girl With reverence
And extend my best wishes
to your dear father

Scene 7

(*the principal's office in Silvia's school*)

HEINZ: (*with a newspaper*)
Here it is
In black and white

PRINCIPAL: I instructed the teaching staff
to observe absolute confidentiality
I regret this indiscretion
A grave error
It's a bit awkward for me too

HEINZ: I'll hang
your regrets

over my nightstand
And your awkwardness
moves me
to tears
My trust abused
grossly
most
grossly
Hours and hours
in this office
with you
What for
I ask you
what for
An affront
A disgrace
You swore up and down
Your word of honor
As principal
of this school
Here read Go on
Your word isn't worth
a thing
Not a damn thing
What are you waiting for then
Put me out
of my misery
and my daughter
my daughter as well
Cornered
finally cornered
He feels as though
there were a thousand bars
and behind those thousand bars
no world
Rilke knew it
Prurient journalism

Leering reporters
From today
a single topic
My wife
she read the paper
this morning
Nervous breakdown
Went into shock
You carry
the responsibility
in every respect
Thank you so much

PRINCIPAL: You can leave my office
at once
if you're going to take
this tone
Not with me
my dear colleague
I fully understand
your agitation
Your manner however
impossible impossible
It's not acceptable my dear colleague
It's just not acceptable Not with me
Pull yourself together
Get a grip on yourself
The language of street kids
A respectable man like yourself
No Sit down
I appeal to your sense of reason
Sit down I said
Actually I should be in class
I'll ask a colleague
(*goes out briefly. On entering . . .*)
Besides the name's been changed
Nobody knows who it's about

even now
and that's what it comes down to
   doesn't it

HEINZ: Reporters are bloodhounds
Papers are shit

PRINCIPAL: There must be a leak
I don't know where
it just happened
The story also has
something positive about it
An outcry
A warning
We cannot
We must not
simply
keep
such a serious crime
quiet
On the contrary
It has to come out
It must be made public
A duty
my dear fellow
especially for us

HEINZ: They'll soon have the name
quick as a flash
Please let's not underestimate
the power of curiosity
A feast
for the masses
In a few days
everyone will know all about it
Pointing their fingers
Stopping and whispering

A raped child
an outcast
My family and I
we'll become famous
All this I owe to you
to you

PRINCIPAL: A misjudgment my dear fellow
You are ignoring the seriousness
    of this as a whole
For the public at large The other
    pupils and their parents
A child molester
A child molester is running around
    free
A pervert An animal
Unpredictable Dangerous Crazy
Quite possibly
he'll grab another child
tomorrow
And the day after
the next
Do you want to be held
responsible for that
I know you a bit oh yes
Drowning in self-reproach
and unable to bear
your own reflection in the mirror
that's my prediction
Just because for once you were un-
    willing to jump over your own shadow

HEINZ: I can't sleep any more
I lie in bed
with open eyes
and I can see
no way out

Why me
Why me of all people
So many
get by
without even
a stumble
Every day
smooth and even
To pick me
out of countless
possible others
I don't believe
in coincidence
They're shoveling
shit on me
Why No idea
It is how it is
They're sticking
the knife into me
I must get through this
I must get through this
In secret
I always believed
in an ideal world
That was a mistake

PRINCIPAL: How is your daughter
Has she even halfway
A stupid question Of course not
Good thing she's going to school
That will give her something else to
    think about
Even before she was a very quiet
a rather shy girl
Hardly any contact with boys
which always surprised me
It's going to be difficult for her

but she'll manage
We will all help each other

HEINZ: She doesn't say a thing
              Doesn't speak a word
              Keeps her silence
              She guards her secret
              like a treasure
              The man wasn't only
              rough with her
              She likes him
              One feels that

PRINCIPAL: For God's sake
              the things you say
              Such fatalism
              She is protecting him
              He has bent her
              to his will
              Who knows with what
              Who knows with what
              sordid tricks
              One can quickly get a child
              on one's side
              You don't have to be
              too clever for that
              But she has to talk to us
              she has to

HEINZ: She doesn't have to do anything
                  Anything
              Just so that's quite clear
              Nobody's going to force her to do
                  anything
              The psychological pressure
              An enormous burden
              For Silvia practically unbearable

We're going to give her time
As much as she needs
I am not
in a hurry
I am not
Only with patience
with thoughtfulness
I won't allow
anything else
The case will
resolve itself
Or maybe not
Or maybe not
She will not be questioned
in my absence
No psychologists
No lawyers
I am the only person
she trusts
I will protect her
I am her father

PRINCIPAL: Fifteen years ago
my daughter
was about the same age
In spite of everything you are
in a way
remarkably calm
and controlled
Who knows how I
If like you I
Presumably
No certainly
quite certainly
I am capable of it
I would have hunted him down
like a cur

beaten him to death
and broken his neck.

HEINZ: We are different
             I respond in another way
             I don't make
             rash judgments

PRINCIPAL: A child
             A girl
             Your own
             daughter

HEINZ: Put yourself
             in his shoes

PRINCIPAL: I will not do that
             With the best will in the world
             I couldn't do that

HEINZ: Of course you can
             Try it
             You won't even
             you won't even try
             How's he supposed to
             defend himself then
             How's he supposed to
             fight back then
             How's he supposed to
             explain himself, then,
             if nobody gives
             him a chance
             He risked everything
             everything
             He still
             hasn't lost
             Or has he

No
not yet
he hasn't
lost yet
He hasn't
lost yet
not
yet

Scene 8

(the family at dinner)

SILVIA: In German
the teacher
wrote
something
in my book
She said
I'm doing well

DANIELA: That's lovely
Show me

SILVIA: *(brings the book)*
No there
on the
next page

DANIELA: I am very pleased that Silvia
is studying well even now
What's that supposed to mean
EVEN NOW

HEINZ: Has she actually written
EVEN NOW

Give me the book
EVEN NOW
That just can't
be true
Studying well EVEN NOW
They all know about it all of them
Why not posters then
banners placards billboards
Why not splash a tin of garish paint
over the child
Put on show at lunchtime
in the middle of the playground
for an hour a day
Silvia What do you say to that

DANIELA: Leave her alone

HEINZ: And underneath the inscription
            VIOLATED

DANIELA: Be quiet

HEINZ: Taking great relish
            in the misfortune of others
            Did I not predict it
            Did anyone believe me
            Nobody nobody Everyone pigheaded
            pigheaded bent on getting their
                own way
            Just eat Finish your soup
            But don't burn your tongues
            Let's act as if we hadn't
            just had confirmation
            that God and the world are fully
                informed
            The sparrows are singing it from
                the rooftops (*It's all over town*)

and only we carry on as if nothing
   had happened
And how is the food Are you
   enjoying yourselves

DANIELA: Let's just be glad that she's good
   that she studies and gets good marks
   We'll buy you a dress Silvia tomorrow
   for doing so well or some tights or
      a sweater
   Do you want more soup

SILVIA: Yes but more noodles please
   Not a dress mummy
   Tights if anything

DANIELA: Has anything come to you in the
   meantime
   Can you remember anything

HEINZ: A little bit of cheese
   A little bit of cheese
   is enough Silvia
   and the mouse
   is in the trap

DANIELA: You are nasty
   nasty and mean
   I'm not going to let myself
   be insulted
   What am I doing to her
   What am I doing wrong
   With who else but me
   should she talk to about it
   I am being neither loud
   nor am I being aggressive
   I don't push her

I don't force her
Now and again
I allow myself
to ask her
But I mayn't
even do that
because he
for whatever reason
doesn't like it
You are overwrought Fine
You are angry Fine
You are in despair Fine
but I am all of that
as well
For heaven's sake
we can't just bury
ourselves up to the ears
in the debris
and wait for better times

HEINZ: This continual dissecting
            This incessant interrogation
            It torments her It hurts her
            Against every basic instinct
            you trample all over your daughter

DANIELA: It's your behavior Heinz
            I don't understand it
            What's the matter
            What has happened
            Why won't you let me
            do as I want
            Why do you constantly throw yourself
            between us like a barrier

HEINZ: Was it dark Silvia
            or was it not

SILVIA: It was dark

HEINZ: Go to your room
             I have to explain something
             to your mother
             (*Silvia goes into her room*)
             The fact is that it was dark
             Do you follow me this far
             (*he turns off the light. Dark*)
             Go on then What's wrong
             Describe me Come on
             Clothes Features
             Color of hair Height
             Age Weight
             Am I a foreigner
             Am I from here
             I don't hear anything
             You are so quiet
             Strange
             Why this
             false modesty
             Why do you hesitate
             Let fly my darling
             This filthy pig
             we've got to get him
             The sooner the better
             (*turns on the light*)
             If we ourselves
             with our adult eyes
             with our heightened
             and subtle powers of perception
             are not in the position
             to distinguish
             one thing from another
             And here is a child
             Rigid with fear

Highly distressed
But that is not enough
Once more a
violence is done to her
Brutal Without any heart
Her head
Her mind
Would she
kindly remember
Provide pictures
Descriptions
detailed accounts
But it's just
not possible
It won't work
She did not
see him
She couldn't possibly
have seen him
The crime was
committed at night

DANIELA: As if I am an idiot
As if I am an idiot
Tries to teach me
as if I couldn't
add
two and two
Up against a barrier
for days
You shut yourselves
off from me
Silence Taboo
Don't touch
Don't disturb
Keep your hands off
The child

of course
I don't blame
the child
But that you
can treat me so shabbily
disturbs me
hurts me
alienates me
You're evading me
You keep out of my way
Like a beaten dog
sometimes
What are you scared of
I really don't mean
any harm
Nor am I asking
too much of anyone
My daughter
has been raped
How soberly
one can say it
Since then
I have had nothing but that
on my mind
I can
think
of nothing else
dream
of nothing
else
You know
terrible
pictures
day
and
night
It haunts me

Won't let go
of me
And then
there's you
you abuse me
treat me like a
stupid cow
and you say in all seriousness
I hurt her
deliberately
I am thoughtless
you say
What's actually got into you
What do you think
you are
Who do you think
you are
My God you are not
above everything
Why don't you
help me
Why do you leave me
so alone

HEINZ: Please forgive me
I am sorry
I really didn't
want to
Calm down
I am sorry
Whatever happens
We two
We'll stick by
each other
yes
(*Pause*)
I have

to do
my utmost
My mind
To seize To grasp
My little head
Look my hands
they're shaking
One can actually
watch
as everything
slips out of their grasp
I can relate to
objects
to form to contour
What I have to deal with here
is amorphous
One can't get hold of it
It slips through my fingers
Wait a moment What
What should I say
Not a slip
Not one slip I
don't want
don't want to
lose everything
(*opens the door to Silvia's room*)
Come Sit down
with us

SILVIA: I don't want
you to quarrel because of me
I don't want you to quarrel
at all
You've got to get on
with each other
You have to be nice
to each other

DANIELA: We'll clear the table
               We might just find something sweet
               for the three of us

SILVIA: As old and as tall
               a bit like
               daddy mummy

HEINZ: She's not going to school
               tomorrow
               I'll write her
               a note

SILVIA: But daddy never
               comes into my room

HEINZ: Like an elephant
               No sense of tact
               Studying well even now
               An impudence

SILVIA: Mummy daddy never
               comes into my room

HEINZ: You could go mad in this house
               Not one second to catch your breath
               If no one asks you
               don't give an answer
               Please we have to
               open the windows
               To a question which hasn't been put
               one does not give an answer
               The air is so thick in here you could
                  cut it
               When was this place
               last aired properly

What do I mean the windows
The doors too
The doors and the windows
Open everything
We must have fresh air
fresh air
Don't you notice
how hot Stinking hot
I'm sweating like a pig

DANIELA: I closed
the windows only
a few minutes ago
Something at least
The height is important
Are you certain

HEINZ: Wanted
the tall stranger
The enemy The criminal

SILVIA: What flower would you like to be

DANIELA: No flower Silvia

HEINZ: Steals by night
through the alleys
Stalks up on
little girls

DANIELA: No flower

HEINZ: The police are after him
We must catch him
This animal This pig

SILVIA: A rose with a thorn

or a blue Forget-me-not

HEINZ: Air air
Open a window
It's close
Terribly close
There's absolutely
no doubt
it's close
hideously close
awfully close in here

DANIELA: If you wish we can
air the place anytime
anytime

HEINZ: And above all the mess in here
Doesn't anyone see Like a pigsty
    everywhere
I insist I insist on cleanliness
You don't put the spoon on the table
The spoon belongs in the bowl
In the bowl I said
You don't throw your bag into just
    any corner
Why do we have a proper place for
    school bags
It belongs there and nowhere else
Do it now
Do it right now
Isn't asked and gives an answer
That's impertinent and stupid
You only answer when you're asked
Do you finally get that
Can you finally get that into
    your head

SILVIA: Yes daddy

DANIELA: Your head Heinz
               Your head will give me
               an answer
               I have a question
               for you

HEINZ: I Me
               A question for me
               Go on Just ask
               Ask away everyone
               Why not Please
               I am at your disposal
               Just ask
               The spotlight
               The spotlight Go on
               On me please On me
               The cross-examination Faster
               Where are my shoes
               Bloodhounds Bloodhounds
               I'll say no more
               Where are where are they
               I must get some air
               Now the conspiracy
               has begun
               No what am I saying
               has gone on for some time
               A man You get
               a man in your sights
               you line him up
               for
               the kill

DANIELA: Be quiet
               Shut your mouth
               Quiet Quiet

Enough Finish
I hear your voice
I hear your words
but I can't
understand a thing
not a single sentence
nothing nothing
it's crazy
What is being talked about
We've lost track
What is being talked about

HEINZ: What about what about
We are talking
You're not
listening to me
We are talking
about fear
about persecution
About manhunts
about lynching
I know what people are like
They are stubborn
Stubborn and stupid
A picture of the villain
They paint themselves
a picture of the villain
and then they let fly
at this picture
I am not blind
To what happens
happens all around me
I stay alert
Notice everything
Precisely quite precisely
Ridiculous Laughable
After all

I am in no way
involved in
this affair
In no way
As if I
As if I
had anything
to do with it
They encircle me
Push me into a corner
They advance
upon me
Even
within
my own
four walls
I'm warning you
Don't go
too far

DANIELA: The pictures
are crooked
The table
I've got to
hold on to it
The ground
is shifting
Silvia go
Silvia go
Go to your room
immediately

SILVIA: I am scared
mummy
I don't want
to be alone
Mummy

we've got to
stay together

DANIELA: There is something
I don't know about
There is something
being kept from me
There's a secret
which laughs at me
from every corner
of the room
The cupboard the clock
the floor the door
the chairs the table
the curtains everything
everything everything
mocks me
Fool
Idiot
Like a cat
thrown
into water
It seems
I should
be ashamed
but of what

HEINZ: I am cold

DANIELA: You wanted to go out
Your shoes Heinz
Put them on then

HEINZ: I don't feel like
going out any more
Silvia please close
the windows

DANIELA: They are closed
             The windows are closed

HEINZ: But the door
             the door is open
             Silvia please close
             the door
             the temperature
             is dropping
             In the evening you can feel
             the autumn
             One shouldn't
             waste heat thoughtlessly

DANIELA: They forecast
             rain

HEINZ: And fog

DANIELA: Fog too

HEINZ: In the
             low-lying areas
             It does you good
             to talk
             things through
             To call things
             by their proper name
             Find common ground
             don't you think

DANIELA: Probably yes
             If one does
             call things by their proper name
             I am going to knit
             Knit and think
             Knit and think

and ask myself
questions
which will be
a wasted effort
because
I don't know
what the answer is

Scene 9

(*Silvia's room. The bed, in which Silvia is sleeping. On the floor Mutzi, a doll. The door is opened softly. Heinz comes into the room. He sits on Silvia's bed. Looks at her. Carefully pulls back the cover. Unbuttons her nightdress. Touches her breasts and caresses them.*)

SILVIA: (Sleepily)
             Mutzi
             Daddy

HEINZ: Don't wake up
             Go on sleeping

SILVIA: Take your hands away daddy
             You mustn't do that any more
             You'll go to jail
             It's forbidden
             Go back
             to mummy

HEINZ: The eyes of the whole town
             are closed
             Only we two
             are awake
             only we two

SILVIA: Not just any man
           You daddy you
           it was you

HEINZ: Shift over to the wall
           Daddy's cold
           Let me in
           That's all That's all
           I'm proud
           of you
           You're brave
           very brave
           We two
           Silvia
           we won't
           give ourselves away

SILVIA: Go to mummy
           Mummy
           is sad

HEINZ: I've only
           come
           to see
           how you are
           Whether you're
           asleep
           Whether you're
           having bad dreams

SILVIA: Your dick
           you want to
           stick it into me
           again

HEINZ: One doesn't say
           dick

SILVIA: We all say
           dick
           in my class

HEINZ: It's nice
           and warm here
           with you

SILVIA: Your hands
           are so cold though
           I just about
           freeze to death
           when you
           touch me daddy

HEINZ: (*puts his hand over her mouth*)
           The ears Silvia
           Think of the ears
           One false ear
           in this night
           one sound too many
           one word too loud
           then it is finished
           then it is over
           They'll nail
           your father
           to the cross
           Beat him
           till he's bloody
           battered and sore
           Do you see
           this hand
           Look
           at it
           Has it ever
           beaten you

Watch out
Be on
your guard
Black and blue
that's
a promise
Don't play
with fire
A tall
dark man
that's all
No one needs
to know more
More
is
dangerous
I love you
Come
touch me

SILVIA: Your dick
is all
bent
and small

HEINZ: You can easily
make it harder
yes like that
that is
good
Close
your
eyes
Think only
of me

SILVIA: You are

                     squashing
                     me

HEINZ: Let yourself
                     go
                     Let's both
                     abandon ourselves
                     I'm already
                     quite dizzy
                     Desire is like
                     a top
                     We're lifting off

SILVIA: I can't
                     breathe

HEINZ: Quick
                     your legs
                     open them

SILVIA: No
                     Please no
                     My feet
                     they're stuck
                     together
                     today

HEINZ: Nothing's stuck
                     Come on
                     open them

SILVIA: Pregnant
                     Daddy
                     You are
                     so heavy
                     Leave me alone
                     Leave me alone

Please
Go away
My feet
Together
Tied together
I don't
want you

HEINZ: And how
            you want
            me
            I have
            always
            been gentle
            with you
            You would like
            to be
            begged
            Then I'll just
            nibble away
            at your
            thighs
            caress them
            and kiss them
            And then
            I will take you
            as I have
            always
            taken you
            (*lies on her*)

SILVIA: Ow you're
            hurting me
            Ow Don't
            Go away
            That tears

HEINZ: Don't yell like that
            Shut your mouth
            Don't spoil
            it for me
            Move them apart
            I said

SILVIA: You can't
            just get in there
            like that
            It hurts
            so much

HEINZ: (*Puts the pillow over her face. Fucks
            her. Comes quickly. Pulls the pillow away*)

SILVIA: Help
            I just about
            suffocated
            You're mad

HEINZ: Are you
            going to
            shut your
            trap
            now
            Are you going to be
            quiet now
            Quiet
            Quiet
            I
            said
            (*rolls off her*)

SILVIA: You just don't
            know
            how it

burns

HEINZ: If you
resist it
then
it hurts
Your fault
If you didn't
freeze up
it would be
quite easy

SILVIA: I'm all
torn apart
down
there

HEINZ: Come on
Nothing nothing
is torn apart
What could
be torn
You're being
pigheaded
pigheaded
and stubborn
It has to
give you
pleasure
You have to
let yourself
go
You can't
do that
Unfortunately
you are incapable
of that

even though we've been
working
at it
for so long
More sensual
Silvia
You still have to
become
far more
sensual

SILVIA: The sheet's
            wet

HEINZ: You've
            wet
            the bed

SILVIA: No
            I
            haven't
            You always say
            I
            wet
            the bed
            But this
            this is
            something else

HEINZ: That
            happens
(gets up. Turns on the light. Goes outside.
Comes back with a glass of water. Pours it
over the spots. Wipes it with his fingers)
            I'll make sure
            that your mother
            doesn't make

too much of a fuss
in the morning
(*lifts Silvia into the bed*)

SILVIA: But I can't
            lie
            in
            the wet

HEINZ: Cover yourself
            well

SILVIA: Where is
            Mutzi

HEINZ: (*turns the light off. Sits down on
            the bed*)
            In the
            darkness
            everything
            changes
            life
            the world
            Every night
            I find myself
            in the grip
            of a dream
            I can't
            resist
            it
            The dream says
            Get up
            Go to her
            Quick
            Move Hurry
            She is already sick with longing
            And in her mouth

> runs the water of lust
> The young breasts they tingle
>   with desire
> They thirst for you Come get up
> Between the thighs a sweat
>   breaks out
> Juicy and hot Get drunk on it
> I hear the voice What should I do
> Unbearable the bad conscience
> Compassion Fatherly feelings in fact
> which change of course mingle
> One is human A man
> At the mercy
> of this inscrutable night
> With force virtually
> it drags me
> from my bed
> into the cold
> I have to come to you
> I have to Silvia
> I love you
> More than any
> other woman
> It is dark
> The darkness
> is my mistress
> because she makes this love
> possible for me

SILVIA: My Mutzi

HEINZ: (*kisses Silvia. Takes her hands. Puts*
          them around his neck. Moves them
          so that they stroke him)
          Come your lips
          Move your mouth
          Be quiet

I heard
something
No nothing
Probably
the wind
Kissing
with the right intensity
has always been
your weakness
You move
your mouth
when you
kiss

SILVIA: My Mutzi
is gone

HEINZ: The wood
sometimes
the doors creak
by themselves
Don't let
your thoughts
wander
Wood breaths
Wood is alive
That's normal
quite normal
What's wrong
with you
You're
rejecting me
You put me aside
like a
broom
What's got
into you

A whore
in a
brothel
kisses better
than you
no matter how expensive
or how cheap
but while I
explain to you
how it works
how one
does it
you are
somewhere else
far away
from me
In your head
no place for me
any longer
I'm not going to be
humiliated
by you

SILVIA: I'm not going
             to bed
             without Mutzi
             She can't
             sleep
             without me

HEINZ: A bundle of rags
             thrown down
             somewhere
             Under the bed
             what do I know
             I'm fed up
             with this

SILVIA: She's scared
            without
            me

HEINZ: The hell
            the bloody hell
            she's scared
            Mutzi Mutzi
            A scrap of cloth
            Eyes of glass
            No soul
            No heart
            I thought
            you were
            big
            a grown-up
            a mature
            woman
            to be taken seriously
            Infantile
            in reality
            A child
            nothing else
            (*tries to kiss her*)
            Don't turn
            away
            Open your mouth
            more
            Your breasts
            The nipples
            They're
            getting hard
            Quiet Listen Noises
            What's happening
            A door
            Footsteps
            quick ones

Someone's
moving through
the rooms
She's awake
She has been
listening to us
Where could
she be going
Delivered
Relieved
Freed
At last
A weight
is lifted
from my chest
Another
bears down
I am
guilty
guilty
A door
slams
shut
I
need
you
My
knees
Hold
me
tight
Come
back
I
beseech
you
Come back

Scene 10

(Silvia alone. She is lying in bed. Darkness)

SILVIA: Mutzi
Mutzi
where
are
you
Come
Come
to me
Cuddling
We love
each other
Wet
you are
wet
You've wet
the bed
all over
from top
to bottom
Don't
cry
There's
no need
to cry
We won't
get cross
Mutzi
make yourself small
Careful
Quiet

Don't
be scared
I'll stay
with you
You laugh
You laugh
We two
Mutzi
we two
we'll
go
away
Just
us
two
To the
lions
Mutzi
and to the
monkeys
and to the
squirrels too
My feet are itchy
(*scratches herself*)
What yours too
Yours are
itchy too
(*scratches Mutz*i)
There
There
There aha
There it's
good
Is that good
when Silvia
scratches
you

(*flings Mutzi against the wall*)
Phew Phew
you stink
Of shit
Of piss
You stink
A child
nothing else
You must
be
more sensual
Be
sensual
right
now
Quiet
Not a word
Not
a single
word
(*lifts her hand*)
Do you
see
this
Has it
ever
beaten you
Black and blue
that's a
promise
(*aims at Mutzi with her index finger*)
Between
the eyes
Blood
Mutzi
Blood
Are you going to

play with me
(*lies on the floor*)
I am
muck
I am
muck
Help Mutzi
my feet
my feet
are stuck
together
I can't get
my feet
apart
any more
Don't
Please
Don't
Don't
Don't
tear them apart
Hands
Everywhere
Hands
It won't
go
I don't
want to
Torn
apart
(*curls up*)
My nose
My eyes
My mouth
All stick
My hands
Stick

Together
Open
them
(*rolls around. Tries to free herself. Pushes
against the wall. Kisses herself. Licks
herself. Strokes herself. Bites herself.
Scratches herself. Beats herself*)
I
am
ugly
At last
so
ugly
that I
disgust
him
that he'll
never look at me
again
that he'll
never touch me
again
that he'll
never
lie on top of me
again
that he'll
never
push himself into me
again
Go away
Please
Leave me in peace
at last
You've
wet
the bed

once again
Mutzi
But Silvia
won't be
cross
She
won't be
cross
Don't be
frightened
Don't be
frightened
(*takes scissors. Cuts Mutzi into pieces*)
We'll
hide
ourselves
Mutzi
We'll
make
ourselves
small
small
very
very
small
And then
a horse
will
come
a
white
horse
The horse
belongs
to us
We'll
sit

on
it
and
ride
away
just
us
two
without
any
saddle
And the
horse
Mutzi
it
knows
where
you
have to go
Simply
away
Far
away

CURTAIN

Friedrich Ch. Zauner

A Handful of Earth
A play in five scenes

Translated by Agnes Bernelle and
Johannes Mattivi

Cast

Rowena Gresham
Charles Gresham
Virgil
Raymond
Selma
Fanny
Miller's voice
Farm hands

The play is set at the turn of the century

The Set

The large parlor in the Greshams' house.

The room is furnished with massive dark furniture which clashes with the rustic architecture. This makes the room look pompous and uncomfortable. Even when the furniture and the piano are rearranged the feel of the room is not changed. A grandfather-chair has had wheels added to make it into a wheelchair. Two portraits of distinguished-looking elegant ladies are the only decoration on the wall. A large map dominates the room. On the map thick red lines represent the constantly shifting borders. The map is worn and yellowed with age. A piece of red chalk is dangling on a string, conveniently ready to use.

Scene 1

Charles is sitting in his wheelchair and seems hardly aware of what is going on around him. Rowena is rearranging the furniture. She is struggling to carry a heavy chair from one side of the room to the other. She checks whether the chair looks better in different places. She is not sure.

ROWENA: (*to CHARLES*) What do you think? (*no reaction*) Doesn't that look better?

She does not seem to expect an answer. After a while she turns the wheelchair around so that Charles faces in the right direction.

ROWENA: I don't know ... and if I move the big cupboard over there ... (*she points*) then where do I put the piano? How was it at your aunts' house? (*tries to remember*) Yes, the big cupboard over here ... (*comes back, gives the wheelchair a thoughtless push so*

*that it moves aside; not with emphasis but in a mat-
ter-of-fact tone).* Oh you . . . you couldn't care less!

*ROWENA starts to move the heavy cupboard by herself.
She is obviously very strong and gives the impression that
she is used to doing everything herself.*

ROWENA: (*walks to the door and opens it slightly*) Raymond! I need you!

*She walks back to the cupboard. She has already moved
one side quite a bit from the wall but realizes that she cannot manage without help.*

ROWENA: (*back at the door, shouts loudly*) Raymond!

RAYMOND enters. He is a calm, introverted young man.

RAYMOND: What?

ROWENA: Where were you?

RAYMOND: In my room.

ROWENA: Are you deaf? Do I have to yell my head off?

RAYMOND: I was reading.

ROWENA: (*grunting*) Uh! (*already back at the cupboard*)
Come on, give me a hand.

RAYMOND: (*annoyed*) Not again . . .

ROWENA: We'll move it over there.

RAYMOND: What's the point?

ROWENA: Just give me a hand! It doesn't look right here.

*They lift the cupboard and move it a bit. Raymond obvi-
ously has more difficulty lifting the piece of furniture than
his mother has. They rest a moment.*

ROWENA: There's more light over there. We'll be able to
see it much better. It cost us enough, after all.

They resume pushing it.

ROWENA: (*gasping*) I paid as much to move this furniture from Salinas as I pay a cowhand for a whole year.

They rest again.

ROWENA: It'll look much better over there.

RAYMOND: Maybe . . .

ROWENA: (*unsure*) Don't you think so?

RAYMOND: I don't know.

ROWENA: I don't know! I don't know! Is that all I ever hear from people in this house? No one ever does any thinking around here! No one ever does anything! Everything is always left up to me. And who do you think I'm doing all this for? For you. For my children. So that one day you can have a better life. Selma is the only person I can rely on.

RAYMOND: Selma isn't here.

ROWENA: I know that. As I said, no one here to help me. Grab hold.

They continue to move the cupboard.

ROWENA: (*while carrying, with strained voice*) I have a letter from her.

RAYMOND: From Selma?

ROWENA: Hey, watch out, don't damage the edge!

They put the cupboard down.

ROWENA: There's no one in the whole neighborhood who could repair such a piece of furniture. The cabinet-maker down in the village is a boozy good-for-nothing. You wait and see, one of these days he'll manage to make even three-legged milking-stools wobbly.

RAYMOND: I didn't damage it.

ROWENA inspects the edge. She runs her finger over it.

RAYMOND: Wouldn't it have been more sensible to empty it out first?

ROWENA: Why?

RAYMOND: It would have been easier to carry.

ROWENA: You're strong enough for that, I hope.

They grab hold of the cupboard again and move it to the wall. On Raymond's side it starts to topple over.

ROWENA: Hey, watch out!

The cupboard is against the wall.

ROWENA: My God, what a dummy you are!

She inspects the position of the cupboard.

ROWENA: A few inches more to the left.

They move the cupboard to the left. ROWENA takes a step back to look at the new arrangement. The wheelchair is in her way; she pushes it aside.

RAYMOND: Can I go now?

ROWENA: You'll just ruin your eyes with all that reading. (*referring to the room*) So, what do you think? (*addressing the father*) Charles? Eh? It looks better now, doesn't it? (*to Raymond*) Since you happen to be around, the piano has to go over there. (*while she is talking she pulls on the curtains a few times*) New curtains wouldn't be a bad idea, I think . . . (*she has picked up the letter*) Have you read it?

RAYMOND: No.

ROWENA: (*reads*) "Dear mother, beloved family! I can only assume that you haven't received my last letter, or is there another reason for your silence? . . ."

She writes well. But, then again, we are paying a lot of money for her education.

RAYMOND: Didn't you answer her letter?

ROWENA: I never had the time.

RAYMOND: In two months?

ROWENA: Well, and then, you know, I'm a bad letter-writer. (*she tries to find a certain passage in the letter*) Here . . . you could have answered her letter as well. Here. It says: "Why doesn't Raymond write anymore? His letters were always so nice." You see? "My friends, too, always liked it when he talked about life on the farm, when he . . ."

RAYMOND: She reads her letters to other people?

ROWENA: Looks like it. . . . "when he talks about the changes. It must be exciting at your place!" Imagine, she says that and she lives in a town! "I'd hardly recognize you and the house. It seems to have gotten so large and elegant. Or was Raymond exaggerating?" She'll be surprised when she comes home next year from school. "I can see the whole landscape clearly before my eyes, the hills in the west, the alders by the ravine where we so often used to play 'mommies and daddies' when we were children. The beautiful horses on the Enfield pasture . . ." (*moved*) She has indeed become a lady but she hasn't forgotten us farmers out here. (*she walks over to CHARLES*) Wouldn't you agree, Charles, not even the aunts could write such letters?

RAYMOND: The aunts don't write us at all.

ROWENA: (*pointedly ignores that remark*) At the end she says we should send her pictures of ourselves. Imagine that! And she asks (*turns to CHARLES*) how father is doing these days.

RAYMOND: I don't know if I'd recognize Selma after all these years even if I bumped into her somewhere.

ROWENA: She has surely changed. Of course . . . but you would recognize her, no doubt, you would see that she is a Gresham like you. And you would see that she is different from all these farm women around here.

CHARLES: (*not immediately and without connection to the previous remark*) You don't know that—what are you talking about?! You haven't seen her since she was fifteen.

ROWENA: She attends one of the best Swiss boarding schools.

CHARLES: (*without connection*) A letter from time to time . . . Words . . . What does she write?

ROWENA: She asks how you are doing.

CHARLES: How can somebody be doing who is confined to a wheelchair?

RAYMOND: Why didn't you send me to school?

ROWENA: What sort of school?

RAYMOND: Any sort of school.

ROWENA: That's different. You're a man. But what would become of a girl in this wasteland out here? Cut off from all culture. What can a girl make of herself here? No company. I told Selma: I'll pay for the most expensive school for you, but don't you dare come back until you are as distinguished and educated as your aunts. (*points at the two portraits on the wall*)

RAYMOND: They've opened a new school in Milford, I read about it in the newspaper. They offer courses

on how to farm, how to achieve a better yield, how
to improve the soil, and all that . . .

ROWENA: (*interrupts him*) If only you wanted, our farm
would offer you enough opportunities to prove that
you've grown to be a man at last.

CHARLES: (*seems not to have listened to the dialogue*) Tell
her that I'm sitting in my wheelchair, that I'm
thinking, that I'm growing old, that I'm thinking
and that I'm watching my decay . . .

ROWENA: Nonsense, you're not older than I am and you
feel splendid.

*She pushes the wheelchair aside and starts to move the
piano.*

ROWENA: (*to RAYMOND*) Grab hold of it. Don't make me
ask you twice all the time. Over there!

*They push the piano to the designated place. She scruti-
nizes the new position.*

ROWENA: (*abruptly*) Did you get the sugar?

RAYMOND: What sugar?

ROWENA: I told you yesterday to get a bag of sugar from
the store in town.

RAYMOND: You didn't tell me that.

ROWENA: Oh, come on! You never listen to a word I say.

RAYMOND: I don't remember you saying anything about
sugar.

ROWENA: Always arguing! Always contradicting! Always
pretending to know better! Do you want to drink
your coffee without sugar?! All you've got on your
mind is reading.

*She is irritated because the room does not look any better
after the furniture has been rearranged.*

ROWENA: (*trying to persuade herself*) Yes, good, it was a good idea to move the cupboard over there. (*silence*) Looks much better now. (*silence*) It gets more light and doesn't look so massive. (*silence*)

ROWENA abruptly turns to CHARLES.

ROWENA: I'm sure you remember, Charles. What did it look like at your aunts' place? It's the same furniture. Even made by the same cabinetmaker! You must remember. Why do you always leave things to me? Why should I always be the only one who cares? (*with bitter scorn*) Your aunts could afford to spend their time embroidering daisies on velvet, playing the piano and reading poetry. I never learned to play the piano. I didn't have the time for things like that. I remember, once I saw these two aunts (*in crudely malicious tone*) well, their carriage-horse bolted. They were traveling without a coachman. Some loud noise must have frightened the horse. They weren't able (*with emphasis*), together they weren't able to grab the reins . . .

Some noise can be heard outside the door. ROWENA is attentive for a moment. When the noise stops, she carries on.

ROWENA: The carriage overturned, they clung to each other and then they were thrown out into . . .

Again some outside noise. She stops to listen. In situations like this she is always fully concentrated.

ROWENA: (*carries on*) They both landed in the ditch, on their starched asses.

She listens, nothing can be heard. She walks out the door, comes back immediately, wide awake, speaks rather softly but with strong intensity.

ROWENA: Push your father into the kitchen.

RAYMOND obeys immediately, does not ask any questions.

ROWENA: You can go to your room and read.

RAYMOND pushes his father outside.

ROWENA: (*following them*) Hey, don't forget to put the book back on the shelf right when you're done with it.

She waits until the door is closed behind Raymond, then she quickly opens the other door.

ROWENA: You can come in now.

The door stays open for a while, then Virgil enters. He has been shot in the shoulder. The wound has been dressed in a makeshift way, but there is still blood on his clothes. He hesitates to enter.

ROWENA: Come on in.

She drags him into the room and closes the door behind him.

ROWENA: Who was it?

VIRGIL: Miller and his foreman.

ROWENA: Did they recognize you?

VIRGIL: No . . .

ROWENA: Are you sure? (*no answer*) Let me see. (*she starts to undo the bandage*)

VIRGIL: Ouch! Be careful! (*he pushes her aside*)

ROWENA: Lie down.

She covers the sofa bed with a blanket first, then she forces him to lie down.

VIRGIL: All because you won't let me carry a gun. Otherwise there wouldn't have been any problem at all.

ROWENA: Hold still. Where did it happen?

VIRGIL: Down in the valley. (*he stifles his pain while his mother takes off the sticky bandage*) By the bend.

ROWENA: On Miller's pasture?

VIRGIL: Yeaaargh. (*the "yes" turns into a suppressed moan*)

ROWENA: Can you move your arm?

VIRGIL: Yes.

ROWENA: Try it.

VIRGIL: I can move it.

ROWENA: Then do it.

She helps him move his arm. This causes him pain, which he tries to suppress.

ROWENA: No bones broken, it seems. (*she continues to take off the bandage*) All because you have sawdust between your ears! How can a man with any brains get the utterly stupid, insane idea of stealing Miller's horses from his own pasture? Didn't I always tell you: further down in the valley! And didn't I always tell you to leave Miller alone, for God's sake! Have I become so old and senile and stupid that nobody's got to listen to me any more?! Why don't I just save my breath? Don't you know that Miller is always watching to find something he can pin on us? Don't you know what sort of lies he spreads about us? He just doesn't have a shred of evidence, that's why (*tears the last bit of the bandage from the wound*) . . . he is so furious.

VIRGIL: I didn't mean to do it, I had already walked past . . . but suddenly this lone stallion appears on the hilltop . . .

ROWENA: That was on purpose, didn't you get that? (*taps her finger roughly against his forehead*) And you,

idiot that you are, were taken in. The wound isn't
that bad after all.

VIRGIL: I was bleeding like a stuck pig.

ROWENA: I'm not surprised. The bullet is still there. (*she
examines the wound closely*) So you think they
didn't recognize you?

VIRGIL: I had my face covered with a piece of cloth to be on
the safe side.

ROWENA: (*not clear whether she refers to the wound or
CHARLES' last sentence*) Mhm . . . well . . .

VIRGIL: They didn't get any closer than forty feet. I turned
around and ran like hell. They shot after me as if
they were hunting a fox. I was hit just when I had
almost made it over the hill.

ROWENA: Did they follow you?

VIRGIL: What do you think? Of course. But, you know, I'm
too fast for them. They didn't catch up with me. And
I threw them off the track as well. I headed towards
the railway and spent some time on the embank-
ment, because there they couldn't . . .

ROWENA: Good. At least you did that . . .

VIRGIL: Then I hid behind a bush.

ROWENA: The bullet must be taken out.

VIRGIL: I can't possibly go to a doctor. As soon as I turn up
there they've got me. The doctor will see right away
that this is a gunshot wound.

ROWENA: Of course, you can't go to a doctor with that.

VIRGIL: I thought it would be best if you give me some
money and I'll go away from here.

ROWENA: A Gresham doesn't run away.

VIRGIL: I'll hide out for a while. Until the dust settles.

ROWENA: Nonsense!

VIRGIL: I'm not about to wait till they put me in jail.

ROWENA: Rubbish!

VIRGIL: It was you who said that Miller wants to pin something on us, he won't give up until he . . .

ROWENA: Miller is a fool! (*walks to the door and shouts*) Raymond! (*she fetches a washbowl with water*) Miller thinks he can set himself up as the number one. He's used to having people crawl to him. Am I a nobody? Just because these fat asses have been sitting on their land for a few generations. (*shouts outside*) And get some rope, too!

RAYMOND's voice: (*from the outside*) What sort of rope?

ROWENA: What sort of rope? For God's sake, rope! Strong rope! From the storeroom.

VIRGIL: What are you going to do? Let me go into hiding.

ROWENA: Nonsense!

VIRGIL: It would be better for all of us. Miller is like a raging bull! Give me some money. You know his reputation. If he's got his mind set on something . . .

ROWENA: (*scornfully*) Eh! Who dressed your wound?

VIRGIL: (*does not answer right away*) Fanny did . . .

ROWENA: Fanny who?

VIRGIL: She's a waitress . . . in town. At the "Coach and Horses."

ROWENA: (*shouts through the door*) Raymond! What's keeping you?

In the meantime she has made arrangements. She has fetched water, bandages, arnica.

RAYMOND enters carrying the ropes. Rowena does not give him time to ask questions.

ROWENA: Tie his legs.

VIRGIL: You . . . are not going to do this yourself?!

While RAYMOND ties VIRGIL'S legs down to the sofa bed, Rowena explains to him what happened.

ROWENA: (*casually*) Virgil was unlucky, he got into a shooting. Some hunters who are roaming around. The bullet is still in his shoulder.

RAYMOND concentrates on tying.

VIRGIL: The old poacher, Joe from Tunbridge, he's been running about with a bullet in his thigh for five years now.

ROWENA: What do you mean "running around"? That's not running! He's hobbling like a cripple!

She is now wholly taken up with what she is doing. The preparations and the operation are carried out without haste, without sentiment and with great precision.

ROWENA fetches the knife and cleans it.

ROWENA: Make the knots very tight.The other arm as well.

VIRGIL: (*whining*) Hey, it's not that bad, it doesn't hurt— I can still have the bullet cut out some time later . . .

He tries to free himself but the knots are too tight. His hatred is directed against RAYMOND, who feels painfully embarrassed by the whole scene. RAYMOND has now also tied down the other arm and is about to leave the room.

ROWENA: (*commanding*) Give him some gin.

Raymond gets the bottle from the cupboard and fills a glass.

ROWENA: More. Fill it up!

RAYMOND holds the glass to VIRGIL'S lips. He drinks.

ROWENA: Drink it!

Some gin runs over his cheeks.

ROWENA: Get it down your throat.

The glass is empty.

ROWENA: Another one.

RAYMOND refills the glass and puts it to VIRGIL'S lips. He cannot drink any more. ROWENA pushes RAYMOND aside, takes the glass away from him and holds it herself. Now, with effort, VIRGIL drinks up the second glass. Raymond tries to sneak out of the room.

ROWENA: (*commanding*) Hold him tight. He mustn't be able to move.

VIRGIL: (*full of fear and helpless rage*) I don't want him here! The ninny! He shouldn't watch this! He's a wimp!

ROWENA: (*shows Raymond the grip*) You have to hold him like that.

VIRGIL: He'll only get sick when he sees the blood.

It is true, RAYMOND cannot bear the sight of blood. He tries to avoid watching and has difficulty fighting his nausea. ROWENA, kneeling on VIRGIL with one leg, makes the first cut.

VIRGIL rears up and screams.

ROWENA: (*to RAYMOND, with intensity*) Hold him tighter, you idiot!

VIRGIL: Stop it, you're slaughtering me!

ROWENA: (*coldly*) It has to be done.

She makes the second cut. Again VIRGIL rears up and screams.

ROWENA: Tighter, God damn it!

RAYMOND desperately holds his brother as tightly as he can, his face turned away. VIRGIL is now screaming incessantly and tries to break free.

ROWENA: (*performing the operation with full concentration*) The bullet is damned deep in the flesh. Thank God, no bones are broken.

She stuffs a piece of cloth into VIRGIL'S mouth.

ROWENA: Bite into it! As hard as you can. Bite into it.

Now the screaming turns into intense groaning. He is still trying to break free. ROWENA attempts to extract the bullet, she is having difficulty, finally she succeeds, triumphantly she holds up the bullet in her blood-stained hand.

ROWENA: There it is! It's over . . . (*with compassion*) It's all over . . .

She fills the glass and holds it to VIRGIL'S lips. RAYMOND needs to vomit, he is feeling sick. ROWENA applies salve on the wound and removes the ropes. VIRGIL rises, his face stained with tears.

VIRGIL: (*with strained voice, towards RAYMOND*) As I said, I knew he isn't be man enough for it.

ROWENA: (*while dressing the wound*) You'll feel better in a minute. It had to be done. You could have gotten blood-poisoning or heaven knows what. Did it hurt very much? You are strong and healthy. That'll heal. You have the constitution of a young ox.

VIRGIL: (*meek and subdued*) I'll never do that again . . . I won't leave the house without a gun again. The swine! They almost killed me.

ROWENA wipes his face. She gives him the bottle.

ROWENA: Go to your room. Get drunk. Sleep. Tomorrow you'll be all right.

Exhausted, the bottle in hand, VIRGIL drags himself outside. When he passes RAYMOND they exchange looks of contempt. RAYMOND lowers his head again; he is still feeling sick. Before he walks out of the door VIRGIL spits into the spittoon beside the door. ROWENA washes her hands.

ROWENA: (*to RAYMOND*) Clear the stuff away.

RAYMOND rests both hands on the sofa bed, his head down; he takes some deep breaths, then he starts to take some of the things outside. ROWENA dries her hands and fetches a deck of cards from the cupboard. She shuffles them with special ceremony.

RAYMOND comes back, pushing his father into the room. Then he takes some more things outside.

His father sits in his wheelchair, hunched over, deeply lost in thought. ROWENA spreads the cards, eagerly waiting to see how they will turn out.

ROWENA: If only one of my sons had a bit more blood in his veins. They are both damn weak-willed Greshams. No guts, either of them. (*addressing Charles*) I don't understand it. Don't we have a right to some happiness? And the spread isn't that good either—

In the meantime RAYMOND lethargically clears away the rest of the things from the room.

ROWENA: If only they had some of my gumption, imagine what they could achieve, especially now . . . Ah . . . With a bit of luck . . . with a bit of brains . . . (*occupied with the cards*) I don't see why unimportant people always have to stay unimportant?! (*to CHARLES*) Virgil's been shot and wounded. Miller is a pain in the neck! If I could get a few hundred dollars together . . . Don't you think we could ask your aunts . . . (*picks up one of the cards*) That means money. (*puts the card down again*) Where from? Just where from . . . I can't expect a single penny from these rotten old aunts. (*she continues to shuffle the cards; abruptly she turns to RAYMOND*) Do you know Fanny?

RAYMOND looks up.

ROWENA: Well?

RAYMOND: She's a waitress.

ROWENA: I know.

RAYMOND: At the "Coach and Horses."

ROWENA: Well, yes. So? Tell me, this "Coach and Horses" . . . what is it like?

RAYMOND: It's a saloon.

ROWENA: What sort of saloon?

RAYMOND: Just a saloon.

ROWENA: What kind of reputation does it have?

RAYMOND: What kind of reputation is it supposed to have? It's a saloon. You meet neighbors. The local people get together when they have business in town or when they are waiting for a stagecoach.

ROWENA: And she?

RAYMOND: She?

ROWENA: This Fanny. Don't be stupid.

RAYMOND: What about her?

ROWENA: What's she like?

RAYMOND: She's nice . . .

ROWENA: (*scornfully*) Nice!

RAYMOND: Friendly. Everybody likes her.

ROWENA: (*scornfully*) Friendly!

RAYMOND: She's really nice . . . Why do you ask?

ROWENA: I mean . . . can she be relied on?

RAYMOND does not understand. ROWENA quickly and carelessly gathers up the cards. Suddenly she is in hurry.

ROWENA: I have to go to town myself.

Suddenly she is very active. She does everything as quickly as possible, yet with full concentration, not nervously. While gathering up the cards she already starts to undress. She always tries to do two things at the same time. She leaves the room.

ROWENA'S VOICE: (*from outside*) Tell Jack to hitch up the horses.

Raymond looks out the window.

RAYMOND: Jack isn't around! He is out in the fields mending the fences.

ROWENA'S VOICE: (*from outside*) One of the hands has to be around!

RAYMOND: Sure!

ROWENA'S VOICE: (*from outside*) Then whoever is there should hitch up the horses.

RAYMOND returns to the window.

RAYMOND: (*shouts outside*) Hey! Hey, you! Mark, hitch up the horses! You hear me? I said hitch up! The small buggy. The mistress is going to town.

ROWENA rushes in. She is half dressed, wearing a dressy skirt. Her girdle is open at the back.

ROWENA: (*while entering*) Hey! Don't shout out the window like a lout! Do me up at the back.

RAYMOND pulls the strings of the girdle tight.

ROWENA: Tighter! Is the skirt all right? Can I go out like this? What do you think? Pull really tight. I won't break. Tighter!

RAYMOND pulls as tight as he can. He puts his knee against her back for more support. The girdle is now so tight that ROWENA is hardly able to move.

ROWENA: (*takes a few deep breaths*) I've put on weight. (*crudely*) Damn!

She wiggles the upper part of her body to adjust the girdle.

ROWENA: Too fat! Too old! Too flabby! Damn!

She takes a quick look into the mirror. Then she puts on her blouse and tucks it into her skirt. In the meantime she is looking for her handbag.

ROWENA: Don't let anyone into the house while I'm away. Understand? (*she is already at the door, turns around*) How do I look? (*she does not wait for an answer*) Don't let anyone in! And don't talk to anyone. Understand? Not to anyone, no matter who it is!

SCENE 2

CHARLES is sitting in his wheelchair. RAYMOND is sitting sideways on the piano-stool tinkling clumsily on the piano with one finger. He plays simple tunes slowly, sometimes he does not know how to continue and changes abruptly in the middle of a tune.

CHARLES: (*talks monotonously, without any particular emphasis, without involvement; sometimes he pauses, he seems to have lost his train of thought*)

I've made plans, you might still find them in one of the drawers . . . of how to irrigate the land. There are some springs further up, did you know that? You would just have to make use of the natural slope. All the small farmers working on their few acres could grow vegetables and sell them in town. The soil is good, fertile. (*pause*) Everything grows upwards from below, it is so natural that we forget about it. Upwards from the mud, the earth, the dirt . . . never the other way . . . only we humans always do everything the other way. (*pause, he takes a few breaths*) Perhaps my system is not perfect, I'm not an engineer, and of course something like that can't be put into practice by a few individuals. All the neighbors would have to work together.

RAYMOND: Something has happened to Virgil, he's been hurt. Mother is doing her best to keep it a secret from us. As if you could keep something a secret that is already the talk of the town. Do you know, father, what a reputation we Greshams have? Why, we can't show up anywhere without having people huddling together and whispering behind our backs . . . When I go to the saloon, nobody wants to sit at my table, apart from . . . Fanny perhaps . . . because she is not from here . . . and since she is a waitress . . . she isn't very much respected by the people either . . . And I hardly go out with the hands anymore . . . I see the farmers standing behind their windows with angry expressions on their faces because they are afraid our sheep could stray into their fields again and they couldn't do anything about it . . .

CHARLES: You have to teach people. They have forgotten that the land is their partner and that it is alive, like the animals, like the human beings. They come from the towns, they have lost their jobs, they are hungry. They think that once they've bought a piece of land they have only to wait until the ripe fruit hangs down into their mouths. You can't learn how to plow overnight. They don't know how to breed animals, how to plant and cultivate trees. (*pause*) The land is good. And there is enough for everybody. (*pause*) You can't just chop down the trees that are in your way and drive the sheep onto the meadows where they eat all the good grass and ruin the soil. You can't just force your will on nature with impunity . . . (*he seems to have lost the thread. Pause*) I don't believe that paradise was only located between the Euphrates and the Tigris. It was once everywhere. And we haven't been driven out with flaming swords, but people have just stopped being aware of it.

RAYMOND: I hope you know how mother raises the money for her wheeling and dealing? She sends Virgil out to steal horses! She bribes the clerk, so that he allows her to look into the land register. The other night I caught her coming home with Virgil, both of them spattered all over with mud. She tried to make me believe that they had made some repairs on the dam. In the middle of the night, without the farm hands. She must think I'm still a child. They had moved boundary stones. They had stolen a piece of land from the neighbors. (*waits for a reaction from CHARLES which does not come*) Now Miller has caught Virgil red-handed . . . Father, why did you let all this happen?!

CHARLES: (*silent for a while, finally*) We got married secretly, your mother and I. My aunts would never have allowed me to marry a woman like Rowena. She was a factory worker's daughter, she didn't have any education—it wasn't her fault—and not a penny of dowry could be expected. I was entitled to inherit this small farm here from my grandparents. It had been leased and was in a terribly dilapidated state. It seemed that we would hardly be able to make enough to keep body and soul together. It is difficult to imagine now what this place looked like then. Your mother possessed little more than the clothes she was wearing, and all we had got from my aunts as a wedding present was their portraits. When we arrived here, it was in the evening, the sun was low, there hadn't been any rain for weeks, the grass was dry, the soil had deep cracks, it almost made me cry. But your mother said: here's a piece of land, we can make something out of it. Her hands were like chisels. We spent our wedding-night repairing the broken windows. The next day we started to change the floor-boards. Since we didn't have any lumber we took whatever wood we found, and we didn't think twice about it. When we were hungry we went poaching or stole eggs from the neighbors' chicken-coops. Two people must have a roof over their heads, they need food and a piece of land under their feet. How were we supposed to survive? Your mother was pregnant with your brother. (*he is silent for a while*) Have you ever watched that? When a bird finds a place with food it takes some of the grains or seeds and flies away. It doesn't take long before you see a whole flock of birds on the place. I don't know how useful it is to ponder over things instead of doing them. There would be so much to do. I wouldn't have enough hands to do it all.

RAYMOND: I would like to go to the small farmers and show them how to improve the cultivation of the land. I have read all of your books and I think . . .

The door opens and ROWENA enters. RAYMOND stops in mid-sentence.

ROWENA: Stop tinkling on that piano!

She slams the piano lid down. RAYMOND has to withdraw his hand quickly to prevent his fingers from being caught.

ROWENA: You can't play it. You'll only ruin it.

She is in a good mood, carrying some parcels under her arm.

ROWENA: Lend me a hand with these. Don't stand around like a stuffed dummy.

RAYMOND lends her a hand. ROWENA starts to take off her shoes. She has difficulty bending over, Raymond kneels down to undo the laces.

ROWENA: I have been to the land registry. I have registered your share of the pasture in your name.

RAYMOND: I'm not twenty-three yet.

ROWENA: Who cares? I'm your mother, I carried you and gave birth to you. You are as old as your mother says you are.

She pulls her blouse over her head.

ROWENA: Untie this instrument of torture.

RAYMOND unties her girdle.

ROWENA: (*takes a few breaths*) Ooh! Ah! That's tight. (*she moves the upper part of her body and frees her breasts with her hands*) Heavens, this thing is suffocating me. Ooh . . . To hell with the guy who invented that. I can't understand why women put up with it. (*she sits down and stretches out her legs*) Well, I can't wear it for a whole day, from morning to night. (*Suddenly she stands up. First she grabs the wheelchair and pushes CHARLES outside, then she comes back, walks over to the map and*

draws a new border with powerful strokes) This is
your land. (*RAYMOND does not react*) Look. Look
at it.

RAYMOND: Oh well, there! It's practically desert. What
grows there, anyway?

ROWENA: What does it matter?

RAYMOND: Mostly weeds. The soil is practically worthless.

ROWENA: (*busy drawing the new lines, finally*) All the
same! It's land! You are entitled to have it. Every
cattle breeder is entitled to his share.

RAYMOND: I'm not a cattle breeder.

ROWENA: And it costs next to nothing.

RAYMOND: I don't have any money either.

ROWENA: (*matter-of-factly*) You must not forget to dig a
well. It'll be enough to knock a piece of pipe into the
ground. As long as it looks like a well. So that you
don't lose your rights.

RAYMOND: If I want a piece of land I'll choose it myself.
And I will certainly not choose such a wasteland,
hardly good enough to feed a goat. The soil is all
sand. The lizards bask in the sun on the stones
there. I know that area. The soil is as barren as an
old woman, there's not even grass enough for cattle.

ROWENA: (*hands him a piece of paper*) Sign it.

RAYMOND: What is it?

ROWENA: The confirmation of a gift.

RAYMOND: What gift?

ROWENA: (*points with her finger*) There. Come on, sign it.
There.

RAYMOND: Why?

ROWENA: To make sure that that land reverts to the Greshams.

Raymond signs the paper.

ROWENA: (*looking over his shoulder*) In case something happens to you . . . You never know, do you? (*tersely*) No, don't enter the date. (*she quickly grabs the paper from his hand*)

RAYMOND: You can have that wasteland right away if you want, you just have to tell me. I don't claim it.

Rowena roughly yet cheerfully taps against his forehead.

ROWENA: Numbskull! Doesn't anything strike you? (*no answer*) Well? (*she leads him over to the map*) Haven't you got eyes in your head? Well?

RAYMOND does not understand.

ROWENA: (*taps the flat of her hand against his forehead*) You still don't get it? Nothing strikes you? Don't you see where that land is? (*she points on the map*)

RAYMOND: It borders the Hanson farm.

ROWENA: And that farm . . .?

RAYMOND: . . . is next to Miller's.

Rowena bursts into coarse laughter.

RAYMOND: (*then*) So what?

ROWENA: (*cunningly*) I thought while I was there . . . I slipped the land registration officer a few dollars, and he let me glance at the register. (*pause, with a delighted grin on her face*) The Hanson farm is mortgaged to the hilt.

RAYMOND: No! You haven't . . .

ROWENA: I had my right of first refusal confirmed.

RAYMOND: Mother!

ROWENA: I can beat the price down. For a few hundred, at most a thousand dollars that place can be mine.

RAYMOND: Don't you ever get enough?! What do you gain from this . . . place?

ROWENA: Hey, now! Just because you haven't got eyes in your head. (*she violently presses his head against the map*) This is where Miller gets the water for his cattle. When I cut off his supply . . .

RAYMOND: You can't do that.

ROWENA: Don't you tell me what I can do and what I can't. In six months Miller will be that small. He'll be lucky if someone buys his useless farm from him. And in the present economic situation I'll be the only one to offer to buy it. Therefore I'll fix the price.

RAYMOND: Doesn't it bother you that this is fraud?

ROWENA: And how do you think the Millers got so rich? Eh? Do you think you can get rich without getting your fingers dirty?

RAYMOND: Stop talking about Miller! Of course, he's a crook. Miller! What do I care about him? I'm a Gresham and I don't want to be ashamed of it.

ROWENA: Sooner or later I could own the largest spread of land in the whole district. Everybody would have to tip their hat when a Gresham walks past.

RAYMOND: And they'll say: Good morning, big-time swindler Gresham. Good morning, land robber Gresham. Good morning, big-time horse-thief Gresham.

Suddenly, to RAYMOND'S complete surprise ROWENA slaps his face hard. Silence. No movement. Then RAYMOND turns around slowly and walks out of the room.

ROWENA: (*with an almost surprised tone in her voice, rather softly*) You are a rebel.

She finishes changing her clothes. Then she starts opening the packages.

ROWENA: (*walks to the door, shouts*) Virgil!

She walks back to the packages. VIRGIL appears in the door, reluctant to enter.

ROWENA: Come in! Don't stand in the doorway like a stuffed dummy.

VIRGIL enters the room.

ROWENA: Close the door.

In the following scene between ROWENA and VIRGIL the incriminating sentences are spoken in a hushed voice.

Several times during the conversation ROWENA listens outside to make sure nobody overhears them.

ROWENA unwraps a jacket and throws it on the table in front of VIRGIL.

ROWENA: Take off your jacket.

VIRGIL: What?

ROWENA: Take it off!

VIRGIL starts to take off his jacket. He does not know why. His wounded shoulder makes it difficult for him. RO-WENA helps him, but she is not very gentle.

VIRGIL: Ouch!

ROWENA: How clever! How cunning! How smart! You had a piece of cloth tied over your face?!

VIRGIL: I swear!

ROWENA: But you had to wear this fancy jacket! (*she rips*

it off his body) This jacket that everybody around here recognizes!

ROWENA: (*throws the new jacket at him*) Put it on! (*referring to the jacket*) This one goes into the fire.

VIRGIL: I could have been miles away now if you had let me.

ROWENA: And let me make this clear: you gave this old jacket away weeks ago.

VIRGIL: What?

ROWENA: Because you didn't like it anymore. You gave it to some drifter who was traveling through and who you felt sorry for. Or even better, you lost it to him in a card game. You don't know his name of course. And you couldn't possibly guess that he was a horse-thief. But all the drifters steal like magpies. Understand?

VIRGIL: Yes.

ROWENA: Good. I'll straighten things out, don't worry. With that waitress as well.

VIRGIL: Fanny hasn't . . .

ROWENA: I had a look at her.

VIRGIL: She's all right.

ROWENA: Do you sleep with her? (*VIRGIL feels embarrassed*) Don't make such a fuss about it, I know what young stallions do. So, is there anything between you?

VIRGIL: Yes.

ROWENA: Hm . . . Nevertheless, it was utterly stupid of you to . . . er . . . to run to the first tart you could think of. You'll never do that again.

VIRGIL: Where else should I have gone? We haven't got any friends we can rely on.

ROWENA: You realize you're at her mercy.

VIRGIL: At Fanny's? She doesn't know anything. She lives in town, how should she . . .

ROWENA: She can put two and two together. She's not stupid.

VIRGIL: She's the least of my worries. She is crazy about me. I can twist her around my little finger.

ROWENA: I think so too. She's no problem. She will want money though. She can have it and then get lost. How much will she want anyway? A lousy waitress . . . a few silver dollars would be a fortune for her.

ROWENA unwraps the second parcel. Without saying a word, yet with some ceremony she hands him a pistol. This is meant as a sort of knighting. His self-esteem is heightened.

ROWENA: You'll have to go out once more.

VIRGIL: (*with emphasis*) Oooh, no!

ROWENA: It'll be the last time. I promise. The very last time. I have a few men at hand, black marketeers trading horses. They'll pay almost any price for good thoroughbreds.

VIRGIL: No, I won't do that any more.

ROWENA: Sh!

VIRGIL: I'm wounded.

ROWENA: You'll just need your ass for riding, and one hand will be enough to hold the reins.

VIRGIL: You're raving mad.

ROWENA: (*hushed, with emphasis*) This is our chance.

The Hanson farm is for sale. We would need less than a thousand dollars. (*points to the map*) This is the area with the springs. Once we have this property we can cut off Miller's water supply.

VIRGIL: Good thoroughbreds are rare.

ROWENA: And that is exactly why we can charge whatever we like for them.

VIRGIL: I won't do that anymore. There is scarcely a breeder left who would still leave his horses outside overnight.

ROWENA: (*softly*) Hey, Virgil? We won't get another chance, will we? I'll have to get that money from somewhere. You think about it.

VIRGIL: Raymond can go, he's never done anything.

ROWENA: Raymond! He's got too much of his father's blood. He wouldn't be any good for that job.

VIRGIL: Now that that story's gone around, they'll wait for me at every corner.

ROWENA: (*tempts him with the gun*) You can defend yourself. (*more self-confidently*) One more time, just one more time. You are a real man, you can be bold if you have to. Sure! By the way, I'm not sure it's wise to let your father see you with that pistol. (*she carries the wrapping out of the room*)

VIRGIL looks at the gun, extends it in firing position, aims at something. He feels very grown-up with it.

RAYMOND enters and takes a book from the bookcase. VIRGIL proudly plants himself before his brother. RAYMOND is not impressed. VIRGIL blocks RAYMOND'S way with the gun.

VIRGIL: Surprised, aren't you? Huh? (*points the gun under his nose*) A real Colt. An automatic.

RAYMOND: Leave me alone.

VIRGIL: Look at it. In case you should one day decide to grow up and be a man.

RAYMOND'S indifference is a provocation for VIRGIL. He aims at his brother.

VIRGIL: Scared, little brother, huh?

VIRGIL levels at RAYMOND, who gets frightened and dodges. VIRGIL follows his movements with the barrel.

RAYMOND: Are you crazy?

VIRGIL: Are you afraid of a bang?

RAYMOND: Are you out of your head? Stop it! Do you want to kill me?!

VIRGIL: How come I always have to do the dirty work? So a wimp like you can sit home comfortably and read your books!

RAYMOND zigzags around the room trying to dodge VIRGIL. VIRGIL follows him and aims at his legs, his arms, his head.

RAYMOND: (*exclaiming while he is running*) Hey! Stop it, you crazy bastard! Leave me alone! This isn't funny!

VIRGIL: (*simultaneously*) Do you want a bullet in your shoulder? This time I'll cut it out myself. So you can feel what it's like.

Suddenly the gun goes off. The bullet misses RAYMOND and hits the wall. VIRGIL and RAYMOND are paralyzed by fear; they did not know that the pistol was loaded.

Rowena rushes in. She heard the shot outside.

ROWENA: Hey! What do you think you're doing?

VIRGIL: (*in a serious, almost soft voice*) I'm teaching him to dance.

ROWENA: Are you crazy? We've got enough trouble as it is.

ROWENA wrenches the gun from VIRGIL, opens it and inspects the barrel.

ROWENA: You idiot! (*points at the bullet-hole in the wall*) Look, it's loaded. Go outside if you want to play with it. You could have hurt someone, you lunatic, or damaged the piano.

Scene 3

ROWENA is setting the table for five. She rushes in and out the room carrying dishes, cutlery, etc. from the kitchen.

ROWENA: (*shouting*) Dinner will be ready in a minute. (*walks out of the room*)

RAYMOND pushes his father into the room, yet not straight to the table.

RAYMOND: (*speaking in low tones*) I found the plans.

CHARLES: (*surprised, delighted*) They still exist?! (*then sceptically*) Ah well ... it's all nonsense of course. As your mother always used to say: crazy ideas! Where did you find them?

RAYMOND: In the attic. (*shows him the plans*)

CHARLES: The idle contemplations of a cripple. Just half-baked foolishness.

RAYMOND: I think they're great ideas.

CHARLES: You don't understand anything about it.

RAYMOND: (*subdued*) No ... you're right ... (*the conver-*

*sation stops as ROWENA enters, and continues set-
ting the table)*

ROWENA: Where's Virgil? (*she does not expect an answer*)
He doesn't leave the house all day, and now it's dinner time, and where is he?

She walks back into the kitchen.

RAYMOND: Father, you know . . . I think someone should
really talk to the new settlers about your irrigation
plans. They should be interested. Surely! They
should be interested in finding ways to stop their
land from drying up in summer just because a few
farmers divert half the water from the spring for
their own use.

CHARLES: Yes . . . that was the idea . . . yes . . . (*enthusiastically*) I marked it out on the plan—you can see
the lines—I marked it out where the land would be
most suitable for pastures, and where to plant fruit
trees, because there is enough humus soil, where it
would be best to plant trees . . .

RAYMOND: You have to talk to people!

CHARLES: You can grow anything you like on this land.
The big farmers could breed their cattle or their
horses, for the small farmers it would be more prof-
itable to grow vegetables or fruit or flowers for the
people in town. Anything will grow in such soil.

RAYMOND: They would understand that.

CHARLES: And there would be plenty for everybody.

RAYMOND: If only someone would explain it to them in
the right words.

CHARLES: Everything in nature follows the dictates of
reason. There is a trace of life everywhere, in per-
petual ice, in the desert. You can grow things even

on a sandy hill, even on a rocky slope. We are just not used to thinking in the right way. We just take and take. Destroy, waste, exploit! As if the land wasn't our life! As if it wasn't entrusted to us, left for a while in our charge, lent to us on condition that we pass it on one day . . .

ROWENA enters; CHARLES immediately stops talking.

ROWENA: (*to CHARLES*) We're having braised beef and beans. (*she continues setting the table*) And boiled cabbage. (*to CHARLES, warmly*) That's your favorite, isn't it? (*no reaction from CHARLES, she does not expect any*) It's time, isn't it, Charles?

RAYMOND: Always beef, beef, beef!

ROWENA: (*harshly*) Nobody asked you!

VIRGIL enters in a state of exitement, looks at CHARLES, hesitates, but can't contain himself.

VIRGIL: (*to ROWENA, in a low choked voice*) Miller wants to press charges against me. He says he recognized me. You know what that means!

ROWENA: (*does not want to talk about it*) Hey! Don't rush into the room with your boots on!

VIRGIL: (*close to her*) I'll go to jail for stealing horses. And perhaps this will bring some other things to light.

ROWENA: First of all take off your dirty boots!

VIRGIL: (*softly*) Miller is serious.

ROWENA: (*softly and intensely*) Who told you that?

VIRGIL: Jack.

ROWENA: (*loudly, casually*) You can't believe a word of what a worker says.

VIRGIL: It's already the talk of the village.

ROWENA: How often do I have to tell you: a Gresham doesn't hang around with cowhands!

She leaves the room. VIRGIL realizes that there is no point in talking. He stands around undecided.

RAYMOND: (*meanwhile talking to CHARLES*) I'm sure if someone talked seriously to these people . . . I can't believe that they wouldn't understand how sensible your plan is.

CHARLES: How do newly-hatched turtles know the shortest way to the sea? The eggs were laid in the sand, the sun hatched them. Hungry flocks of birds are waiting for the moment they come out. Suddenly it happens. Masses of little turtles are running, struggling, stumbling to the sea. The shortest way. I read it in a book. Years ago. This image hasn't left me since. Not one of the tiny turtles runs in the wrong direction. Not one of them. How do they know their way? Why do humans know so little?

RAYMOND: I think you're wrong, father. Didn't mother and you set off like these turtles? Set off on a trail you hadn't walked before? Nothing could stop you and here you are. If people didn't know that there was a place just for them, for which they would take responsibility . . .

CHARLES has taken RAYMOND'S head into both hands.

CHARLES: Wake up, little one . . .

He shakes Raymond's head.

CHARLES: You . . . are too much like me . . .

ROWENA: (enters carrying the soup-tureen. Virgil stops her at the door; the following dialogue is almost whispered, but intense.)

VIRGIL: Give me 200 dollars. That'll be enough for the time being, afterwards I'll make my own way.

ROWENA: If I had 200 dollars I'd think of a better way to spend them.

VIRGIL: 100 dollars then . . . Aren't I worth 100 dollars? 80? Damn it all, you could spare me 80 dollars. For Christ's sake! They'll catch me.

ROWENA: What proof have they got?

VIRGIL: Proof! Miller saw me!

ROWENA: Did he? He thinks he saw somebody with a cloth over his face wearing a jacket like the one you used to have.

VIRGIL: Miller won't give up that easily.

ROWENA: What can he prove without witnesses? These are just his own unfounded allegations. Because he's jealous of my success. Anyone can see that. He's blinded by jealousy. Because he's afraid that I, a mere woman, can beat him at his own game.

VIRGIL: Let me go away. It's my neck that's at stake.

ROWENA: Who do you think you are, you wimp! You weakling! Worried about your precious little hide! The house of Gresham is at stake! Don't forget that. And I'm the one who is responsible for seeing that everything is in order here. This is my house. This is my family. Do you think I'm going to let anyone come along and take you away and lock you up? Nothing is going to happen, you hear me, nothing at all! (*loudly*) Take your places for dinner! (*to VIR-GIL*) It's not for nothing that I bribe the police every month.

VIRGIL: You underestimate Miller. If it . . .

ROWENA: And you underestimate me. (*loudly*) Dinner's ready!

VIRGIL: It would be better if for some time I . . .

ROWENA: (*to VIRGIL, loudly*) Did you wash your hands?

They are all standing around the table, except for CHARLES who is sitting in his wheelchair. There is an empty place.

ROWENA: (*says the prayer routinely*) Oh Lord, bless this simple meal, the cattle, the house, and the people who live in it.

All: Amen.

ROWENA dishes out the soup. VIRGIL makes a gesture to show that he is not hungry, ROWENA fills his plate anyway.

ROWENA: Don't wait, the soup isn't as hot as it was.

They eat in silence.

Nobody notices that the door has been opened, Fanny is standing outside. She is unsure about whether she should enter or wait outside.

FANNY: Sorry . . . I . . .

All look up and stop eating. Nobody gets up. After a while ROWENA resumes eating, the others follow.

FANNY: I've come at an awkward time. I'm sorry.

ROWENA: So you are . . .

FANNY: Yes, madam. I'm Fanny Fillingham.

ROWENA: Fimming. . .

FANNY: Fillingham.

They continue eating.

FANNY: (*unsure how to behave*) You left a message, madam . . . that I should come and see you.

ROWENA: Yes. Right. (*to CHARLES*) Don't you like the soup? Charles? (*no answer*) Don't you like it?

CHARLES: I do.

ROWENA: We have plain food. Unsophisticated. (*looks at her while eating*) Not like in the fancy restaurants in town.

FANNY: That's probably . . . healthiest, anyway.

ROWENA: Plain farmer's fare. As it suits farmers. The land doesn't yield more, anyway.

FANNY: You don't have to say that, madam. As if one didn't know.

ROWENA: You are quite mistaken, Fimm . . .

FANNY: (*quickly*) Fillingham.

ROWENA: Fillingham, hard work makes a hard life. (*to VIRGIL*) Don't slurp. I've told you a thousand times: don't eat like a pig. (*to Fanny, with an undertone*) Damn difficult to teach these rascals some manners. This is Virgil, my son. You know him?

VIRGIL looks up for a moment. She nods to him, smiles, he lowers his eyes immediately.

FANNY: Oh yes, . . . we know each other.

ROWENA: This is Raymond.

FANNY: Hello, Raymond.

RAYMOND: Hello, Fanny.

There is another pause.

FANNY: (*just to say something*) Why don't you come to the saloon any more, Raymond? You haven't been there for quite a while.

VIRGIL: (*to RAYMOND*) Ho, ho. Look at our little one.

RAYMOND: (*to FANNY*) I . . . I've been quite busy lately.

VIRGIL: Still waters run deep. (*to FANNY*) Say, did he proposition you? Huh? (*bursts into crude and self-confident laughter*) My little brother? Did he?

ROWENA: (*calling to order*) Don't make so much noise at the table! Eat!

They eat in silence.

ROWENA: (*after a while, talking over her spoon*) You work as a waitress, Fimm. . .

FANNY: Fillingham. Yes, madam.

ROWENA: Good job?

FANNY: Could be worse.

ROWENA: Reasonable pay?

FANNY: Thanks. What with the tips and all . . . You know, I don't ask much, I get by and I can't complain.

ROWENA: You see a lot of things . . . in a bar, I imagine?

FANNY: Oh yes, madam. Sure.

ROWENA: Things that are better not talked about . . .

FANNY: Yes, that too.

ROWENA: What I mean to say is if a guy gets drunk, for example, or if he . . . gets involved in something . . . there's no need to broadcast it all over town.

FANNY: We don't wash our dirty linen in public.

ROWENA: (*not quite satisfied with the answer*) That's right, that's how it should be.

The dinner continues, Fanny shifts from one foot to the other.

RAYMOND: (*quietly to his mother*) Ask her to sit down.

Rowena ignores him. They continue eating.

ROWENA: What do people say about the shooting that happened recently? (*no answer*) A serious business that was ... Tell me frankly. What have you heard? Don't worry, you can tell me.

FANNY: The talk is that ...

ROWENA: That what?

FANNY: ... that it was your son Virgil.

VIRGIL: (*to his mother, quietly*) You see!

ROWENA: I see, so that's what they're saying in town.

FANNY: Yes.

ROWENA: (*directly to FANNY*) And what do you think?

No answer. Virgil gets up and is about to leave the room.

ROWENA: You stay where you are.

VIRGIL: I'm full.

ROWENA: It's rude to leave the table before everyone is finished.

VIRGIL: I have to ...

ROWENA: Sit down.

VIRGIL: I have to ...

ROWENA: (*quietly*) And keep calm.

VIRGIL: What is this! I have to go.

ROWENA: You've still got your boots on! Didn't I tell you to take them off. (*towards FANNY*) He's always messing up my good floors with his dirty boots ... These men never show any consideration.

VIRGIL: How am I supposed to take them off? With my shoulder in this condition.

ROWENA: Raymond.

RAYMOND understands. He helps VIRGIL to take off his boots. VIRGIL is seated. RAYMOND steps over his leg and VIRGIL puts his other foot on RAYMOND'S behind.

Meanwhile:

ROWENA: (*to FANNY*) Do you like the town?

FANNY: Oh yes.

ROWENA: Well, Ashford is not exactly the big wide world.

FANNY: I think it's a nice little town.

ROWENA: To be honest . . . it's a miserable hole.

FANNY: Yes, I suppose it is, madam.

ROWENA: I'd imagine that a girl like you would like to get around. See bigger places. Huddlestone. Where things are going on. Greenfield. Full of life and action. A place where you can get somewhere. I understand well enough, I'm not yet too old to understand. Places with night clubs where the customers are distinguished gentlemen and not loutish country bumpkins. A good clientele.

FANNY: I'm not that kind of girl.

RAYMOND takes off VIRGIL'S second boot. In the process VIRGIL kicks him so hard that RAYMOND stumbles and falls at FANNY'S feet.

VIRGIL: (*crudely*) Look at that, you have a Gresham at your feet.

RAYMOND gets angry. Yet he controls his anger, throws the boot into the corner, and sits down at the table.

RAYMOND: Sorry about this, Fanny.

They eat.

ROWENA: Er . . . Miss . . . Fimm. . .

VIRGIL: (*with emphasis*) Fanny Fillingham.

Pause. ROWENA looks at VIRGIL. She eats.

FANNY: I've picked an awkward moment for my visit. Perhaps I could . . .

ROWENA: How much would it cost?

FANNY: Would what cost?

ROWENA: Moving.

FANNY: Moving? Where to?

ROWENA: To Huddlestone. No, Greenfield would be better.

FANNY: I have no plans to move.

ROWENA: Of course it won't be cheap. But then, what is cheap nowadays? The fare, accommodations, expenses until you can find a decent job.

FANNY: I don't understand, madam.

ROWENA: I think . . . it would easily take . . . (*eats a spoonful while scrutinizing FANNY*) . . . fifty dollars. (*eats another spoonful*) Sixty?

FANNY: If I really wanted to move away from Ashford, it wouldn't be a question of money. I have some savings.

ROWENA: How much?

RAYMOND: Mother!

ROWENA: I know one shouldn't ask things like that.

FANNY: 635 dollars.

ROWENA: (*impressed*) 635! Well done! Do you earn so

much in your business? Well, it probably depends on whether you know how to treat your customers right . . .

RAYMOND: Mother, please . . .

FANNY stands around embarrassed. She does not dare to leave. Silence. They continue eating.

ROWENA: (*to RAYMOND*) Have you started digging for water yet? On your land?

RAYMOND: It's not my land.

ROWENA: It's registered in your name.

RAYMOND: No, I haven't.

ROWENA: Then start as soon as possible. You know that otherwise your registration lapses. (*to FANNY*) I try to teach my sons to be economically minded. These are tough times. You haven't bought yourself a section of land?

FANNY: No.

ROWENA: Of course not. Why should you.

She stands up and begins to stack the plates.

ROWENA: You want to be free, free to move . . . Don't you? Who can say after all where one will end up in the course of time.

She carries the plates and the soup tureen into the kitchen.

RAYMOND: (*to CHARLES*) Aren't you feeling well?

CHARLES does not answer. RAYMOND pushes the wheelchair away from the table. He covers CHARLES' legs with a blanket. FANNY takes the opportunity and moves a bit closer towards the table and VIRGIL. The following dialogue in hushed tones.

FANNY: How is your shoulder?

She touches him gently. VIRGIL winces.

FANNY: Does it still hurt?

VIRGIL: No, no, it's getting better.

FANNY: Are you angry with me?

VIRGIL: Why should I be?

FANNY: Is something wrong with you? If you are worried about Raymond . . . I like him, I really like him, but there's nothing between us.

VIRGIL: (*with self-confident laughter*) Of course not . . . With him! (*lowers his voice, points over his shoulder*) It's just, she doesn't like people to talk about it.

FANNY: I know what your mother is getting at . . . Tell her not to worry. I would never let you down.

At this moment ROWENA enters with the main dish. She has overheard the last sentence. FANNY immediately takes a step back and stands at the door, unmoving as before.

ROWENA: Charles, don't you want anything else to eat?

Raymond approaches the table.

RAYMOND: I don't think father is well.

ROWENA: I hope we're never worse.

She fetches plates from the cupboard. As she walks past FANNY she secretly hands her a purse. FANNY does not want to take it, yet already holds it in her hand.

FANNY: (*baffled*) What's that for? What is this supposed to mean?

ROWENA: Come on, dinner is not over yet. (*quietly to FANNY*) Nobody messes with the Greshams!

The meal continues. FANNY does not know what to do. Nobody talks, nobody takes notice of FANNY, only RAYMOND sometimes secretly glances at her. Suddenly the door opens.

In the doorway stands SELMA with a suitcase in her hand. Nobody notices her arrival.

ROWENA: (*noticing SELMA*) Well, I never . . .

CHARLES: (*stops eating*) This is . . . if I'm not completely mistaken . . .

ROWENA: (*exclaiming*) Selma!

VIRGIL: Little sister!

They all dash towards SELMA. FANNY is pushed aside.

CHARLES: Is it really you?

ROWENA: (*embracing her*) Selma, child!

SELMA accepts the enthusiastic reception lethargically. Only now does RAYMOND take her suitcase.

RAYMOND: (*to FANNY*) This is my sister Selma. She is back from her boarding school.

SELMA looks pale and ailing. She's wearing make-up and urban-style clothes which set her apart from the others. Despite her sensual appearance she always seems strangely listless, lifeless, and bloodless; except for rare moments when abruptly a greedy zest for life bursts out from deep within her.

VIRGIL dashes towards SELMA and lifts her up with his good arm. He is joyful, twists SELMA around and has, like the others, completely forgotten about Fanny.

VIRGIL: Selma! Well, what a surprise! I almost didn't recognize you. Now, what do you say?

He carries her around, twirling in high-spirited mood, laughing. SELMA remains stiff as a puppet.

VIRGIL: You are as light as a feather. Girl, you don't weigh anything at all.

SELMA: (*referring to VIRGIL'S arm*) Are you hurt?

VIRGIL: Oh . . . nothing serious . . .

ROWENA: (*drags SELMA away to interrupt the dialogue*) Have you finished your school yet? Tell me. You are coming back in the middle of the year. I thought you had at least another term?

SELMA adjusts her dress which VIRGIL has rumpled.

RAYMOND: You are really finished with everything?

SELMA: (*simply*) Yes.

RAYMOND: (*to FANNY*) Selma has been to a finishing school.

ROWENA: (*puts her arm around SELMA*) Come here, come closer. Where is your luggage?

SELMA: (*points to the suitcase*) There.

VIRGIL: Is that all you've got? (*lifts her suitcase slightly and drops it again*)

ROWENA: Come on, child, sit down. You look worn out. Did you have a tiring journey? (*SELMA does not sit down*)

VIRGIL: Tell me, little sister, how was it? What did you see out there in the big world? Come on, sit down and tell me!

SELMA: Raymond. (*she talks to RAYMOND in a low voice; she seems refined, cultivated, urbane, in language and behavior like a stranger*) You have grown.

VIRGIL: (*breaking in*) And me? Eh? Haven't I grown since we last saw each other? Say, Selma! (*over the top, jokingly showing his height*)

SELMA: (*seriously, quietly*) Of course, Virgil. You too. Of course. Is this your bride?

VIRGIL: Er . . .

ROWENA: (*breaking in*) You will want to freshen up. Or —
or do you want to take a little nap first? You look
tired. We are just having dinner.

RAYMOND: (*hasn't stopped looking at SELMA*) You have
changed a lot. Beyond all recognition. If I had
bumped into you in Huddlestone I would have addressed you as "madam." No kidding.

*He laughs. SELMA smiles and strokes his head. Mean-
while FANNY has left the room unnoticed, leaving the
purse on the piano.*

*SELMA walks over to her father, CHARLES does not react
immediately. He looks at her for quite a while.*

ROWENA discovers the purse on the piano.

ROWENA: What a bitch. (*gazes after her through the window while she puts the purse in her pocket*) This
Fillingham. Mhm . . . mhm . . . Not as easy as I
thought. I'll have to think of something else.

SELMA: Hello, father.

*She takes both of her father's hands, bends over and sits
down on the floor in front of him. She lowers her head.*

RAYMOND: Father, it's Selma. (*his father does not react*)
She's back from her boarding school.

CHARLES: Are you ill?

ROWENA: Selma has had a tiring journey.

CHARLES: (*takes her had in his hands and raises her face
up*) How old are you, child?

SELMA: Twenty-one.

CHARLES: Sweet twenty-one . . .

ROWENA: Stop this silly fuss, Charles! You don't have to
ask your own daughter's age, do you?

SELMA: How are you, father?

CHARLES: Poor child . . .

ROWENA comes over and draws SELMA away.

ROWENA: (*to SELMA*) Come and sit down. You must be
hungry.

She leads SELMA to the table.

SELMA: (*surprised*) Did you know I was coming?

CHARLES: How could we?

ROWENA: Of course not.

RAYMOND: You should have written. We would have
picked you up in the carriage.

SELMA: The table is set for five.

RAYMOND: Mother always does that. Every day.

ROWENA: You are part of the family, after all. Even when
you are not here. Sit down, child. Eat.

SELMA: That's very kind of you, mother, but I am not hungry.

RAYMOND: How slim you are.

ROWENA starts filling SELMA'S plate.

SELMA: (*politely*) Thank you, mother, really not. I couldn't
eat a thing. But . . .

Rowena fills her plate anyway.

ROWENA: People must eat. We live in the country. You'll
be blown away by the wind.

SELMA: What I would like is . . .

ROWENA: Yes?

SELMA: Something to drink.

ROWENA: Of course. How stupid of us to forget that! But . . . we haven't got much in the house. How about some fruit juice? You are probably used to far better stuff.

RAYMOND: Our fruit juice isn't that bad.

SELMA: (*sitting with her hands in her lap, her legs together, her head very often slightly lowered*) A little whisky would be nice.

There is a short pause of surprise. SELMA looks up for a moment.

VIRGIL: A drop of what?

ROWENA: (*then*) Oh, sure . . . It . . . We've only got homemade gin. That'll be too raw for you, too strong, I suppose.

VIRGIL has already fetched the bottle and a glass. He fills the glass. SELMA hesitates, then she takes the glass and drinks it down in one swallow. Everybody is waiting for her to choke or cough. She does not cough. She lowers her head for a moment, then she looks up, smiles innocently. First Virgil, then ROWENA and RAYMOND start laughing.

VIRGIL: Well done, little sister. (*slaps her on the back*) Another one?

ROWENA takes the bottle from VIRGIL'S hand and puts it back into the cupboard.

ROWENA: You have a fine opinion of your sister!

VIRGIL touches SELMA'S face with his fingers.

VIRGIL: Say, is that the fashion in town now?

He laughs while he follows the line of the make-up with his fingers.

VIRGIL: Look! (*shaking with laughter*) She's painted her face!

ROWENA: (*drags VIRGIL away from SELMA, who doesn't feel secure*) Selma, I'm glad you're back. You can help me teach these ruffians some manners. Come on and eat, my child.

SELMA picks at her food out of politeness, in a slightly affected manner. She only takes tiny pieces. Everybody watches her, which increases her insecurity.

SELMA: (*with a friendly smile*) I don't want to be impolite, mother, it tastes excellent. I know you are a great cook. It's just I'm not a bit hungry at the moment.

ROWENA: She's become every inch a lady. (*with playful exaggeration*) I should have hoped so too, girl! I wouldn't have liked to throw my good money down the drain. (*she takes SELMA'S hands*) Such hands. Do you see? Hands like parchment. Well? Selma is every bit as cultivated as the aunts.

RAYMOND: (*pushes his way close to SELMA*) Tell me, what was it like in school? Say a sentence in French. What did you learn? Drawing?

VIRGIL: (*laughing coarsely*) In any case she has learned how to paint her face.

RAYMOND: I have read almost all the books you sent us. Especially the ones on agriculture. Oh, they taught me a lot of new things. Perhaps I didn't understand all of it.But now you can explain it all to me.

ROWENA: Agriculture . . . Do you think Selma was in a school for farmers?! You really are a dolt. (*violently taps her finger against his forehead*)

RAYMOND: I'm interested in the other things as well. Everything. Music, for example.

VIRGIL: (*to SELMA*) Did you notice? Mother's bought a piano. Just for you. We weren't even allowed to touch it.

ROWENA: I'll say not. You and your clumsy paws!

RAYMOND: Maybe you could teach me some melodies. We've even got some songbooks.

SELMA has taken RAYMOND'S hands and holds them.

RAYMOND: Look here, this is Schubert. I can only read the words, unfortunately I can't read the music.

SELMA: I'm sure you'd be able to play the piano well, you have nice soft hands.

VIRGIL: That's because he doesn't do any work.

VIRGIL is searching through SELMA'S luggage.

ROWENA: (*reserved*) And you . . . are finished with your school?

SELMA: Yes.

RAYMOND: You don't have to go back to your boarding school any more?

SELMA: No.

ROWENA: And school's finished now? Just like that, in the middle of the term?

SELMA: Yes . . .

ROWENA: How does that work? I had to send the money for the whole year in advance.

SELMA: That's the way it goes . . .

VIRGIL has discovered SELMA'S cosmetics. He grabs a lipstick.

VIRGIL: Look at this! Hey! What is it?

SELMA: (*calmly*) A lipstick.

VIRGIL: Is that the sort of thing they use in town these days? Wow! That would be something for our little boy Raymond.

He jumps on RAYMOND and tries to paint his face. RAY-MOND manages to escape, VIRGIL runs after him. They knock over some chairs. Their mother steps in and restores order.

ROWENA: Hey! You wild young stallions! That's no way to behave in front of Selma! Stop it! What will she think of you! Put the chairs back properly.

While RAYMOND is putting the chairs back, VIRGIL is again busy searching through SELMA'S suitcase.

ROWENA: (*to SELMA*) You see . . . you'll have your work cut out for you. Until these louts finally . . .

VIRGIL has discovered a perfume spray.

VIRGIL: (*boisterously, holds it up as if it were a great discovery*) And this here?! Ooooh!

ROWENA: Leave Selma's bag alone. Those are her private things. You know you shouldn't do that, for Christ's sake!

VIRGIL: What's in there?

SELMA: (*to VIRGIL, calmly*) Perfume.

VIRGIL sprays some perfume in front of his nose, smells it and starts to spray wildly about the room.

VIRGIL: Perfume . . . Mmmmmmmh. What a nice smell! Mmmmmh . . . Say, what do call this smell?

SELMA: Rosewood.

VIRGIL: What a time you must have had in town, eh?

VIRGIL sprays the perfume all over himself under his arms, into his trousers, between his legs. He does it with grotesque exuberance. In all this hurly-burly SELMA remains calm, looking tender, lost, helpless, fragile and strange.

ROWENA: (*to VIRGIL*) Don't you think you are behaving like a fool?

VIRGIL comes over to SELMA, puts his arm around her and kisses her on the cheek.

VIRGIL: We won't tell anyone we are related. OK?

SELMA: What happened to your arm?

VIRGIL: Oh . . . that's nothing.

SELMA: My poor brother.

VIRGIL: Oh, that was just Miller, the asshole, he caught me when . . .

ROWENA: (*interrupts him*) It was an accident. Such things can happen in the country. It seems you have completely forgotten what really goes on out here. I hope you are not too disappointed and will get used to living with us again. But tell us about yourself, child, we are all curious. You haven't said anything.

VIRGIL has already gone back to the suitcase. Now he pulls out some pieces of sexy underwear.

VIRGIL: (*holding an embroidered garter in his hand*) What do we have here! Wow . . . look at this! How do you wear a thing like this?

He holds the garter to his body and dances around until ROWENA takes it away from him. She puts it back into the suitcase. In the meantime VIRGIL has grabbed a pair of lacy underpants and behaves in the same way with them. ROWENA tries to stay serious, yet cannot quite keep a straight face. Even RAYMOND is laughing.

ROWENA: That's enough now.

Every time she takes a piece of underwear away from him

and puts it back into the suitcase, VIRGIL has already grabbed another piece and continues his show.

ROWENA: Stop it, you fool! Put it away! Leave it alone. That's not yours. Don't you see you are making a fool of yourself? You should show some consideration for Selma, you numbskull!

The show is over. VIRGIL puts the last piece of underwear back into the suitcase.

VIRGIL: Did the pupils in your school wear that stuff?

SELMA: Yes.

RAYMOND: Come. (*takes SELMA by the hand*) Play something for us. (*leads her to the piano*) What do you think of the idea, father? I am sure he would love to hear something too. When he was young his aunts used to have musical evenings once a week. They invited their friends and neighbors, didn't they, father? They served wine and home-made cakes. And now we could start doing that here as well. (*he sets the piano-stool in place for her*) Please.

SELMA: I don't know . . .

ROWENA: Selma will be too tired now. You shouldn't rush the child. She'll play something for you tomorrow when she has had some rest.

RAYMOND: (*forces SELMA to sit down*) Should I get the music for you? What would you like?

SELMA: Oh no.

RAYMOND: It doesn't have to be a concert, just play a few notes, so at least we can hear what our piano sounds like. Nobody has played it since it's been here. Apart from when I sometimes . . .

ROWENA: All you can do is tinkle, you with your— (*stops talking because SELMA starts to play*)

First SELMA sits motionless for a few moments, then she starts to play. She plays a jazzy, honky-tonk popular tune with professional skill. Her facial expression and her pose, however, do not in the least correspond to the music. Her body does not move, her face gives the impression of complete absent-mindedness. At first everybody is taken aback. They had expected to hear a sonata. Even CHARLES lifts his head and turns around. VIRGIL is the first to react, he starts to stamp his feet in time.

VIRGIL: *(loudly, merrily)* Hey! That's my kind of music! It's not like it was at the aunts' though.

RAYMOND: *(taken aback)* Yes . . . it almost sounds like the music they play at the cattle market in Ashford . . . but . . . *(more relaxed)* Oh yes, she plays well.

VIRGIL twists and turns and claps his hands, suggesting some sort of dance. Gradually RAYMOND joins in the rhythm.

VIRGIL: Hey! What do you say to that! Isn't she great, our sister! Terrific!

ROWENA: She has learned something. *(tries to relax and take a positive view of the performance)* I have to admit, she knows how to play.

VIRGIL: *(in motion)* You bet! Wow . . . And how! I should never have thought it of our little sister. What do you say? Eh?

VIRGIL is dancing with increasing excitement. Every now and then he lets out loud cries and shouts of glee. He urges ROWENA to dance with him. At first she is reluctant. After a while even RAYMOND can be persuaded to join into the dance. They are dancing some sort of grotesque folk dance.

VIRGIL: That's the stuff! On we go! Come on, come on, step to it! That's music! Go on, little sister, don't stop!

The excitement increases, the dance becomes more sweeping and grotesque. Laughter, noise, movement.

SELMA remains unmoved. She plays her tunes with tremendous speed and rhythm, with skill, yet without involvement. As the bustle reaches its climax a volley of shots cracks through the window without warning. The noise of splintering glass. SELMA is the first to react. She quickly ducks under the piano, curls up and keeps still. The mother drags her two sons to the floor looking for shelter. The noise of gunshots and splintering wood. ROWENA crawls over to CHARLES's chair and pushes it against the wall. The shooting stops as abruptly as it began. Silence. Nobody moves for some time. ROWENA stands up first. Cautiously she peeps out through the window.

ROWENA: (*swearing*) Bastards! Murdering bastards!

SELMA comes up from under the piano and sits down on the stool. She does it in the same unmoved manner as she played the piano. ROWENA checks that nobody is hurt. VIRGIL stays under cover longest of all. He has suffered the biggest shock.

ROWENA: (*self-controlled*) It's all right . . . It's all over.

VIRGIL fetches his rifle, rushes to the window and aims.

VIRGIL: Where are the bastards? I'll get them! I'll pick
   them off, one by one! Cowards! Assholes!

ROWENA: (*calmly*) Stop it. (*takes the rifle away from him
   and puts it back in the cupboard*) Now things are
   getting serious! Very well! (*to SELMA who is still
   sitting at the piano*) You took it well, girl. (*with re-
   spectful approval, yet also with uneasy surprise*)
   You didn't even scream.

She checks again if CHARLES is all right.

ROWENA: Are you all right, Charles? (*runs her fingers*

through his hair) Nothing happened, nothing happened to you. You see?

She starts to gather up the pieces of broken glass.

ROWENA: (*gazing out of the window*) You won't get me. Not as easily as that! Fools! Hah! Learn to shoot first. (*gathering up pieces*) Now he is getting serious. Very well. I'm prepared. (*discovers a bullet-hole in the cupboard*) Just look at that! The bastards. That was Miller.

RAYMOND: How do you know it was him?

ROWENA: It was him.

RAYMOND: How can you be sure?

ROWENA: (*gathering up pieces*) He must have found out that I've taken an option on the Hanson farm. All right, Miller, if that's the way you want it! I'm not afraid. First I'll cut off his water supply. Then I'll have him on his knees. The great Miller! (*when passing the piano she gives SELMA a quick hug*) Not a nice welcome for a lady. You really took it well, girl. (*then with sudden determination*) Tomorrow we'll put a gate up on the drive. Nobody is ever going to come onto my land with a gun again, no matter who it is. Nobody is going to get the better of us.

Without any apparent order she has now gathered her family around herself.

Scene 4

Sunday.

From outside the low voices of the laborers can be heard. They are singing melancholy songs. SELMA is sitting by the window, as usual in a stiff, puppet-like pose. She is embroidering daisies on velvet. VIRGIL, in another part of the room, is cleaning his rifle. RAYMOND is dozing on the couch. ROWENA takes an old book from the cupboard. She tries to find a certain page. She hands the book to CHARLES who is sitting hunched over in his wheelchair.

ROWENA: Father, will you read us the Sunday psalm? (*admonishing*) Raymond.

RAYMOND sits up. CHARLES has difficulty holding the heavy book. He reads with effort. Sometimes he makes long pauses at inappropriate places.

ROWENA: (*points to the relevant passage*) Here, father.

CHARLES: Lord, thou hast been our dwelling place in all generations. Before the mountains were brought forth . . . (*pulling himself together*) or ever thou hadst formed the earth and the world . . . thou art the everlasting God and world without end.

ROWENA: Virgil! Will you listen to your father! Leave that gun now, you ape!

CHARLES: Thou turnest man to destruction; and sayest . . . Return, ye children of men. For a thousand years in thy sight are but as yesterday . . . when it is past, and as a watch in the night. Thou carriest them away as with a flood. (*pause*)

RAYMOND: What's the matter with you, father?

CHARLES: They are as asleep: in the morning they are like grass . . . (*seems to have lost his place*)

Rowena takes the book from him.

ROWENA: Let me read. (*reads*) . . . In the morning it is green and grows; in the evening it is cut down, and withers. For we are consumed by thine anger, and by thy wrath are we troubled.

CHARLES sometimes mumbles half a sentence or a few words along with ROWENA'S reading.

ROWENA: . . . our secret sins are revealed in the light of thy countenance. For all our days are passed away in thy wrath: we spend our years as a tale that is told. The days of our years are threescore years and ten; and if by reason of strength they be fourscore years, yet is their strength, labor and sorrow;

Every now and then she casts a quick look to make sure that everybody is paying attention.

ROWENA: . . . for it is soon cut off, and we fly away. Who knoweth the power of thine anger? even according to thy fear, so is thy wrath. So teach us to number our days, that we may apply our hearts unto wisdom.

She sits quietly for a while, then she closes the book. After that she sits a little longer lost in thought. Then she regains her usual energy and puts the book back into the cupboard.

ROWENA: What do you think, Selma . . . shouldn't we move the cupboard to this wall?

SELMA looks up. She does not say a word.

VIRGIL: Just leave the damn furniture where it is!

ROWENA: Somehow it doesn't look right here. Do you think it would look better over there, Selma?

SELMA: (*continuing her embroidery, without involvement*) Yes. Yes, it's possible.

ROWENA: You think so? You've seen the nice apartments of the people in town, of the cultured people. How are they furnished? (*to RAYMOND*) Come on, give me a hand!

RAYMOND: Virgil can give you a hand.

ROWENA: He? How could he? Virgil's only got one good arm.

VIRGIL: I'm more useful with one good arm than that wimp with two!

ROWENA and VIRGIL carry the cupboard.

RAYMOND: (*meanwhile to SELMA*) Didn't you bring any books?

SELMA: No. I'm sorry, Raymond. (*runs her fingers through his hair*) I didn't think of that. And then, I didn't have enough time in the rush of departure. Please forgive me.

RAYMOND: That paper by Selmor would have been interesting, his views on rearing cattle.

SELMA: What a pity. Why didn't you tell me?

RAYMOND: I meant to. But we all thought you wouldn't be back for another year.

ROWENA: (*to SELMA*) Move your chair away from the window, will you?

SELMA: Why?

ROWENA: The cowhands. They keep staring at you through the window.

SELMA moves her chair a bit.

RAYMOND: (*to SELMA*) Tell us about your school. What were the teachers like?

SELMA: They were nice. What are they supposed to be like?

ROWENA: Sometimes I wonder if this is really the same furniture as the aunts have. I think that crook of a carpenter cheated me.

RAYMOND: I would have liked to go to school as well.

ROWENA: What would have been the use? Besides, I couldn't afford these exorbitant school fees for . . . for all of you.

VIRGIL: Raymond would also have liked to learn how to embroider such nice flowers on velvet.

ROWENA: (*to SELMA, almost pleadingly*) Well? Say something! What do you think of the room now?

SELMA: Yes. It looks nice.

ROWENA: You think so? And the piano? Over here?

SELMA thinks about it.

ROWENA: When you hold your head like that you look like one of the aunts. (*to her sons, comparing SELMA'S profile with the portraits of the aunts at the wall*) Doesn't Selma look like a spitting image of them?

CHARLES: You think so? I don't.

ROWENA: Sure. She just moved her head, that's why you can't see it.

CHARLES: What does it matter anyway?

ROWENA and VIRGIL carry the piano.

SELMA: (*running her fingers through Raymond's hair*) What silky hair you've got.

VIRGIL: (*puts the piano down*) That's the only place he's got any hair at all. (*approaching RAYMOND, puts his hand to his face*) Nothing there! (*pretends to open his trousers*) And nothing there. (*laughs crudely*)

RAYMOND roughly pushes him aside. VIRGIL is surprised, stands still for a moment. Having an injured arm, he cannot defend himself.

ROWENA: (*intervening immediately*) Hey! Hey! Break it up! I don't understand why you are always fighting.

Why can't you behave like human beings? You are brothers. (*walks over to CHARLES*) Talk to them, father, if you speak to them they will listen. Tell them that they are of the same blood. (*to her sons*) Both of you are Greshams, don't forget that! (*to Charles*) Why don't you tell them, father, what it means to be a family.

Together with VIRGIL she continues to move the furniture.

RAYMOND: (*to SELMA*) You look so pale all the time. I remember, once you were a happy girl. You were joyful then and carefree.

SELMA: Was I? I was still a child then. We can't expect to be happy forever, can we?

The piano is now in its designated place. ROWENA has discovered a scratch on the cupboard.

ROWENA: Just look at this! That damn Miller! He is going to pay for that, you can never get that right again.

SELMA: The hands sing well, don't they? (*she secretly pours herself a glass of gin and drinks it quickly; she tries not to be seen by anybody, yet ROWENA has been watching her*) Why are they sitting outside? Why don't they come in? We could make some music together.

ROWENA: None of the hands has ever set foot inside this room, and I'm not about to start letting them now. I don't want them ruining my floor with their muddy boots and cracking their dirty jokes in here. One doesn't mix with the hands, something always rubs off. They are good workers, that I grant you. If they weren't, I'd kick them out straight-away. But one simply doesn't mix with them.

SELMA: (*to RAYMOND*) What do you usually do on Sundays?

RAYMOND: (*does not understand*) What do you mean?

SELMA: And in the evenings?

RAYMOND: We sit together. Sometimes I go to town. To the "Coach and Horses." I haven't been there for ages.

SELMA: Aren't there any parties around here?

RAYMOND: What sort of parties?

SELMA: Parties . . . private parties. Where the neighbors get together, where you exchange the latest news, sing songs together, have a drink and a dance.

RAYMOND: I can't dance. Where could I have learned to dance? At the Smiths' and at the Hammonds' over on the other side of the hill some local boys and girls do get together every now and then on weekends. So I've heard. But we never get invited.

ROWENA: And we don't go in for that sort of thing anyway. All they want is to show off, and with what? They probably don't have more than a few dozen half-starved cows on their pastures.

RAYMOND: Down at old Maggie's place, I don't know if you remember her . . .

SELMA: Wasn't her husband a smuggler?

RAYMOND: That's the one. But he's dead now. He got involved in a shooting with the coast guard and a bullet struck him down. She has opened a dive of some sort in her house.

SELMA: So there's a lot going on there?

RAYMOND: Oh well. There's a lot of drinking and gambling. I've never been there myself. It's mostly the hands who go there and a few whores from Huddlestone.

ROWENA wants the conversation to stop. She leads SELMA over to the map.

ROWENA: You probably haven't taken a close look at that yet. That's all our land now. (*proudly follows the border line with her finger*)

SELMA: Oh, it seems like an awful lot!

ROWENA: It is a huge area! The second largest farm in the district. Only Miller owns a few acres more. (*grinning*) Who knows, one day the whole district could be called Gresham country. The council is selling land to new settlers. You should apply for your share soon.

SELMA: But I'm not a new settler, I was born here.

ROWENA: They're not going to be all that strict about it. And the whole thing will cost you next to nothing. As soon as I get to Ashford I'll have a word with the land commissioner. He owes me a favor anyway.

SELMA: Thank you, mother.

ROWENA: It'll be best if you take this piece of land here, (*points at it*) it's next to Raymond's. It might not be worth a lot . . .

SELMA: Doesn't matter, mother.

ROWENA: . . . But (*with emphasis*) it borders our sheep pasture. And if one day you get married . . .

SELMA: (*walks away from the map*) Oh, mother . . .

SELMA sits down on her chair again and resumes her embroidery. RAYMOND takes a book of music from the cupboard and carries it over to SELMA.

RAYMOND: Could you play this for me?

SELMA looks at the music with a helpless expression. Then she looks at RAYMOND.

RAYMOND: Not now. Some time when you feel like it. It's Schubert.

SELMA lowers her eyes and carries on with her embroidery.

RAYMOND: (*after a moment*) You can't read music? (*not reproachful, more with surprise*) You must have learned that in school.

SELMA shakes her head in a barely perceptible way, continues embroidering.

VIRGIL: Leave Selma alone with your nonsense! You heard how well she can play!

ROWENA has started to gather up the washing for the next day. SELMA'S underclothes are part of it. SELMA notices that. She stands up immediately and walks over to her mother. She tries to remove her things. It is too late.

ROWENA: (*with hushed voice*) Explain this to me, child—

SELMA: (*softly, yet with unusual determination*) I'll wash my own things.

ROWENA: I just want to soak it all first, we'll wash it tomorrow and put it out in the sun to bleach. Tell me, child . . . is something wrong with you? Are you ill? How else am I to account for that?! That discharge? Say? The doctor in Ashford is an old boozy quack, but perhaps you should try in Huddlestone. You could go to . . .

SELMA: We should agree, mother, that we each mind our own business.

Outside the singing of the hands stops abruptly. Everybody looks up irritated, especially ROWENA and VIRGIL. Rowena walks to the window. There is an immediate tension in the room.

VIRGIL: Hey! Hey! (*quietly*) That's . . . That bastard actually dares to come here. It's Miller.

ROWENA: I can see that.

VIRGIL: (*grabs his rifle*) What does he want here?!

ROWENA: (*wary*) We'll see.

VIRGIL: Don't let him in! (*levels the gun, resting it on the window-sill, aims outside, yet stays under safe cover*) Let him have it!

ROWENA: You won't do anything at all.

VIRGIL: I'll shoot that bastard down like a rabbit!

ROWENA: (*violently taps her finger against his forehead*) I wish you had a few more brains in your head! Brains instead of sawdust!

VIRGIL is standing at the window, hidden behind the curtain, so that he can look out without being seen from the outside.

ROWENA: (*to the others*) Keep calm. Don't panic.

VIRGIL: Hadn't we better hide?

ROWENA: You are all staying here. And especially you! Today is Sunday. This is our house. We live here and we are going to stay here. Just let me see the person who is going to stop us.

VIRGIL: (*gazing outside*) He's actually getting closer. He's got nerve.

MILLER's voice: (*shouts*) Gresham! (*after a moment*) I must have a word with you! Hey! Gresham! I know you are home!

ROWENA appears in the window.

ROWENA: What do you want?

MILLER's voice: Gresham!

MILLER is not visible, only his shadow is looming vaguely.

ROWENA: Stay where you are!

MILLER: I have to speak to Charles Gresham.

ROWENA: Speak, Miller.

MILLER: Are you the master of the house? I've come here to take a known horse-thief before the judge.

VIRGIL reacts.

ROWENA: Where would you find a horse-thief in the Greshams' house? If you can prove—and I say prove—that one of my hands has committed such a crime, he'll get the punishment he deserves. I don't need any judge for that.

MILLER: I'm not talking about one of your hands.

ROWENA: Then there's nothing to discuss.

MILLER: I've come for your son—Virgil Gresham.

ROWENA: Since when are you the Sheriff?

MILLER: We have been suspicious of you, Rowena Gresham, for a long time now. And of your brood too. When you arrived here, not much more than twenty years ago, you didn't have a penny in your pocket.

ROWENA: Take care, Miller, what you wish on others may come back to haunt you.

MILLER: We couldn't stop wondering how you were able to raise all that money to buy more and more land. Now at last we've got the evidence. Your son has been caught red-handed. He's a thief, he was after my horses.

ROWENA: My son? I have two sons, which one of them is supposed to be a thief?

MILLER: Virgil Gresham.

ROWENA: Virgil hasn't left the house for days.

MILLER: I can swear to the contrary, and Robert, my foreman too.

ROWENA: And what evidence can you produce that it was
my son Virgil?

MILLER: Everybody knows his fancy jacket.

ROWENA: What nonsense. None of my sons has a fancy
jacket.

MILLER: Everybody in Ashford knows that jacket! It's
known all over the district.

ROWENA: It's quite possible that Virgil once had such a
jacket. He gave it to a poor tramp a long time ago. If
you are looking for a horse-thief with a colorful
jacket, you are looking in the wrong place.

MILLER: I've got more proof. He has a gunshot wound.

ROWENA: (*talking back over her shoulder*) Show yourself
in the window. (*VIRGIL does not dare to do it*) Come
on! Show yourself! Move your arm. And smile while
you are doing it.

*VIRGIL quickly shows himself, he moves his wounded
arm, ROWENA assists him in a rough manner, he tries to
suppress his pain.*

ROWENA: Does he look wounded?

MILLER: You are a clever woman, Rowena Gresham, cunning and greedy. But unfortunately you don't know
when to stop. Take care that you don't bite off more
than you can chew. They tell me you've taken an option on the Hanson farm.

ROWENA: What if I have?

MILLER: It was agreed a long time ago that that farm

would be merged with the Miller farm if it were ever put up for sale.

ROWENA: Do you have any written proof of that?

MILLER: So far nobody has ever thought it necessary to make a fuss about signatures. Between honest people a word and a handshake have always been good enough. Every man in the whole district would have respected such an agreement.

ROWENA: I'm not a man and definitely not every man.

MILLER: It's not the Hanson farm or the Teignmoor you want. The land is practically worthless. I know what you're really after. Power. And every means is right for you. Your ambition drives you to want more and more. You just want to outsmart everyone. But you don't know the rules of the game here. If you interfere with the old water rights, then God help you.

ROWENA: We'll cross that bridge when we come to it.

MILLER: Listen, Rowena Gresham, I'm going to make you an offer! Just one, and I'm only going to make it once. You waive your right of first refusal on the Hanson farm, and I will not press charges against your son.

VIRGIL: That's it, very good. Now we have him.

ROWENA: Miller! Just because I'm a woman, you think you can take me lightly. I'll be glad to do business with you. Let's talk about your pasture which soon won't have enough water. I might buy it off you before it dries up completely. But only if the price suits me, Miller.

MILLER: (*angrily*) We'll put a stop to you and to the whole Gresham gang! Don't be too sure of yourself, just because you see me standing like a beggar in front of your window now. I can put your son in jail, and I swear to God, I'll do it. Don't trust your luck too far. (*goes away*)

VIRGIL: There he goes, the coward. You should have let me shoot that asshole down.

ROWENA: He has challenged me. I hope I didn't talk too big. (*shouts out the window*) Pete. Hey, Pete. The option is going to lapse in a week's time, how am I going to raise the money in time? (*hissing through her teeth*) I'm surrounded by weaklings. What they won't give, you simply take. Everybody goes by that rule. So far no one's gotten big without getting his hands dirty.

RAYMOND: Why didn't you accept his offer?

ROWENA: What sort of offer was that? Eh? (*starts to change her clothes*) Why should I have agreed to that?

VIRGIL: For my sake. After all, I'm risking my ass.

ROWENA: Oh no. Don't you understand? If I give up my option, what do I have over him? Men don't keep their word either.

VIRGIL: Miller is serious, eh! I should have shot him while I had the chance. That would have made one witness less.

ROWENA: And created five more. The hands out in the yard. Stop behaving like an idiot. (*shouts outside*) Pete, hitch up, quick.

SELMA: What are you going to do, mother?

VIRGIL: That guy is going to turn me in to the police, don't you see that?

ROWENA: Yes, yes, yes, yes . . . So Miller comes here and puffs himself up. (*she shows it: she puffs herself up, her arms slightly stretched out sideways, with her lips she snorts a raspberry*) But in reality he is already that small. (*shows the size with a thumb and a finger*) And he knows it! (*to VIRGIL*) Hey! Don't stand around like a stick. Go and get dressed, you are coming with me!

VIRGIL: Do you think I'm crazy? I'm not putting a foot outside the door.

ROWENA: Go and get dressed. While I sort things out in town you must get hold of that Fillingham woman.

VIRGIL: What?!

ROWENA: He thinks she's his trump card. Tell her to pack her belongings. And to take all her money, you hear, and not forget her savings book.

VIRGIL: Why?

ROWENA: You're going to marry her.

VIRGIL: (*protesting*) You must be crazy.

RAYMOND: You can't do that, mother!

ROWENA: (*still changing her clothes*) Do you have a better idea? Eh? Then tell me! I'm listening. When she's your wife no court in the world can force her to testify against you.

VIRGIL: Fanny won't let me down.

ROWENA: Are you so sure about that?

VIRGIL: I'd swear to it.

RAYMOND: She surely won't let him down.

ROWENA: And if she has to appear in court? And if she has to swear an oath? You say she is such a good, honest, decent person. Would she commit perjury?

*ROWENA keeps leaving the room for a few moments to fin-
ish getting dressed.*

RAYMOND: But he's not in love with Fanny.

ROWENA: He sleeps with her, so he can marry her.

VIRGIL: Hold on! That's a different story. You don't have to
   go and marry a girl just because of that.

*SELMA, who has been embroidering her flowers all the
time, looks up in alarm for a moment. Yet, she immediately
lowers her eyes again and carries on with her needlework.*

RAYMOND: You're going too far!

VIRGIL: You just shut up!

RAYMOND: Fanny is a decent girl.

VIRGIL: Aha! Now I understand! (*plants himself in front
   of RAYMOND in an ironic and provocative manner.
   RAYMOND does not shrink back*) Look at our little
   one!

RAYMOND: Must you drag everything and everyone
   through the mud for your greedy and insatiable
   ambition.

VIRGIL: Didn't you sleep with her? Eh? He didn't succeed!
   I'm not surprised, little one, you're not yet man
   enough for her!

RAYMOND: And you . . . you horse-thief! Boundary-stone
   mover! Smuggler! Fence! What are you that you
   think so much of yourself, that you think you are so
   good? You're just one of the kind people spit at.

It seems that the two brothers are about to start a fight.

VIRGIL: (*to RAYMOND*) I don't want her. You can take her
   if you want her so much. Go ahead and have her.
   You can marry her, all right, and I'll keep on satis-

fying her for you. If you ask me nicely. I don't want her. Why should I?

ROWENA separates them.

ROWENA: Do you think I would have wanted someone like her for your wife? I'd rather have seen you marry the daughter of some fine gentleman from Ashford. But there's no other way, or do you know a better solution? It's your stupidity got you into this pickle. And again it's me who has to get you out of it. Sooner or later you, being a Gresham, would have been able to marry a woman from one of the best families. But what can I do?

RAYMOND: Stop fooling yourself, mother, in the respectable houses a Gresham wouldn't even be allowed into the hallway.

ROWENA: (*to VIRGIL*) Come on, you dummy! Get dressed! (*to RAYMOND*) Just you wait and see. They'll be lining up just to be invited for a cup of tea in our house. (*to VIRGIL*) Now hurry up, you lazy lout.

VIRGIL: Fanny is nice but she's not the sort of woman you want to marry.

ROWENA: She won't say no, will she?

VIRGIL: Of course she'll take me. She loves me.

ROWENA: You got yourself into this mess. Now do you want to leave it like that? It's the only solution. I happen to know a priest who will put up the bans without asking questions. We will have to give him a generous donation though . . . Everything costs money, nothing is free in this world. If he can put up the bans on Sunday . . . The wedding could take place as early as Monday. Miller won't get scheduled in court before Monday. I bet anything on that.

RAYMOND: (*to CHARLES*) Father! You're not going to let this happen!

ROWENA: (*to SELMA*) I'm sorry, child, it's not the proper way, but what can I do?

RAYMOND: Father.

ROWENA: Leave your father out of it. (*to CHARLES*) Life is tough out here in the country. I wish I could spare him all that.

RAYMOND: You heard what they're going to do. Don't let them do it. I beg you, father! Say something for a change!

ROWENA: (*softly to SELMA*) In this world one has to be tough. Either you make it to the top or people walk all over you. Do you think Miller is a man of honor? Don't you think he would try every trick in the book? The world is a place where stags rut, one stag governs the whole herd, the others can go and run their antlers against a rock till they bleed.

RAYMOND: (*shaking CHARLES who seems to be asleep*) Father, you can't just pretend you are asleep. This is your business too. We are your family, it concerns us all. We'll all have to answer for it. (*without stopping, quietly, as with surprise*) he is dead . . .

ROWENA: (*it is not clear whether she has heard him*) Leave your father alone. He needs his sleep. You know . . . you shouldn't bother your father with problems like that.

RAYMOND: (*shouting*) He's dead!

Silence. Shock.

RAYMOND: (*loudly*) Can't you hear, are you deaf, are you stupid? Are you blind? Haven't you got eyes in your head? Father is dead.

ROWENA: (*motionless for a while, then*) Nonsense. He's asleep. Or pretending to be. All his life he's been shirking responsibility. (*shaking him*) Charles! Can you hear me? (*examines him more closely*) Charles . . . (*lifts up his head which falls back on his shoulder. Gradually she realizes that Charles is really dead*) My God! (*slowly closes his eyes*)

RAYMOND: You've killed him! With all your crooked dealings which he couldn't bear and couldn't fight against, you with your . . .

ROWENA: (*loudly, for the first time really loudly*) Shut your mouth! (*RAYMOND shuts up immediately; after a moment, more softly*) Haven't you got the slightest sense of decency?

They all stand in embarrassed silence. Nobody knows what to do, it is up to ROWENA to react.

VIRGIL: What are we going to do now?

ROWENA: I don't know. I don't know. I don't know. I don't know. I don't know. For God's sake, I don't know either. At least I could have been spared that. Really, I could have been spared that. As if I didn't already have enough trouble! We have to lay out his body. Clear out the small room. Poor Charles . . . I never believed he was really ill. I always thought he was only pretending . . . to keep himself out of everything.

RAYMOND has slipped out of the room unnoticed.

SELMA: How peacefully he has fallen asleep. I hope I can have the good fortune to pass from this world like that one day.

ROWENA: Virgil, push two tables together in there and cover them with a black cloth. Selma . . . show him how to do it. Your father was such a good man . . .

gentle, far too gentle. A kind-hearted man. He wasn't a hard worker though. He never was. He scarcely would have been capable of providing the food for the next meal. A dreamer, that's what he was. But he has given us a respected name.

SELMA: Poor mother. It must be terrible for you.

ROWENA: You remember where we keep the candles?

SELMA: How many?

ROWENA: As many as you can find. All of them. And don't forget the candlesticks.

SELMA leaves the room, VIRGIL comes back. There is movement, yet quiet and mechanical. SELMA re-enters with the candles.

ROWENA: Take them into the parlor.

SELMA exits.

ROWENA: We have to wash and dress him. Get the black suit from the wardrobe.

VIRGIL goes. SELMA re-enters.

VIRGIL'S VOICE: Where is father's suit?

ROWENA: In the wardrobe! The black one. His wedding suit.

VIRGIL comes back with his father's suit.

VIRGIL: This one?

ROWENA: (*she fetches the crucifix*) We'll put the crucifix near his head. And we need flowers. Try and find some flowers somewhere. Raymond can . . . (*without any transition to VIRGIL and SELMA*) Where is Raymond?

SELMA: (*calmly*) Raymond? He's gone.

ROWENA: (*speechless*) What do you mean, gone?

SELMA: (*repeating Raymond's words, she does it in a soft voice, her head lowered*) He said . . . you make everything vile and dirty . . . he said he wants to be respected by people, he said . . . he can't go on living here like this . . .

ROWENA rushes out of the room, comes back after a short while.

ROWENA: He's left all his things—he'll be back!

SELMA: He said he wouldn't.

ROWENA: Of course he'll be back.

VIRGIL: How far can he get? Without a penny.

SELMA: He said that he wants to go and talk to the to the small farmers . . .

VIRGIL: (*surprised*) Why? What does he want from them?

SELMA: He wants to help them improve their land . . . He wants to show them father's plans, show them how to irrigate the land . . . and how to lay out gardens . . . I wish him luck.

ROWENA: But he had everything here with me that he could possibly want.

SELMA: (*quietly*) Yes.

ROWENA: The idiot . . . the dreamer! Trying to run away . . . He's lost his nerve. He'll never make it on his own. (*to SELMA*) Bring in the crucifix and put it near your father's head.

SELMA does so.

VIRGIL: If that idiot thinks he has to run away, why doesn't he go to town then? To Greenfield . . . or south or across the border . . . where something's happening . . . I would try to make big money. It's money that buys you respect. Why go to the farmers?

ROWENA: Leave me alone. Please, leave me alone for a moment.

VIRGIL takes the suit into the chamber. ROWENA is now alone with CHARLES.

ROWENA: (*very softly, simply*) Poor Charles. I would have loved so much to arrange a funeral for you as befits a Gresham. Eight pallbearers. And the bells ringing for one hour. The aunts would have had to come. They couldn't have stayed away, after all you are their brother. Poor Charles . . . You've died at the wrong moment. Everything in your life you did at the wrong moment. But I have to . . . I have to get Virgil out of his mess first. I can't let them throw him in jail. You wouldn't want that either, would you? You wouldn't just let it happen. I can't think of any other solution, we will have to bury you secretly, here at your home. The wedding, we couldn't possibly . . . All we can do is wait until the period of mourning is over . . . Oh, I feel so sorry for you. Living with me wasn't always easy, I know. I was never really able to show you but . . . I loved you. There was so much we had to build up, we had to have a house, we had to try and be somebody in this world, we had to make a home, a home for the children— And it's all so difficult, so damn difficult . . . Where have we gone wrong? You . . . you would have known so much better, you were wise, but you never said a word. And we, we always do things the wrong way— Raymond's run away from me . . . and with Selma, I know, it hasn't gone the way I wanted. (*silence*) The child's got problems . . . (*silence*) And you . . . you sneak out of your life like a thief at night— quietly . . . like you've been all life, quietly . . . without any fuss . . . you just steal away . . . Poor

Charles. And we . . . we haven't even got the time to mourn our dead properly . . .

She has started to cry. She is crying silently. The tears are running down her cheeks. She does not even attempt to cover her face with her hands.

Scene 5

SELMA is alone in the room. She is decorating the table, but she is not very good at it. Every now and then she takes a sip from the gin bottle. Although she is alone she does it in a furtive manner as if somebody might see her. She seems excited. Sometimes she peeps out of the window.

She wears a dark, yet sophisticated low-cut dress. She wears make-up. Her cheeks are reddened.

SELMA: (*looking out of the window again, talking outside*) Can you see the carriage yet? (*the answer is incomprehensible, then*) Sorry, I can't tell you that either. (*listening, then*) Oh yes. (*she gives a short laugh, withdraws from the window, then returns to it*) You are Jack, aren't you? And that strong fellow there, that's Pete?

She stays at the window for a moment. She is flirting a bit. Then she starts rearranging things on the table just to keep herself busy. Suddenly she realizes that a few more glasses are needed. She puts them on the table.

There is some noise outside the door. Immediately Selma rushes to the door and opens it. FANNY and VIRGIL are outside.

SELMA takes FANNY'S hand immediately. She acts sentimental with a slight touch of hysteria.

SELMA: Welcome to the Gresham Household! (*she throws*

her arms around FANNY'S neck, apparently having to fight back her tears) Now I have a sister as
well. (kisses FANNY on both cheeks) I'm so happy!
(she releases FANNY from her embrace but holds
her hands tightly)

*ROWENA appears in the background. She cannot enter the
room because the others are blocking her way.*

ROWENA'S VOICE: Come on, Selma!

SELMA: (throws her arms around FANNY'S neck again) I
wish you the best of luck. (releases FANNY from her
embrace) All the best, from the bottom of my heart
. . .

FANNY: Thank you, Selma.

*ROWENA pushes through into the room. She does not like
all the fuss.*

*SELMA now embraces VIRGIL. ROWENA tries to drag
SELMA into the room but SELMA resists.*

SELMA: (to VIRGIL) And now you are really a man. A
proper married man. (she has tried to say this in a
slightly humorous tone) All the best for you as well,
brother! (kisses him) You have a beautiful wife,
treat her well. (kisses him, then releases him. Not
speaking directly to VIRGIL and FANNY; trying to
make it sound easy and funny but not really suc-
ceeding) And a whole room full of handsome,
strong, healthy, little Greshams!

*ROWENA starts to change into everyday clothes right
away. She sometimes leaves the room while doing it.*

*VIRGIL wants to enter the room. FANNY holds him back.
He looks at her uncomprehendingly.*

FANNY: (quietly) Please . . .

VIRGIL: (does not understand) What?

FANNY: Please, Virgil! (*looks at him*)

VIRGIL: (*turns away*) What do you want?

FANNY: (*quietly*) You have to . . . carry me over the threshold.

VIRGIL: What for?

FANNY: It's the tradition in my family. Please . . .

VIRGIL hesitates for a moment, then he lifts her up, FANNY puts her arm around his shoulder, smiles. He carries her into the room. ROWENA has come in again.

ROWENA: (*urging*) That's enough. The hands are watching.

FANNY: (*while VIRGIL puts her down*) It brings good luck.

VIRGIL: You don't honestly believe that, do you?!

FANNY: (*kisses him happily*) I don't know. I can't really say if I believe in it. But I know that I wish to be happy. With you. Yes, that's what I wish for us, a whole lot of happiness. (*discovers the empty wheelchair*) Where is your father?

ROWENA: (*notices the table*) Hey, what is that supposed to be?!

SELMA: I wanted it to look a bit festive today . . . in honor of the occasion . . .

ROWENA: (*already at the cupboard*) You know we don't want to make a great fuss.

She takes the cards from the cupboard and starts to spread them out. SELMA has filled three glasses. She passes one to FANNY, one to VIRGIL. She keeps one herself.

SELMA: (*lifts the glass*) Here's to you both.

She drinks first.

ROWENA: (*watching the spread of the cards*) Diamonds!

Look at this spread! Diamonds throughout. Diamonds! Money! (*has watched the drinking ceremony, quickly, with one look*) I think you should take a bottle of gin to the hands outside.

SELMA: Oh yes.

FANNY: Or we could invite them inside to celebrate with us.

ROWENA: (*as if she had not heard*) They're good workers, I'll give them that!

SELMA: I'll take care of it.

ROWENA: Take a bottle from the lower shelf. It's only the first run but it contains more alcohol.

VIRGIL loosens his clothes.

SELMA: Why are you changing?

VIRGIL: We always do that.

ROWENA: That's a custom in the Greshams' house.

VIRGIL: We also do that on Sunday after mass.

FANNY: I just thought . . . because we are celebrating today.

VIRGIL: I don't feel comfortable in this tight stuff. Do you mind?

FANNY: (*laughing*) No, I don't mind. (*then, easily*) As long as you don't have any worse habits!

ROWENA: Diamonds! I've never seen anything like this before . . . A whole load of diamonds! Just look at it! Everything seems to turn out well in the end. I wouldn't have dared to dream of that. (*turns the cards*) And now it's become reality.

SELMA: (*at the cupboard looking for the bottles*) Oh sure.

(*has not really listened*) I think Fanny is going to be a good wife for our Virgil.

ROWENA: (*irritated*) What? (*then*) Well, of course. She is ... (*arranging the cards with concentration*) She is. A few spades always have to be in the spread, of course ... It wouldn't be right without them.

SELMA has secretly taken two bottles, she tries to smuggle them out of the room hidden under her arms.

SELMA: Well, I'll go and take the gin to the hands outside.

VIRGIL has noticed the second bottle.

VIRGIL: What! Two of them?

SELMA: (*quickly walking on*) Mother says so! (*she quickly leaves the room*)

VIRGIL: They'll just want to get drunk at our expense.

ROWENA: (*does not look up from the cards*) Of course. Let them get drunk. I don't mind!

Outside the hands break into shouts of joy when SELMA brings the gin.

ROWENA: (*arranges the cards*) Look at this! Let them get drunk in honor of the occasion. That's okay. After all, some things are going to change for them as well. (*concentrating on the cards*) I've never had a spread like this before!

FANNY: (*to VIRGIL*) Raymond wasn't at the wedding. Where is ...

VIRGIL: (*gesturing to her to be silent*) Shhh!

FANNY: Why wasn't he there?

VIRGIL: Don't ask so many questions.

FANNY: You don't think Raymond is upset, do you?

ROWENA is getting restless, abruptly she stands up, walks over to the window, looks outside.

ROWENA: (*shouts sternly*) Selma!

She goes back to her cards.

VIRGIL: (*meanwhile, in a soft voice, with a sidelong look at his mother*) Raymond's run away, his name won't be mentioned in this house ever again. Understand?

ROWENA: Oh yes. This is a good spread. Diamonds . . . they've never let me down. Good . . . good. I've got to take a risk. But I'll succeed in the end!

FANNY: (*to VIRGIL*) When are we going?

VIRGIL: What do you mean?

FANNY: Or are we having the wedding party here? I don't mind.

VIRGIL: Of course we are staying here. What do you want to do? It's all so . . . We are . . . It's not the time now for a real celebration.

FANNY: I mean . . . it's customary at least to invite a few friends and . . .

ROWENA: That's the first lesson you'll have to learn, Fillingham . . .

FANNY: (*not aggressively, simply*) My name is no longer Fillingham, I'm a Gresham now.

ROWENA: A Gresham—you'll have to earn your right to that name first. (*turns round to FANNY*)

FANNY: I'll do my best.

ROWENA: (*concentrating on the cards again*) Then you have to understand that we have a great deal of respect for work here and not a lot for celebrations. You are not in your bar any more.

She starts to gather up the cards.

FANNY: (*quietly*) Oh yes, I know that. But don't worry, I'm used to hard work. I've had to look after myself from the time I was fourteen. I'm not like you might think I am, madam. You just don't know me yet. (*trying to get VIRGIL'S support*) Virgil? I became a waitress because . . . there was no other job for me. But I'm not the sort of person who gets familiar with customers if you think that. Virgil, help me, you know it's true. No one can say a word against me in that respect. You can ask anyone in town. If you want.

ROWENA: (*puts the cards back in the cupboard*) I've already done that, girl, what do think? (*walks up to the window, glimpses outside, sternly*) Selma!

She walks out of the room.

FANNY and VIRGIL are alone. Embarrassment, silence.

FANNY: (*then, without emphasis, just to start a conversation*) Where is Raymond? Tell me honestly.

VIRGIL: (*annoyed*) He's gone.

FANNY: Where to?

VIRGIL: How should I know? Do we really have to talk about him? Mother doesn't like it. For God's sake, don't mention his name in front of her.

FANNY: (*thoughtfully*) I still have to get used to a lot of things. I'm afraid . . . It's all so strange for me. I hardly know your family. I know you. And Raymond a little. He used to come to the "Coach and Horses" quite often. Raymond is a nice fellow. I like him . . . but . . . it all happened so quickly, I can still hardly believe we are married. (*tries to approach him, he moves back*) You know how I feel? As if my alarm clock could go off any moment and my landlord will shout upstairs: Get up, Fanny! Rise and shine! Scrub the floor! Wash the glasses!

She stands by his side, takes his arm.

FANNY: Say it! (*looks at him*) Come on, say it . . .

VIRGIL: What? (*wants to shake her off*)

FANNY: Is this your bad arm? I'm sorry. For me it was like a bolt from the blue. Say it. Oh, my silly little boy! Don't give me that desperate look. What do you think I want to hear? That you love me . . .

VIRGIL: (*turns away a bit*) Of course I do. After all I married you, didn't I?

FANNY: When I started to work at the "Coach and Horses" and I saw you for the first time . . . I remember exactly . . . I noticed you right away. Of course, then I had no idea where you came from, who you were, I didn't find that out till much later. I never told you, but I crossed my fingers behind my back that you would sit at a table I was waiting on. It worked, but you never took any notice of me. I liked you from the very first moment. How is it possible that you see someone for the first time and take to him right away? You don't know this person, don't know anything about him, but still you fancy him immediately. As if you had known him in a previous life, and suddenly, without warning you meet him again, face to face. At that time . . . I wouldn't have dreamed that it would be you, the stubborn skirt-chaser Virgil Gresham, who would marry me of all girls. You have to say it. Please . . .

VIRGIL: If it means so much to you. I love you.

FANNY: (*puts her arms around his neck and kisses him*) Is it really so difficult for a man to say these three little words? And I love you. (*kisses him*) From this moment we are really husband and wife. You know, I would have stayed with you even if you hadn't married me. I mean, you see how stupid I am . . . two people are husband and wife from the moment they really love each other . . .

ROWENA: (*enters, has heard the last sentences to VIRGIL*) This Fillingham, is she really that naive? Or has she read too many novels?

She crosses the room in one move without stopping. Walks towards the window.

VIRGIL has freed himself from Fanny's embrace. Fanny stands isolated.

ROWENA: (*to VIRGIL*) Go and bring her luggage inside. (*goes to the window, looks outside, then*) Selma! Hey! Come back inside. How long are you going to stay out there?

During the whole scene the muffled laughter, singing, and shouting of the hands can be heard from outside.

VIRGIL enters with the suitcases, he puts them down carelessly. One of the suitcases flies open. While stuffing the clothes back in VIRGIL discovers a wedding dress. He pulls it out. FANNY is embarrassed, she cannot stop VIRGIL.

VIRGIL: Hey! Now look at this! (*holds the dress up*) That's a real wedding dress! Hey!

ROWENA gives it a quick expert look.

ROWENA: (*partly with irony, partly with respect*) Lace! What do you say to that!

VIRGIL: (*laughing*) She was prepared!

FANNY: Please . . . Virgil . . . stop it . . . You didn't want to have it that way, but I always hoped to have a white wedding one day.

VIRGIL: It wouldn't really be proper: one can't really say you're still a virgin! *(laughs)*

FANNY: Give it back! *(upset, tears the dress from VIRGIL'S hand and stuffs it back into the suitcase)*

VIRGIL: Come on! Don't be so upset. I was just kidding.

SELMA enters slightly tipsy. She has enough control, however, not to let it show.

ROWENA: *(suspicious, quietly, annoyed)* Did you drink some of that gin? *(Selma does not answer)* That was first run!

SELMA: I couldn't refuse, I would have insulted the hands.

ROWENA: More than 70 percent alcohol.

SELMA: Just a little glass.

VIRGIL: *(to SELMA, he has not heard the previous short dialogue)* Just imagine, she had everything prepared: wedding dress, veil, etc. . . .

SELMA: Only a white wedding is a proper wedding. A coach and four white horses. And relatives and a lot of friends. A proper church and the bells ringing . . . *(she says this rather harshly, yet has to fight back her rising emotions)* And girls in white dresses . . . carrying the veil . . . and scattering flowers . . . music . . . dance . . .

FANNY: *(harshly)* To be honest, I had a different idea of this day as well.

ROWENA: Let's come down to earth again! You've made it, Fillingham! You wanted to have Virgil, now you've got him. You've struck it lucky. So you can be satisfied.

FANNY: Well, of course, I'm not ashamed . . . I wished to become Virgil's wife, I dreamed of it. I didn't imagine, I never for one moment imagined that it could come true. I made this wedding dress myself on my days off, while the others went out dancing. I saved up money for my trousseau because I haven't got anybody to pay it for me. I put every penny aside because I knew it would look bad if I moved into my future home poor as a beggar.

ROWENA: A few hundred dollars, my God! Don't make such a fuss about it.

FANNY: Tell me, how many daughters of middle-class families in Ashford do you know who would bring in more dowry?

ROWENA: (*with a dismissive gesture*) Middle-class families!

FANNY: I dreamed of marrying Virgil. But not just to become a Gresham as you might think. The Greshams are not so respected that everybody is lining up to be one of them.

ROWENA: Mind your language! Who are you to talk like that?

VIRGIL: Come on, mother, don't get so upset.

ROWENA: I want to set the rules out clearly. (*to VIRGIL*) You are a weakling! (*to FANNY*) Let's say it straight out, what sort of husband do you think would have been fit for someone like you? A lousy farmhand with scabies, working for starvation wages, and you would have had half an acre for a cow and two pigs so you could get your family at least a warm meal a few times a week. You would have raised half a dozen kids, hardly knowing how to keep them alive. Instead, you made lace for your wedding dress, slept around a bit, and then, before you could say Jack Robinson, you had parked your big ass on a stretch of land so large you can't cover it in a day's journey.

SELMA: Come on, stop fighting. This is not a day for fights. Sit down. Sit down. Let's drink a toast to the new couple.

She rushes into the kitchen and returns with a cake.

VIRGIL: Hey! A cake! Where did you get that from?

SELMA: I made it myself.

VIRGIL: You? (*laughs*) You made a cake?! Is it edible? I can hardly wait to find out.

ROWENA: (*reprimanding*) Stop fooling around, you lout! Of course Selma can cook. She learned it in school.

SELMA starts slicing up the cake.

SELMA: Oh . . . I'm afraid it hasn't risen . . .

She cannot decide whether to hand out the pieces anyway. VIRGIL bursts out laughing.

ROWENA: Give me a slice. Let me taste it. (*tries a bite*) Mmmmh. Yes . . . not bad. You must have forgotten to cover the baking tin with paper. (*to the others, as an excuse*) Selma doesn't know how to handle our oven yet. She's only used to these modern stoves. Like they have in town now.

Silence. Eating. Virgil does not even try to pretend that he likes the cake.

FANNY: (*to be polite*) That was really a nice idea of yours, Selma, to make a cake. Thank you. I think it tastes really good.

SELMA: (*sceptically*) You think so?

FANNY: You have to give me the recipe.

SELMA: Thanks. (*then, humorously*) It will go down easier with a drink.

VIRGIL: (*abruptly*) Hey! Did I hear right? Didn't you say: the largest stretch of land that you can't cover in a day's journey?

ROWENA: (*proudly*) I did say that!

VIRGIL: And Miller?

ROWENA: It's not worth mentioning that name any more. Miller is finished. He's a worm. Pretty soon you will see him kneeling on our doorstep begging for some water for his cattle. While you were driving to church I exercised my option on the Hanson farm.

She walks over to the map and pointedly draws a thick new borderline.

VIRGIL: Well I never! (*laughs*) You are really clever! How did you manage that? I'll be damned! How did you raise the money for it?

ROWENA: (*drawing without watching*) She had a savings book with 635 dollars. You show a Hanson such a sum and he'll agree to any deal.

FANNY: And nobody felt the need to ask me?

ROWENA: I have a few ideas about how to raise the rest of the money . . .

FANNY: And I don't have any say in it? It's my money.

ROWENA: Am I throwing the money away on drink or what? My money! My money! It was the chance of a lifetime. Shouldn't I have taken it? I won't get another chance to stand up to this Miller. Or did you want to spend your few dollars on ribbons and lace?

SELMA: Oh mother, it's not worth . . .

ROWENA: (*to FANNY, close*) You said you wanted to become a Gresham. Fair enough! Why should it bother you then if the Greshams get the biggest name around here, perhaps one day even in the whole district?

FANNY: It is my money.

ROWENA: My money!

FANNY: At least you might have asked me first.

ROWENA: Oh, milady wants to be asked first! All right then, I'm asking you now. The contract's been signed, the price has to be paid within three days. Satisfied? Oh, and I daresay you'll want to be there when I put the money on the table. Because I could be swindled. Because all of a sudden I am too old and too stupid to do it on my own! That's what you think, don't you, my little waitress? You come into this house and before you even settle down you're already the boss here! That's probably the way you imagine it. Sure. It's all so easy. You sleep around a bit, and keep your eyes open, and wait for your chance, and then presto chango, you are somebody!

VIRGIL: Mother, it's not worth fighting over!

FANNY: Apparently it has never crossed your mind that someone might want to marry your son just for love.

ROWENA: Well, the Greshams' property hasn't exactly been an obstacle to your love.

FANNY: Land and property! And the house! And possessions! That's obviously all you ever think about.

SELMA: (*helplessly*) Don't you think you might try to get along with each other today? You've still got plenty of time for arguing.

She fills the glasses and tries to get the others to drink. She drinks herself.

FANNY: I was afraid I wouldn't really be welcome here and I knew I had to expect a lifetime of work. But I'm not a cow that you can put in your cowshed and milk every day. We can leave all this to you, all your grand property, every inch of your "largest stretch of land." If Virgil agrees, it's all right with me. Just keep it all, sit on it, and be happy! If it's all right with Virgil we could move somewhere else right now, on the spot, and start all over again together. I'm prepared to do that. Yes, I don't deny it, I wanted to marry Virgil. When all of sudden he turned up and asked for my hand . . . I would have followed him blindly. If he had said, look, I can't marry you officially but I love you, I would have been like a wife to him. If he had said, look, my mother doesn't approve, so let's move somewhere else, I would have gone with him. We are young, we are strong, and we can make a living, no matter where we are. And hopefully without being hated by everyone. Now I'm beginning to understand why Raymond's run away from you.

ROWENA is furious but she softens her voice.

ROWENA: Is this waitress really that stupid or is she just pretending? (*pause*) Virgil would never have volunteered to marry one of your sort.

FANNY is thunderstruck. She turns to VIRGIL expecting his protest. VIRGIL turns away.

ROWENA: Miller would have gotten a summons to force you to appear in court as a witness. It was the best solution for all of us. Virgil is in the clear, I own the Hanson farm, and with the water rights I am going to cut Miller down to size. And you . . . after all you have no reason to complain either. You wanted to have Virgil . . .

FANNY: That's right.

ROWENA: You are his wife now. What more do you want?

FANNY: (*after a long pause, she has difficulty controlling her voice, then, as a provocation*) My wedding celebration, that's what I want to have now.

She leaves the room. Embarrassed silence.

SELMA: Was that really necessary, mother?

ROWENA: That's what she wanted! You heard it with your own ears, I won't stand being insulted by a cheap—waitress. (*takes a few deep breaths*) Who knows, it might be best to set the record straight right from the start. One day she would have found out the truth anyway.

FANNY comes back, the cowhands appear in the doorway behind her.

FANNY: Come inside! Don't be afraid.

The hands do not dare to enter, they remain standing in the doorway embarrassed.

FANNY: We are celebrating a wedding! Everybody is to have a good time today! I need people to rejoice with me. Come on in!

ROWENA: It is most unusual here to allow hands into the front room.

FANNY: I too have to get used to a lot of things I've always thought were unusual. (*to the workers who are still standing in the doorway*) Come on! Go ahead! Come on in, you're all invited.

She grabs one of the workers and drags him into the room.

The second one stands there embarrassed. Then she drags the second one inside. The others follow slowly, shyly.

FANNY goes to the cupboard.

ROWENA: Hey, hey!

FANNY: (*to the hands*) This is a large farm, the Greshams' farm, it's just recently become the largest around. Be proud, you are working on the largest farm in the area. One day it will be one of the largest in the whole district. (*to ROWENA*) Or am I wrong? The Greshams know how to keep house and how to live. In this house you don't want for anything.

She looks for glasses, ROWENA stops her from entering the side room.

ROWENA: The hands have already had enough gin! I won't allow this house to become a saloon. We have never been given to celebrating.

FANNY: Then it's about time some things changed.

FANNY distributes glasses and gin among the workers.

ROWENA: (*to VIRGIL, quietly*) She is quite capable of causing us a . . .

VIRGIL: What can I do? She doesn't know anything.

ROWENA: Talk to her.

VIRGIL: What can I say to her?

ROWENA: She's your wife.

FANNY: Talk to me. Do you always have to wait till somebody tells you what to do?

VIRGIL: So what! (*turns away*) What's all this to me anyway!

FANNY: Come on, fellows, drink! It looks as if there are not enough glasses, so this house is still not that big after all. You don't mind drinking from the bottle, do you, men?!

The hands stand around undecided and embarrassed.

FANNY: Don't be shy! Come on, drink! A toast to the bride! I've hit the jackpot, I've married the heir of the Gresham farm. It's the chance of a lifetime, let's drink to it!

The workers start drinking, yet still with reluctance.

FANNY: Go ahead and play some music, don't be shy! Pete. I know all of you, Jack, Tom, Josh. I remember you from the time when I was nothing more than a waitress at the "Coach and Horses." I remember you were quite different then.

She pulls a harmonica out of one of the hands' pockets, puts it to his lips, and tries to get him to play. The other hands take out other instruments or quickly get them from outside. Gradually the sound of the music grows fuller.

ROWENA: I knew it! I figured this Fillingham for a bitch! (*to VIRGIL*) Why don't you do something, you weakling? Why don't you stop her?

FANNY: (*busy filling the glasses, only half turning around*) He's not used to making his own decisions. He's used to obeying. (*to the hands*) Drink! There is enough gin, it doesn't matter that it is moonshine. We can all drink ourselves to death if we feel like it. (*again towards VIRGIL*) You'll have to tell him exactly what he's supposed to do. And to say. And to think. Then he will do it, and say it, and think it. He was supposed to marry me, and he did, didn't he? (*to the workers*) Who is going to dance with the bride?

Everybody hesitates, so FANNY grabs the person next to her with determination. The music is still very soft and slow. FANNY dances with the worker, the others make room for them, they form a semicircle and watch the dance.

SELMA sits alone in her chair, separated from the others. When she drinks she always pours down half a glass without pausing.

VIRGIL keeps his distance from the group, he remains close to ROWENA.

At first the music is melancholy, sentimental, the dance is not more than a gentle swaying. Gradually the atmosphere livens up. The other hands start sneaking looks at SELMA. Very slightly, at first almost mechanically, Selma starts to move her body in time with the music.

ROWENA: When I think back how it started with Charles and me . . . Charles hardly dared to tell his aunts. With the only silver dollar I had left I bought our wedding rings at Greenbaum's. Simple cheap rings. No gold. I'm still wearing mine. (*she sometimes pauses in her speech, watching throughout what is going on around her.*) It was on the 17th of September.

One of the hands is flirting with SELMA. When he asks her to dance she turns him down. He starts to dance awkwardly with another worker. VIRGIL fills a glass for him and SELMA.

ROWENA: We spent our wedding night here in this house. Not a single window that wasn't broken. Holes everywhere in the floor. Poor Charles was so sweet and timid . . . so considerate, and his head full of dreams. To know him was to love him. He was a good man. And life wasn't easy for him. Why is it always the good people who have to suffer?

VIRGIL is hanging around the table, SELMA'S attention is more and more drawn to the hands.

ROWENA: I knew the aunts would never have allowed Charles to marry me. We couldn't expect any help from their side. We knew that. And I didn't have anything. The only silver dollar I had . . . I had spent on the wedding. That night Charles and I swore to ourselves that we would make it in life. I have made it. I feel so sorry that he couldn't live to see it . . .

One of the hands takes heart and approaches the table to ask SELMA to dance. He does it in a clumsy way, afraid to be turned down. Therefore he almost looks more at RO-WENA than at SELMA. ROWENA shows her disapproval.

ROWENA: (*reprimanding*) Selma!

She cannot stop SELMA, however. In a strange, almost impersonal way SELMA gives herself over to the rhythm. Her dance is different, her movements are lascivious and do not fully correspond to the serious rural character of the music. The workers are all after the chance to dance a few steps with SELMA, she lets them, but basically she dances by herself. Gradually the music grows faster and more intense. They start to feel the alcohol, the hands grow more relaxed, there is a lively atmosphere and laughter which often bursts out suddenly and contrasts to ROWENA'S speech.

ROWENA: Eventually we had to tell the aunts. There was no way around it. Charles didn't dare to speak to them. So I went alone. They received me in their kitchen. Like a servant. I told them how things were and that I had become a Gresham as well. The fine ladies listened to my story. In their kitchen. Their faces stony. They offered me some tea and biscuits. I couldn't eat a thing. (*she keeps surveying the scene, sternly*) Selma!

The dancing has become hectic and exuberant. Finally everybody stands in a semicircle, laughing, shouting, and clapping to the increasing rhythm. SELMA dances in the provocative, yet mechanical and unemotional style of a night-club dancer. The farmhands change positions, so ROWENA'S view is blocked.

ROWENA: *(her tone gets harsher)* Oh indeed, they were very courteous, these Gresham ladies. Extremely courteous. *(while saying this she cranes her neck and twists her head, yet still cannot get a good view)*

VIRGIL follows the scene with interest. Under different circumstances he would have joined in.

ROWENA: And they addressed me with "Miss Rowena." When they said goodbye they handed me ten dollars. They paid me off like a whore. And I said thank you to those ugly goats! Neither of them would shake my hand. I slammed the door, my face burning with shame. I was choking with anger. I flung the money back at their feet through the kitchen window. Let them choke on it, I thought! These assholes! I, Rowena Gresham, would show them! And I have. I've made it. I've got what I wanted, what a pity that Charles didn't live to see it. I own property now that stretches further than the two old goats could walk on their own two feet.

A sudden scream from FANNY. The hands are startled. The dancing stops. The music gradually fades out. When the hands start moving to the sides, the door comes in sight. VIRGIL jumps up and dashes to the cupboard where he keeps his gun. The door pushes open very slowly. It is RAYMOND leaning against the jamb. He looks badly injured, covered in blood, so beaten up, he can barely stand. It takes quite a while for everyone to overcome the shock.

The hands helplessly pull back towards the wall.

ROWENA: Raymond . . .

VIRGIL: Raymond? Who's done that to you?

RAYMOND: (*making a great effort to speak, in a toneless voice*) I . . . only wanted to help them . . .

FANNY: What happened? Raymond, how did you . . .

RAYMOND: I wanted to explain father's plans to them.

VIRGIL: Give me their names, I'll shoot the bastards.

RAYMOND slowly slumps to the floor in exhaustion.

FANNY: For God's sake, Raymond!

FANNY wants to rush to his assistance.

ROWENA: (*determined*) Oh no! He left the house alone, so he can come back in alone.

FANNY does not know what to do. She does not dare to help RAYMOND, she stops halfway.

FANNY: You look terrible. What did they do to you?

RAYMOND: They wouldn't listen to me.

FANNY: He can't stand up.

ROWENA remains stiff, motionless. RAYMOND starts to drag himself through the room towards ROWENA, very slowly, on all fours, with his last ounce of strength and with supreme effort.

VIRGIL: (*serious, moved*) They're going to pay for this.

RAYMOND has crawled a short distance, has to rest.

FANNY: That's enough, mother!

Rowena remains motionless.

The hands start to slip out of the room quietly and disgusted. RAYMOND pulls himself up again, inch by inch he struggles to crawl towards ROWENA.

VIRGIL: Who did that? I'll shoot the swine!

SELMA: (*to one of the hands*) Pete! Quick, ride to the village and get the doctor!

FANNY: Do we have medicine?

RAYMOND crawls towards ROWENA, slowly and with effort.

FANNY: For God's sake! (*to ROWENA*) He's your son!

RAYMOND has reached ROWENA, he collapses at her feet, she bends down.

ROWENA: Yes, he's my son. (*helps him to stand up*) He's my son again.

This is a signal for the others. The spell is broken, everybody is getting busy fetching water, bandages etc.

A gin bottle is snatched from one of the workers' hands, the gin will be used for disinfection. RAYMOND'S wounds are uncovered, his shirt is cut open, more wounds appear underneath.

VIRGIL pushes his father's wheelchair onto the scene. All together they lift RAYMOND into the wheelchair. They do it very carefully. The workers remain standing along the wall motionless. Although RAYMOND tries not to scream, it is apparent that he is in great pain.

ROWENA: How could this happen?

SELMA: Careful! You're hurting him!

VIRGIL: Who did it?

FANNY: Pete is already on his way for the doctor.

ROWENA: He's young and strong. He'll mend again.

SELMA: We have to dress the wounds.

ROWENA: Wounds heal.

FANNY pours gin into RAYMOND'S mouth.

ROWENA: Don't worry, you're home now.

RAYMOND: (*simultaneously*) I wanted to show them how to irrigate their land.

ROWENA: Don't talk, you mustn't exert yourself.

The following speeches are delivered almost simultaneously:

RAYMOND: (*has difficulty talking, but keeps on without interruption*) Father's plans are good, I know it. They are good.

ROWENA: (*in between*) You'll be well again.

RAYMOND: They beat me up.

ROWENA: (*in between*) We are all together again. That's all that counts. What a pity that Charles is not here to see it . . . I've bought the Hanson farm, we've made it, do you hear, Raymond, old Hanson's farm. And Virgil . . . he's out of trouble.

RAYMOND: I wanted to show them where to dig a channel. But they beat me up and wouldn't listen to what a Gresham had to say. They would rather keep scratching in the dry soil.

ROWENA stands towering in the middle of the scene, RAYMOND is lying half across her lap, the family members arrange themselves in a group around her, forming a pyramid.

ROWENA: It's all right now. Hush. Don't talk, you mustn't exert yourself. You are at home, that's the main thing. Nobody can fight us now. Hush. Forget what happened. Hush. All the small landowners, the riff-raff, Miller, the judge, the neighbors, they no longer matter. We've made it, Raymond, we've made it, we've arrived, now we are somebody . . .

CURTAIN

Elfriede Jelinek

President Evening Breeze
A Dramolet based freely on Johann Nestroy

Translated by Helga Schreckenberger
and Jacqueline Vansant

Act One

Evening Breeze and his daughter Ottilie are sitting in a South Sea islandesque jungle stage set. However, they are dressed like Europeans, with subtle accessories, a mixture of South Sea folklore, feathers, nose rings, etc. Ottilie is very overdone, but likable. Both are chewing human shank bones, blood running down their chins.

OTTILIE sings:
Come on in, dearest friends
We'll wring your necks with our bare hands.
Oh go on, eat that sausage.
Stuff your face, that's our adage.
Come on join us, tourists with your Kodaks
Wandering through our stomachs.
Our stomachs, they'll be churning.
Our stomachs, they'll be yearning.
So come along, we crave your meat.
We're in seventh heaven only when we eat.
The Yugos and the darkies, they're so tempting.
We scarf them down without sampling.
Our plates we smear with mustard and herbs.
Straight off the packing we eat the Serbs.
Oh, the shit'll hit the fan!! Aren't we too much?
Quick, give us your little hand!! Crunch! Munch!
Up there behind the little door there's plenty of drink to
    guzzle.
Come on. So join us, it's no big puzzle.
Our cute mountains and valleys, they're up for sale.
Hey go on in, looky, looky!
Here's our meat grinder!
Don't be coy, come on in!
Well, ladies and gents:

There'll still be wine
And you'll be dead and gone.
You'll be eaten up, cooked or raw.
And there'll be beautiful dames
And you'll have bit the dust.
'Cause foreigners taste the yummiest.

There'll still be wine
and you'll be dead and gone
We have an appetite, but we are not contrite.
And there'll be beautiful dames
And you'll have bit the dust.
'Cause on our kind, we do not dine.

OTTILIE: Oh, Daddy, I'm really quite desperate. I'd really like it if you were the president of our people! And you know, you could ride the street car for a reduced price. My girl friends would be so impressed.

EVENING BREEZE: Go on, you silly puss. . . . I'd have to work all the time. . . . no more holidays, why that wouldn't be Fiji-islandesque at all! Man doesn't live by work alone, he has to eat, too.

OTTILIE: But Pepi's Daddy is a president and everybody knows him. Pepi is always teasing me because of it.

EVENING BREEZE: Doesn't it count for anything that I'm the head of the Council of the United Figi-Islands? I was handpicked especially for the job, there's nobody worse right now.

OTTILIE: But Pepi's daddy . . . ,

EVENING BREEZE: And what's more, I am the biggest meat exporter . . . and my cute little blood banks are all over the country . . . At every beautiful overlook, a little blood bank . . . our discretion is a matter of course, of course.

OTTILIE: Ah, come on, Daddy! I'd be so proud of you . . .

EVENING BREEZE: Go on! . . . Flatterer!

OTTILIE: But Daddy the tourists who visit us, you just can't bump them off and debone them, Daddy. Promise me you won't, okay! They come because of our climate and then they don't want to go back home anymore because it's so beautiful here on our island.

EVENING BREEZE: But only last year one wanted to leave.

OTTILIE: That's right. But we didn't let him out.

EVENING BREEZE: My brave people managed to nab him right at the border and we locked him up. And then I've locked up my people one by one.

OTTILIE: You shouldn't lock everybody up. Daddy, that's just not done. You've got to let out a few so they can welcome our guests!

EVENING BREEZE: Our economic strength is based on the cooperation between corporations and the incorporated. Why in the world do they have to slip so far into our jungle?

OTTILIE: When you've become president, then you can't can the foreigners anymore.

EVENING BREEZE: Then where are we going to get our famous canned goulash from? In the entire Fiji-Federation there's none better!

OTTILIE: You've got to let them leave, Dad! Think about it. Then they can tell everybody what a magnanimous president we have. And you are such a wonderful daddy. (*She kisses him and smears him with blood.*) And you were such a good husband to Mom before her finger accidentally got caught in the sausage grinder.

EVENING BREEZE: And she got pulled in all the way. You know Mommy had gotten a little too fat at the end!

OTTILIE: Oh, Dad, I just want you to become president. That would be enough for me. And Mommy would have been so happy, too.

EVENING BREEZE: But little princess, why when everything's so comfortable as it is right now? I'm just not ambitious. And I don't even want to think about the campaign that I'd have to run in order to get elected.

OTTILIE: It's not a trifle to address the savages with "sir!"

EVENING BREEZE: Then they would have to return the honor.

OTTILIE: And every year we would send cultural emissaries to the neighboring islands so that they would know what culture is and how to recognize it.

EVENING BREEZE: And I'm supposed to pay for that, too, right?

OTTILIE: You'll see, Daddy, you'll like it when you're president.

EVENING BREEZE: But now for today's burning question. What are we going to eat for lunch?

OTTILIE: There's still a little of the young native left over, a piece of rump roast and the last bit of bottom round. And then there're still some leftovers from last week's tourist sausage.

EVENING BREEZE: First, I'll call them my dear compatriots on television and then I'll eat them or save them for later.

OTTILIE: Yeah, television, that's a must, Daddy.

EVENING BREEZE: Did we really eat that much, Otti? I feel so stuffed.

OTTILIE: You know that not many of our neighboring tribe are left anymore. I hardly see any of them when I climb up the mountain and peer down into the valley.

EVENING BREEZE: Then we'll stock up on tourists. We call them a shady lot and scarf them down to the last bite!

OTTILIE: Now, now, Daddy. Who are we going to sell our cans and sausages to if there are no more foreigners left because we've eaten them all and who are we going to use for our sausages if we've already scarfed them down?

EVENING BREEZE: My little princess understands the meaning of enterprise. Bravo!

OTTILIE: Listen, Daddy, the natives are to be spared starting right now. Then if we don't eat them anymore they'll be so thankful that they'll elect you on the spot.

EVENING BREEZE: Not bad. And at the same time curious.

OTTILIE: And as for your campaign I'll voluntarily give up chocolate. And you won't even have to give me an allowance anymore, Daddy!

EVENING BREEZE: Until the election I'll limit myself to foreigners! Our Grand Yoohooers will surely want me. You can always count on them if something's brewing up against foreigners.

OTTILIE: Right you are, Daddyo!

EVENING BREEZE: Some of the natives are so tough that we have to cook 'em for days. I think foreigners are tenderer. They also have culture, although theirs is not as good as ours.

OTTILIE: In any case, they're not used to people like us!

EVENING BREEZE: Anything we can get abroad, we'll process. From now on we're against foreigners, little princess, am I right?

OTTILIE: Exactly. You'll look out for our prosperity. Daddy, you'll do fine!

EVENING BREEZE: And if I get a native by mistake?

OTTILIE: Just don't be so clumsy! You can say the native we're eating is actually a foreigner in disguise and then be done with it.

EVENING BREEZE: You're a clever girl! You take after humble ole me!

OTTILIE: First, we'll eat those in prison. They'll last for a while. They'd never elect you anyway.

EVENING BREEZE: All I want is my peace, little princess.

(OTTILIE *covers him with kisses*): Oh, my daddy can't deny me anything. (*She jumps on his lap.*)

EVENING BREEZE (*is moved and pets her*): If only your Mom could have seen this!

(*Thunder and lightning. A huge can labeled "Vienna Potpourri" descends. The lid lifts off and stays open. LIZZY, EVENING BREEZE'S wife, who had died in an accident in the sausage grinder, emerges. She's wearing a pastel-colored robe—preferably mint green or something like it—as if she were on her way to the Opera Ball. Huge vegetable parts shoot out from around her out of the can. LIZZY emerges as far as her hips and sings a beautiful song.*)

Vienna blood, Vienna blood.
It's hot stuff, it's hot stuff . . .
From the mountains to the valleys
You see bones in all the alleys.
The bones, over the shoulder, are divested
Who was before, is no more, but digested.

Vienna blood, Vienna blood.
Sausage, pork and kraut fill our gut!
Smoked ham, roasted meat do us proud.
Who tastes no good get's kicked out!
Or we'll ask him to dine
On some goulash and some wine.
Who's been served, who wants more?
No one checks graves anymore.
If someone's missing
So what, that's just tough luck.
We'll eat him all spiced up.
So he's at ease
Now at least
In a bed, soft and cozy.
On we'll mosey
With song and fun
He has his peace.
Let the music never cease.
Vienna blood, Vienna blood.
It's hot stuff, it's hot stuff.
If you stroll along the river
You'll get hit till you shiver.
A little hand from the ground,
It comes out, pulls you down
By your coat, by your feet,
Chase it off, and toute de suite.
For the tourists we go all out
So they don't turn around
And take off heedless, bound
To where no past can be found.
On no cathedrals can they dwell.
But that's all just as well
Since we've got 'em, yeah we've got 'em.
It's not us, it wasn't us.
If someone makes a fuss
He'll be eaten straight away

Keeping trouble here at bay.
But we, we're playing with fire.
To sell our souvenirs, who can we hire?
'Cause our people, we preserve in sauce.
Yes, yes, just follow your snozz.
There they are, all of them
For whom no one ever gave a damn
'Cause they never once complained.
At least not to me, not to you.
So we never had a clue.
Hurry,
Hurry,
Vienna blood,
It's hot stuff, it's hot stuff.

Act Two

(*EVENING BREEZE, at a podium, with a television in front of him. The screen is turned towards EVENING BREEZE. A short distance away, some savages are carrying placards with unflattering sayings about EVENING BREEZE on them. OTTILIE is sitting beside her father.*)

EVENING BREEZE: Dear fellow citizens, it's me, your future president. (*Booing comes from the TV.*) Let me share with you: The time is ripe.

OTTILIE: Hello! The corn bins are full, the election is a done deal. Food is cheap here compared with any place else. (*Booing comes from the TV.*)

EVENING BREEZE: I'm now speaking to you, dear islanders. But I forgot what I was going to say. *Booing.*

Ottilie (*softly*): Daddy, you wanted to say that you'll be

president for all Grand Yoohooers, big and small, all are yours, no matter what each tastes like.

EVENING BREEZE (*loudly*): I'd like to be president for all Grand Yoohooers. (*Terrible booing.*) My people don't want to listen to me. They are completely uneducable. I'll have them canned immediately and I'll mail-order new ones from a neighboring island. They're not as belligerent. They're easier to govern.

OTTILIE: First, you take them out of the jungle and then they thank you with a slap in the face.

EVENING BREEZE: Without me they would eat each other raw. Thanks to my sausage empire they are being processed into pâté à la parisienne. Why should I make such huge sacrifices? (*Booing.*)

OTTILIE: Daddy, maybe your people are angry at you because you have canned so many eager, industrious people and exported them.

EVENING BREEZE: Oh, I completely forgot about that.

OTTILIE: If you forgot it, then I forgot it, too, Daddyo. (*Booing.*)

EVENING BREEZE: I'll show them what a president is. We savages have our culture, too.

OTTILIE: I'm afraid they aren't listening to you, Daddy.

EVENING BREEZE: But speechmaking is an old savage custom and I hear even the civilized are imitating us! (*Booing.*)

OTTILIE: Bravo, Dad. Don't show no fear! We'll eat the foreigners first, and then after the election our islanders. You have fattened them up so nicely during your campaign so they would vote for you. (*Booing.*)

EVENING BREEZE: That doesn't help. It seems to me they don't want me and yet I love them to death. I can't sleep at all because I'm constantly thinking about ways to serve them best.

OTTILIE: What are you going to do now?

EVENING BREEZE: I forgot.

OTTILIE: Well, I've had my fill of people who always find something to criticize.

EVENING BREEZE (*sings*):
To be president would be fine and dandy.
Oh, as a president I'd be one of a kind.
I could eat my people just like sugar candy
And then put them out of my mind.
If some hick visits from across the sea
I'll gobble him up, what's it to me?
Your president's greatest talent:
Eat'em and forget'em.

OTTLIE joins in the chorus:

Your president's greatest talent:
Eat'em and forget'em.

(*Angry booing is coming from the television*)

EVENING BREEZE: I'm clueless, my little princess.

OTTILIE: They're ingrates.

EVENING BREEZE: Those are foreign trouble-makers. Meat like that you can only throw away.

OTTILIE: Surely, this angry mob is mostly foreigners. Should we wrap them up for later?

Sings:

The songs of my youth, give me again
The sweet songs of my homeland.

She yodels.

EVENING BREEZE: I won't tolerate anything foreign

anymore. Another St. Bartholomew's Night would be great!

OTTILIE: No pain, no gain.

EVENING BREEZE: Hello, my people! I promise you a warm meal every day made from undesirable persons who come to us from abroad. (*Booing.*) By not asking where the food comes from we are solving our food problems with style.

OTTILIE (*screams*): Be reasonable, people. (*They both duck behind the orator's podium when they are bombarded with objects.*)

EVENING BREEZE: Don't be rash. Don't look for trouble! Don't get me upset! Or even the fattest citizen won't taste good anymore.

OTTILIE: You can't make an omelet without breaking eggs.

EVENING BREEZE: As the call, so the echo.

OTTILIE: Miserable riffraff!

EVENING BREEZE: Miserable pigs! (*The booing and throwing of objects gets so bad that EVENING BREEZE and his daughter have to flee. They run away.*)

Intermezzo

(Sad and disheveled, *OTTILIE sits down on a tree trunk, HERMANN, in a gray business suit and an attaché case, enters. He is a young man dressed to the nines.*)

HERMANN: What do I see? A beautiful savage? I would marry her without a second thought. But why don't you cultivate your appearance any better, Miss?

OTTILIE: State the reason for your coming here or else I'll be forced to call the meat inspector. Hold it, just a minute. It seems to me I now loveth a foreigner. What kind are you?

HERMANN: Maybe you can deduce the answer from this biographical sketch which I invented myself. *(He removes papers from his attaché case and recites):* My birthplace, as well as my early childhood are unknown to me. My memory goes back to the age of four where the employers in my day care spanked me terribly because I wanted to found a new party. Better young than invalid. Ciao! My best wishes.

OTTILIE: You expected everything to be a lot easier, didn't you?

HERMANN: Difficult, it's not. You take a handful of people, carry them away, and position them there where you need them. You just can't forget where they are.

OTTILIE: That's true. That's my father's cardinal mistake. He always forgets everything.

HERMANN: Because you'll need them to applaud.

OTTILIE: That's exactly what's happening on my father's island kingdom where he wants to become president.

HERMANN: What do I hear? Count me in. I'm a specialist, I'm his man. I specialize in unresolvable problems, I assure you.

OTTILIE: Just be careful that you don't become one of our specialties with a little pepper and garlic and coriander. Why doth my heart beat so quickly?

HERMANN: Could you bring a bit of chocolate?

OTTILIE: Daddy takes a handful of people and then turns them into a roast or freezes them. We have to do that because of our climate. What's left over is exported.

HERMANN: Do I understand correctly? He eats those who don't want to vote for him?

OTTILIE: And the others, too, only a little bit later. Do you get my drift? What beateth so loudly in my bosom?

HERMANN: I don't give a fig.

OTTILIE: Not that I would object, but it's about time we had a little more culture here so we can hide behind it in an emergency.

HERMANN: Beautiful lady, do I dare?

OTTILIE: You want to marry me: what an idea!

Hermann (*aside*): That's all I need. (*Aloud.*) As his son-in-law, your honorable father wouldn't eat me, would he?

OTTILIE: As the main speaker of the day he will say that he wouldn't even spare his own son-in-law because he is for moral rejuvenation and against corruption, you understand?

HERMANN: But will it be any fun for your honorable Daddy if he is president and there are no more people to rule over?

OTTILIE: Exactly, everyone will say we are cannibals and nobody will listen to our music anymore, and why do we have it anyway. Why did we swallow the bitter pill?

HERMANN: Hold it, I've got an idea.

OTTILIE: What do you know, handsome stranger, that you want to marry me?

HERMANN: Bring your honorable father out of the jungle. I volunteer to run his campaign for him.

OTTILIE: Do you want to ask for my hand in marriage? Be careful. He hasn't had his snack yet. Could be, he won't think twice about swallowing your hand, too.

HERMANN: Nobody will be able to touch him anymore.

OTTILIE: How will that happen?

HERMANN: He'll only have to say that he forgot everything.

OTTILIE: Ah, go on. He does that already.

HERMANN: Then everyone has to forget, too.

OTTILIE: And how will that happen?

HERMANN: By eating the others, too! Very simple, your honorable father will be president. That's as sure as the amen at the end of a prayer and I'll be his son-in-law. (*He covers OTTILIE with kisses.*)

OTTILIE: The question is if anyone will remain alive on our beautiful island kingdom. Holdari.

HERMANN (*sings*):

Swear to me that you're mine alone.
Swear to be true until you're gone.
Swear that in death I'll be missed.
Swear to me that you've never been kissed.
If I help your father's plan
Then I want to be your man.
Let's marry on beautiful Lake Atter
So the stories of your father's past no one will utter.
That's a lot of work you know.
Where your daddy's concerned, no one's gung ho.

OTTILIE (*sings*):

Well, honey, what will become of the two of us?
Come, let's take pictures, don't make a fuss.
To win the election, you I will happily wed.
And then we'll invent some story about good old Dad
Who isn't and never has been a hero.
But as his in-law you'll make mucho dinero.
Because nobody could tame you, dear wild-boy,
At least with an insurance company you'll find employ!
And so that my father's son-in-law gets paid double
You'll even get disability without any trouble.
In our little garden we can plant lettuce and broccoli.
In addition, we'll have the sausage monopoly!
They all have to elect Daddy, each in his modest way.
We'll raise the price of blood sausage right after election
day.

both:

Each in his modest way
Each in his modest way.

HERMANN (*sings*):

It could be something special because my love is quite in-
sane.
Let's watch what we are doing during the campaign.
Let's keep on our toes! Let's cover our behind!
Afterwards we'll have peace of mind, we'll have peace of
mind!
The prices of the competition sink while ours soar,
The people, they cheer, no meat stinks no more.
Those living in the past come to ask: Are we your fools?
Daddy says, come on, lies are the rules!
Someone slips, there are a few more accidents,
And so the story ends
And so the story ends! . . .

OTTILIE (*sings*):

Someone slips, there are a few more accidents

And so the story ends!
But we're not spoiled, so no offense!

HERMANN: It doesn't matter. We'll just get people from a neighboring island. We have a lot of beautiful beaches, unpolluted air, green meadows, wonderful forests, cultural offerings.

OTTILIE: Outstanding idea! We'll use foreigners to make up a people for our president.

HERMANN: Consider these scenic temptations . . . Wonderful! And what's more, friendly people whose last remains can be used in gastronomy.

OTTILIE (*hugs him*): Oh, if you can do that, I'll belong to you for eternity.

HERMANN (*aside*): And if I don't like her anymore I'll eat her according to the local custom and get me a new model.

OTTILIE: Dearest.

HERMANN (*aloud*): And now get my future father-in-law! And then we'll present ourselves to the foreign visitors at the famous Opera Ball. There won't be any riots anymore, I assure you.

OTTILIE: How do you plan to manage that since you're not an elected representative?

HERMANN: First, your honorable father will become president and then I can represent him.

OTTILIE: How clever of you.

HERMANN: You couldn't have found anyone better.

OTTILIE: I'll go and get Daddy now.

HERMANN (*covers her with kisses*): How pleasant that we're not disturbed by masses of people. But soon there'll be an incessant stream of tourists. You'll see, little wifey.

OTTILIE: Great. Next week the president of the neighboring island is coming for a state visit. And we'll need a polite president to receive him.

HERMANN: Exactly, if we don't have a people, then at least we need a president who can receive the V.I.P.s. And we need the V.I.P.s so we have an occasion to serve our people in sour dressing. Ciao! Your humble servant!

OTTILIE: Dearest! You talk as if you've always lived here.

(*They start to kiss each other wildly.*)

Act Three
Family Photo

(*The president in front of the TV screen. Behind him, the young couple, OTTILIE and HERMANN, who applaud enthusiastically at whatever the president says. Beside them, a picturesque group—the president of the neighboring island, FRANZ JOSEF APERTUTTO, with a small contingent. All are dressed extremely festively, although a bit exotic because of Vienna's Opera Ball. APERTUTTO'S contingent is waltzing, the Danube Waltz of course, its melody drifts softly from the TV.*)

EVENING BREEZE: As president elected by a clear majority I welcome you, dear Franz Josef Apertutto, on the occasion of this unique celebration of the founding of our culture. Take care that you don't fall.

APERTUTTO: Many thanks, my esteemed equal. It's logical that I'm here. We produce useless things and we sell them to you.

EVENING BREEZE: If only the civilians could hear us now!

(APERTUTTO *sings in Bavarian dialect*):

I come from far away, I travel a lot,
Diplomacy, a game to be sure it is not!
I had to come back from the dead,
'Cause there still lies a lot of work ahead!
Once our countries were quite unique,
Now there's no difference of which to speak.
Still they won't listen to me,
I promised the East a good match, you see,
Despite the new union, it never ends!
I even procured a few fat loans for my friends.
Instead of a reward I was cast aside.
As soon as one gets what one wants, one's dissatisfied,
Your only duty is to buy, buy, buy!
But don't underestimate me, be aware:
In your sausage empire I have a share.
So don't underestimate me, be aware:
In your sausage empire I have a share.

So live and be happy, I advised them,
Add to it a few beers and roasted ham.
Some eat here, others there,
And when they're fat, they'll get caught unaware.
My trip has led me to the other side
While real estate prices have gone skyhigh,
Too bad, it just wasn't possible then,
Otherwise, I would have sold real estate like Neu-
schwanstein over
And over again.
Friend, you don't need to complain
You've got fresh air and many a pretty mountain.
Everything can be sold, everything is good.
You really are a gorgeous neighborhood!
One country is here, another's over there—
We even have two, a beautiful pair.
One person wants this, the other that—

Once at least they differed a tat,
Unfortunately, only I myself am departed,
Oh, on this earth you'll never be rewarded,
As soon as one gets what one wants, one is dissatisfied,
Your only duty is to buy, buy, buy!
Hello!

EVENING BREEZE: Bravo! Bravo! It was a pleasure.

APERTUTTO: Let's be brief! I'm really looking forward to the meal afterward.

EVENING BREEZE: First an erudite speech! I invited you to the grand opening of this coffee house for TV. I now declare this coffee house open. We savages have our culture. It's an honor. Elected is elected.

APERTUTTO: I also cut the ribbon on something last week. It's not very tiring and it's a hell of a lot of fun.

EVENING BREEZE: Yes, grand openings go quickly here. But afterward I can't remember what I opened up. It's anybody's guess. Elected is elected.

APERTUTTO: Well, watch it on TV afterward, then you'll remember!

EVENING BREEZE: You joker, you! Stop it! What a savage doesn't know, won't hurt him.

APERTUTTO: I have a terrible suspicion in my heart. A handful of my people have disappeared again. Those who ventured too far from our shores.

EVENING BREEZE: I have no idea what's become of your Apertuttos. In the end, they'll be on my back and we'll have to eliminate them. In any case, my Grand Yoohooers are at home in bed where they belong. They don't belong on the street!

APERTUTTO: Oh, that's why we haven't seen any of them.

EVENING BREEZE: Yes siree. Because they're sleeping. At this late hour! Really! Here I am and here I'll stay, here I eat and here I barf. (*Note: not to be said: Thank you, Rühm!*)

APERTUTTO: But this morning when the red carpet was rolled out for me I didn't see a single inhabitant then either.

EVENING BREEZE: Loitering on the streets! No way! That just isn't done! Things can happen so easily. Why don't you eat and drink with your people!

APERTUTTO: Please, don't go to any great expense on my account!

EVENING BREEZE (*aside*): If we fatten him up now, he'll taste all the better later. (*On the sly he feels to see whether APERTUTTO is fat or not.*) My fellow eaters: Elected is elected!

APERTUTTO: As a gift I brought a little progress along. There in the pot, it's in there. You just have to heat it up! But don't forget it! Otherwise it will cook down and then there won't be anything left.

EVENING BREEZE: Later, later . . . First try our young islanders in apple sauce.

APERTUTTO: I have to say, a wonderful recipe!

EVENING BREEZE: Delicious, try it with a little bit of horseradish. Just don't forget that you have to forget him right away. Otherwise he'll weigh heavily on your stomach for a few days.

APERTUTTO: Be careful that the same thing that happened to me doesn't happen to you. You could be discovered by civilization at any time! Just look at me!

EVENING BREEZE: A little progress wouldn't be bad. So my people could enjoy it. And afterward we'll enjoy the people. Baste with juice every fifteen minutes without fail! My fellow eaters: Express yourself well! Otherwise there'll be trouble.

APERTUTTO: Great! Anywhere else it's expensive.

EVENING BREEZE: Do you know my son-in-law? Bow, boy! It's for a good cause! Today he's being served our latest state visitor. And the next time, he'll be offered himself if he's not good to my little princess! The best thing to do is to lard him up, or what do you think, Hermann, my boy? You have to eat more as long as you still can, right! Elected is elected! An island kingdom for a horse.

OTTILIE *and* HERMANN: Bravo, Daddy! Long live our Daddy! Bravo!

(EVENING BREEZE *bows flattered*): We'll set it up so that no one will have anything to say about us. Here I am and here I'll stay. Here I piss and here I barf!

APERTUTTO: How do you mean that? You know, I really think our relationship is still too delicate.

EVENING BREEZE: There you're right! Delicate. *Aside*: With a banana sauce, yum . . . And my son-in-law telleth me that the butchers are already hanging around at the borders. That's our very special specialty. Those from abroad are practically jumping right into the cans. They just can't wait.

HERMANN *and* OTTILIE: Bravo, Dad! Yoohoo!

APERTUTTO: You could at least let out a handful of people. It looks nice at a state visit when they stand around and yell as if they're burning at the stake.

EVENING BREEZE: And that's just where they belong.

APERTUTTO: For a head of state of my international stature, four or five measly men could easily stand around and wave a few banners.

EVENING BREEZE: But only if they quiet down right

away. My fellow eaters: Express yourself clearly when you're talking to me.

APERTUTTO: Too bad that those abroad don't understand a word we're saying.

EVENING BREEZE: It's just that we speak to them in the language of music. We yodel, we fool around, we rage like hawks. On skis, right! And then we watch ourselves on TV. If you don't have any citizens left, then you have to watch yourself, right. Elected is elected.

APERTUTTO: Crafty! And clever! And afterward you forget everything!

EVENING BREEZE: We are an easy-going people. At night we stay at home.

APERTUTTO: Tell me, who are those two young people on TV? (*Both stare at the screen.*)

EVENING BREEZE: I forgot. *He's sharpening his knife.* Elected is elected.

HERMANN and OTTILIE: Come on, Dad! Not us, we're your own flesh and blood.

EVENING BREEZE: All the better you'll taste to me. All the easier to digest. And now to my diet.

HERMANN *and* OTTILIE: But, Daddy, you can't do that!

EVENING BREEZE: I won't go to any expense because of them. I have to offer my guests something during this international event.

APERTUTTO: We Apertuttos tend to be nationalistically inclined. When nobody understands you anymore, that's nationalistic.

EVENING BREEZE: If you have a culture which everyone understands, that's international. Here I eat and here I barf.

APERTUTTO: That wasn't necessary. Thank you anyway.

EVENING BREEZE: We can't be indifferent to what people abroad say about our cuisine. That attracts foreigners who themselves only want to eat and drink. Elected is elected. (*He suddenly attacks his daughter and son-in-law. Fighting, pushing, shoving and screaming ensues. Apertutto looks on. His subjects are waltzing.*)

APERTUTTO: I'm as hungry as a bear.

EVENING BREEZE (*grasping for air*): Help yourself. Don't be shy. Next time, it will be your turn. I hope you have enough relatives on your island kingdom.

APERTUTTO: I'm as good as related to all of my subjects. Unfortunately, I can't forget them. Day in, day out, they eat me out of house and home.

(*APERTUTTO jumps into the fray, breathing heavily. EVENING BREEZE and APERTUTTO sit down on top of the young people. Suddenly, a white bear appears from the jungle and pats both rulers on the shoulders. They're startled and jump up. HERMANN and OTTILIE are able to escape hand-in-hand. The bear embraces EVENING BREEZE and APERTUTTO in friendship.*)

EVENING BREEZE: Jesus, my holy bear! With all the commotion I forgot about him. Elected is elected.

APERTUTTO: My God! What a savage custom! How easily you forget something important.

EVENING BREEZE: I forgot my holy bear. I didn't bring him his bowl today. Now he's pretty angry.

APERTUTTO: We've been found out. Talk nationalistically to him. Surely, he'll understand you. At least one person should understand if you speak nationalistically.

EVENING BREEZE: We've been found out. Violence is violence.

THE BEAR: Hello, here's my card! (*With a bow he hands over his business card.*)

APERTUTTO: A charming war cry, I have to admit. . . Nice manners! I must take my leave.

THE BEAR: I'm from a television company abroad and want to buy the TV rights from you for the next five years. It's like this, on the other side of the big pond people want to see this ball from now on every year. Good day. Don't pass up such an opportunity.

APERTUTTO (*to his contingent*): Let's go! Let's go! People, we've been found out. TV cameras are here. I'd like to greet all my friends, subjects, survivors, and citizens of my island. Good day, hail myself! It doesn't make sense to hang around any longer. (*He lines up his contingent.*)

EVENING BREEZE: Jesus. They're watching us from abroad. Just a minute. Please wait. (*The bear starts eating EVENING BREEZE.*) My bear's gone crazy. And I even let him graduate from high school. Violence is violence.

THE BEAR (*while eating*): And your famous New Year's Concert, too. The New World wishes to admire it every year anew. *He eats EVENING BREEZE.* They haven't seen anything like it.

EVENING BREEZE (*gasping for air*): Hold it! Don't you know me anymore, buddy ole pal, little bear! *Already halfway disappeared into the bear.* Why don't you wait? Why aren't you dressed nationalistically? How could we have realized that you're from TV? You must have a tie some place. Sir, behave yourself! We're not in the jungle!

THE BEAR: I never had the pleasure of being introduced to you, sir. (*He eats him.*)

EVENING BREEZE (*half suffocated*): Where would we end up if even animals only wanted eat and drink. What was I going to say?

APERTUTTO, his contingent and BEAR together: He forgot! (*The bear eats the last remains of EVENING BREEZE.*)

(*OTTILIE and HERMANN return cautiously. All are waltzing around the satiated bear who is now sitting on the floor and they are singing*):

Happy is, who forgets
What can't be changed anyway.
Eat the bride
Don't be shy
Eat the groom
There's lots of room!
Eat everyone
Clever and dumb!
Watching themselves on TV.
With an appetite so strong, take your people along.
Even the poorest dude takes pride in becoming food
For a certain gent with a cannibalistic bent.
Happy is, who forgets
That which still can be changed. . . . etc.

(*The curtain slowly falls.*)

Peter Rosei

Blameless
Drama in four acts

Translated by Heidi L. Hutchinson

319

Cast:

RITA
OSCAR
AGNES
ROBERTO
MARTHA
TONY

Vikings
The young Keats
Keats' interpreter
Gentleman in Elizabethan costume
Old man
Director
Guy
Warrior
Samurai
Windsurfers

The Have-Nots

ACT ONE: ON THE BEACH

(*Reef, bar*)

(*Lights up gradually*)

VOICE: And I saw another mighty angel come down from heaven, clothed with a cloud; and a rainbow was upon his head, and his face was as it were the sun, and his feet pillars of fire; and he had open in his hand a little book; and he set his right foot upon the sea, and his left foot upon the earth, and with a loud voice, as when a lion roareth. And when he had cried, seven thunders uttered their voices. And when the seven thunders had uttered their voices, I was about to write; and I heard a voice from heaven saying unto me, Seal up those things which the seven thunders uttered, and write them not. And the angel which I saw standing upon the sea and upon the earth lifted up his hand to heaven, and swore by Him that liveth for ever and ever, who created heaven, and all the things therein and the earth, and all the things therein, and the sea, and all the things therein, that there should be time no longer.

RITA (*approaches, calling*): So, are you guys coming? How much farther do you want to go?—I'm ruining my nails. I'm not the Botticelli Venus, you know.

OSCAR (*enters slowly*): I feel like I'm in a movie.

(*They continue walking.*)

AGNES (*on the reef*): I'm so scared, Roberto.

ROBERTO (*climbing*): Up on the rocks, come on up on these rocks, you hear? Don't be such a chicken! It's only water, you know. I'm right here.—And what's that down there?

AGNES: A shell.

ROBERTO: Isn't it beautiful.

AGNES: I'm so scared.

ROBERTO (*reaching for the shell*): It's humongous!

RITA: Look at that, there's one single rock in this bay, and that's where he has to drag the poor kid! I just don't get it. Isn't that idiotic.

OSCAR: For the longest time I've felt like I was in a movie. The ocean there in front of us with its sky-blue waves! The red-orange cliffs over there. The white sand at our feet. Tell me, Rita, isn't it beautiful?— The sand looks like it's been combed by the sea. You can just imagine dolphins and sea monsters living down there in the depths. And the sun! The sun, the sun, the sun.

RITA: I'd rather know what he thinks he's doing with my little Agnes.—Look, now the stupid ocean has gone and splashed water all over my dress!

OSCAR: That won't hurt you.

RITA: Okay, I'm going to get a drink now!

(*They exit.*)

VIKING (*approaches slowly along the beach, talking*):
. . . how I found places of suffering on many ships, got to know the terrible, rocking sea, where often I was assigned the depressing night watch in the stern of the ship, when it drifted close to the rocks. The cold penetrated my feet, bound in cold shackles by the frost. Deprivation sighed hotly in my heart.

On the inside, hunger wore down the spirit of a man weary of the sea. People living well on land cannot have any idea how I, poor soul, spent the winters on the ice-cold sea like a banished man, without loving relatives, hung with icicles, as hail showered down around me. I would hear nothing but the roaring sea, the ice-cold water. Occasionally I had the song of the swans to entertain me, the call of the cormorant and the screech of the plover in place of the laughter of men, the singing seagull in place of mead. (*exits*)

TONY (*at the beach bar*): Let me tell you, all day long these fools talk about nothing but the wind! As if there couldn't possibly be anything more interesting! Well, okay, it pays my rent. Did Rita's husband really die in a plane crash? You can't live on love alone.

MARTHA: If you ask me, I kind of like the surfboards. Flights of fancy! I like the rainbow stripes more than anything. And muscular calves. Make me another drink, will you, Tony?

TONY: There they go again, the fools, running across the sand. As if they were heading for the arms of a beautiful woman.

MARTHA: Your life here is like a dream, Tony. On a fairy-tale bay. And then your real estate! All you need now is the right woman. And you might drink a little less.

TONY: You're worried about me, Martha?

ROBERTO (*on the reef*): I love you, Agnes. I love you.

AGNES: But think of Mama, Roberto. And who would support us?

ROBERTO: That's what I used to think. For the longest time. I was wrong! It was a mistake. I am an interior designer. And now I am laying my heart at your feet.

AGNES: No, don't! It'll fall in the ocean.

ROBERTO: I love you. I love you.

THE WINDSURFERS (*milling about*): Would you take a picture of us? A picture for back home! For our home movies? For our videotape? The boards on the right? The boards in the middle? The boards on the left?

RITA: Smile, please! Keep smiling. Good! That's right! Excellent! The stupid wind's ruining my whole hairdo.

OSCAR: When you look from this side, the windsurfers almost look like golden beetles running across the sand, or like the tears of a madman. I once saw a painting by Füssli, in Zürich, and on it Puck was weeping in his donkey head.

RITA: Tony's beach bar is right up there.

OSCAR: The high-rises of La Salita are getting higher and higher. Like a snow-white wall. Like the Matterhorn. Well, at least they stay in the background. Martha and her shell necklace must be there about now.

THE YOUNG KEATS (*accompained by his INTER-PRETER enters from stage left with his hair unbraided, and recites*):
Bright star! would I were steadfast as thou art—
Not in lone splendour hung aloft the night,

And watching, with eternal lids apart,
Like Nature's patient, sleepless Eremite,
The moving waters in their priestlike task
Of pure ablution round earth's human shores,
Or gazing on the new soft fallen mask
Of snow upon the mountains and the moors—
No—yet still steadfast, still unchangeable,
Pillow'd upon my fair love's ripening breast,
To feel for ever its soft fall and swell,
Awake for ever in a sweet unrest,
Still, still to hear her tender-taken breath,
And so live ever—or else swoon to death.

KEATS' INTERPRETER: What he's trying to say is this:
Bright star, if I could only be like you, looking down,
always alert, watching the earth, the snow, the
mountains, the valleys. No, but I'm even more
steady and more constant than you, lying here in
my lover's lap. This is where I'd live forever, or die.

(*they exit*)

MARTHA (*flirts with TONY at the beach bar*): The walls
are much too thin! You'd be surprised, Tony, how far
away they can hear me!

TONY: I'll tape us with the camera, Martha.

MARTHA: In your dream villa? In the swimming pool?
Look, you can undo this in the back—with your
hand—with your bronze hand, Tony. Would you let
me kiss your gold bracelet, Tony?

RITA (*approaches*): Well, thank goodness my ex at least
left us a villa, and the stocks. I wouldn't know what

to do otherwise—you know how I am—with Agnes, my sweet little brat.

OSCAR (*following her*): We're packed in just as tightly in the vacation condos as we are at home in the apartment house. Martha's right about that! With the few measly bucks that I make.

MARTHA: Hi, you two! Are you talking about money, or about beauty and art?

RITA: So, how's the flirting going?

MARTHA: Tony wants to show me his villa. Imagine.

OSCAR: Everything feels like a dream today. The sea is sighing with its saxophones.

MARTHA: I believe you. Except instead of today you should say always! I'm so sick of your pointless declarations about God and the world; all the alleged books, the novels, the poetry you never write, never will write. You wanted to be famous, you promised me, on our wedding night. "Martha, I'll fly you to the stars, to the peak. Take my hand!" Rosy, in all colors, you painted everything for me—a cherub here, an angel there, with vases full of flowers, palaces, where fountains bubble into ponds. And what became of it? I ask you? A beggar! A companion I put up with! A social case!

TONY: Leave him be! Let's go out in the motorboat, okay? My waiters can take care of things here. Madame Rita, help yourself!

(*TONY and MARTHA exit.*)

OSCAR: You are stabbing me right in the heart!

(*The stage darkens slowly.*)

MAN IN ELIZABETHAN COSTUME: I am Thomas More

and am now going to recite an appropriate passage from my world-famous book "Utopia": The middle portion of the island of Utopia is rather wide and stretches out to about two hundred miles, and the greater portion of the island is not much narrower than that. But toward each end, the island begins to narrow. These ends form an arc about five hundred miles in circumference and make a bay. The whole island looks something like a new moon. The ends of the new moon are divided by straits which are about eleven miles in distance. The straits then empty into a vast expanse. As the winds are kept off by the land which surrounds it, the bay is more like a smooth lake than a choppy sea. Consequently, the bay turns the whole center of the land into a harbor which permits ships to move in every direction. This is, of course, most convenient for the inhabitants. The entrance into the bay is made difficult in certain places by the currents and in others by reefs. In the center of the entrance, a large rock formation protrudes, but since it can be clearly seen, it is not dangerous. This large rock formation has a tower built on it, and the tower is occupied by a garrison. Other rock formations are hidden and therefore dangerous. (*exits*)

(*The beam of the lighthouse light falls on the beach bar.*)

OSCAR: These people here have big social problems. Living in cardboard boxes! Illiteracy! Crime!

RITA: You worry too much.

OSCAR: When you think that any minute an oil spill could happen. Or a reactor meltdown, maybe?

MARTHA: What's that over there, Tony? (*points*)

TONY: Something is moving on the cliffs, a dark spot.

MARTHA: Jesus—it's Agnes with Roberto!

TONY: When it comes to business, that Adonis is a double zero.

MARTHA (*bent over*): May I take it out? May I kiss it?

TONY: Now I feel like I'm in a movie.

AGNES (*on the reef*): Yes. Yes. Yes-yes-yes-yes-yes!

ROBERTO: I can see the windsurfers out on the glittering bay. Straight ahead! Swift as arrows! There they go! Ahoy! Like happiness itself. Like the transcendental career. Full bore! Long live love!

AGNES: I'm going to tell my girlfriends. Can I tell my girlfriends?

ROBERTO: That reminds me of a little analogy. It's from Wittgenstein. From *Wittgenstein*. It is not the sound track that accompanies the film, but the music, get it? The sound track accompanies the film strip. The music accompanies the film. Film strip—sound track, music—film! What corresponds to the film strip and what to the sound track? Language accompanies the world.

OSCAR (*at the beach bar*): Here come some guys with wooden clubs from the trash dump.

RITA: Give me another Martini, waiter.

OSCAR: The Have-Nots! From the dumps at La Salita! The Have-Nots are coming.

(*Shouting in the distance.*)

AGNES: Mama!

ROBERTO (*approaching*): Rita! I was only showing Agnes the cliffs.

(*The Have-Nots appear in the background, armed with clubs.*)

TONY (*lying flat; he surveys the situation*): Those bastards!

MARTHA: Do you love me?

(*Shouting. Blows with clubs. Violence, in which TONY and MARTHA also get caught up. Only OSCAR escapes into the approaching darkness, out of which the moon soon rises. An OLD MAN with a long white beard walks with OSCAR along the beach.*)

OLD MAN (*explaining*): In the earth's interior there are several rivers, one of which is the Acheron, which flows through many wild regions, but above all, it flows underground until it reaches the Lake Acheron, taking most of the dead souls with it; and after they have remained there for their designated amount of time, some longer, some shorter, they are sent away again to beget the living. Now, as soon as the deceased have arrived at that place, those who have led a good and saintly life are separated from those who haven't. And those who appear to have led a mediocre life go down to the Acheron, get on the boats that wait for them there, and ride them down to the lake.

OSCAR (*leaves the OLD MAN behind, continues on, climbs onto the reef, in the dark*): Here I stand, lonesome as a motherless child. What have I gotten out of life, anyway? As a man I am bankrupt. And in other ways as well. All day long I have felt so unreal. Really! I'll try it. Thanks, Plato. I still have death! (*jumps*)

ACT TWO: IN THE TELEVISION STUDIO

VOICE (*modulating*): On the beach! On the beach. On the beach. On the beach. On the beach? On the beach!

OSCAR (*stands, bent over a piece of equipment, with his back to the audience*): I think we'll take this one. The last one, Martha. What do you think? We can push open doors and windows with this one.

MARTHA: So this is your world, Oscar: the production room of the television studio! We've known each other this long, and you've never brought me here! How everything glitters!

VOICE: On the beach.

OSCAR: That's it! It's got to pursue them, pursue, pursue, pursue them, into their innermost being, into their innermost dreams.

MARTHA: My insides are like a murky, dark river, upon which the white feathers of birds float. Kelp grows in the water. You can't even see the bottom, the water is so dark. It's getting wider, this river.

OSCAR: You trying to ruin my whole day, first thing in the morning? I really have more important things to do than to argue with you. We're working on a new series here.

MARTHA: The other day we were in the Luna Park, remember? We rode the bumper cars and the merry-go-round. It was a beautiful fall day. On top of the merry-go-round there was a statue of the goddess Fortuna; she was scattering fruit and bright-colored flowers from a big basket. I wished we could just keep on riding around in a circle forever.

OSCAR: But that's just what we're doing.

MARTHA: I'm crazy about you, Oscar!

OSCAR: I'm hot for you, too. For your breasts.—Look, I may be my own boss here, but I still gotta be on the ball. The viewer numbers, the print media. The reviews, the sponsors. What's in and what's out. The ratings. Once you're in the meat grinder, no one's going to toss you a line. Steel wheels!

MARTHA: When you talk to me like that, I don't know what to say. I just don't understand it. I only understand the language of love. Your face is shining way far away from me. Bright and beautiful. I can almost see it up in the clouds, your face. In a heavenly window. Do you want me?

(*TONY enters.*)

OSCAR: Ciao, Tony. You're in early.

TONY: I pulled an all-nighter. I've got nothing but ghosts waiting for me at home, anyway. Is there any whisky around here? Quick!

OSCAR (*conjures up a bottle out of one of the drawers*): Here.

TONY: I've lost my gold Rolex. Has anyone seen it? How about you, young lady? A gift from my ex-wife Rita.

OSCAR: Her name is Martha.

MARTHA: I'll be going now. I'm going to town, walk around, maybe do a little window shopping. Check out the spring fashions!

OSCAR: Ciao.

TONY (*sits*): Every time I sit down at my desk, it's the same thing: I'm at the end of my rope. Okay, okay! I give up! But then no one'd better blame me for—dammit! My words are crumbling into pieces! My words are ripping apart in the wind. Like in the Chandos letter by, by Hofmannsthal.—How about a scene in a snowstorm, in winter, where instead of snowflakes dollar bills flutter down toward our hero out of the ice-cold stratosphere?

OSCAR (*to MARTHA*): He's having trouble coping with the separation from his ex-wife. And yet she left him everything. Hundreds of thousands! In bonds. In stocks. Surprised, huh?

TONY: Creatively speaking you are a complete flop, she shouted, a complete flop! And she took my daughter away from me.

OSCAR: Agnes?

MARTHA: I'm leaving now, Oscar. I'm going to town, window shopping.

OSCAR: Ciao, Martha.

MARTHA: You're stabbing me right in the heart! (*exits, weeping*)

TONY: You know Agnes, too?

OSCAR: I'm thinking he's the total tycoon, the king of the petroleum industry, young, stylish, polished. He's cleaning up. He lives in a high-rise, suspended, with its illuminated windows, above the bay and the harbor with the docks, the piers. Of course, he's a kind of Numero Uno. He looks down from his loft to the ocean. In his tailored business shirt. With a Martini glass in his hand. The ocean is his lover.— What do you say?

TONY: Should he be drinking? Does he have religious hallucinations? Is he a closet leftist? We could maybe model him after Lord Jim, Fletcher, maybe nobility, and as a pure capitalist. Instead of the South Sea beach we'd have the East Side or Sankt Pauli, with all the tin cans, whores and homeless—he should be at least a little rundown. Those people are incredibly athletic.

OSCAR: A scene where the vodka runs down his hairy chest, in the bathtub—he's blond like me—his nipples, the vodka!

TONY: Of course he has a vacation home. And not a dump, either. It's got to be an ocean-front property. Way outside of town, beyond all the sewage treatment plants, the high-voltage towers, seagulls screaming. There he sits, in his villa with the stairway leading down to the sea, between palms and holly bushes. And either he's on the phone, or tearing open letters and telegrams, or he's calling to his secretary, "Have the cables arrived yet? Did you pick up the mail? Any faxes?" He looks out over the threatening ocean waves. To the ships in the distance, sailing into the night under burning clouds.

OSCAR: Wow, Tony, thanks a lot! This is gonna be big!

TONY: It's about a dame, natch, a dream girl. Shall we toss in a loser, too? That'll provide the story line. You gotta figure on twenty episodes!

OSCAR: The tycoon and this other guy, they know each other. They've been in the same line of business for a long time. A laid-back type, with sideburns, a touch overweight, stocky, graying (*describes TONY*) A good buddy, a . . .

TONY: You're such a total amateur, Oscar.—He's an underworld taxi driver. The hero and him, they've known each other a long time. Since they were kids. They are even sort of friends. Go fishing together. Surfing. In the sun.—The taxi driver reads books, and in fact is highly intellectual; that's why he's got no money. Always eats at McDonald's.—And in the end he gets eaten by sharks. They find his chewed-up body out near the lighthouse. In the mud.

OSCAR: And the shark represents jealousy!—I just

thought of a wonderful scene in a church. This is earlier on: He is praying, to God! It's real bright. Between gigantic candles, with the wax streaming down them.

TONY: And the woman is tall, suntanned, and moves beautifully. She has a daughter, and the two of them are at the beach with one lover.

(*ROBERTO enters.*)

OSCAR: Hi!

TONY: Ah, the producer. What have we done to deserve this honor?

ROBERTO: Good morning, gentlemen! How are things going? I see you're already hard at it.—All I ask is: no political criticism! People are sick of it. And besides, most of them think we're already living in paradise. We wouldn't want to burst their bubble.

OSCAR: Well, I certainly didn't have that in mind. We're writing a modern-day fairy tale, right?

TONY: Maybe we could fix it so that at the end all of humanity is driven to the brink of destruction: environment, pollution, nuclear, whatever. In a stranglehold! Like the lemmings into the Maelstrom, down the drain. Out on the coast. Holocaust! Do you know Poe? Nothing but criminals.

ROBERTO: Doesn't move me, to tell you the truth. The end of the world as an orgasm substitute for the impotent. No Utopias, please, positive or negative. What did trying to save the world ever accomplish? Go for the little causes, please! Taxes, herpes, obesity.

TONY: I don't give a shit if everything goes to the dogs. I really don't care. It was just a suggestion, after all.

ROBERTO: By the way, here's the contract. Your signatures, please!—See you at tennis?

OSCAR: What? Is that all?—I've joined the club now, too.

ROBERTO: Tony gets more.—And please, no unnecessary provocations: no general strikes, rape of minors, race riots. Keep to the stuff that happens around here! Just a tip. Ciao! I have several more people to see. (*exits*)

OSCAR: A hacker? We could use one of those, too, as the friend.

TONY: Do his debts drive him off the cliff? Or fraudulent bankruptcy? Because he's impotent? He can't make love? He has no feelings for his fellow man. He's long since dead.

OSCAR: That reminds me that I need to balance my checkbook.

TONY: He was running after a thousand dames at a time, in droves, en masse. Until he finds the big shell on the beach.—That's how the loser meets up with the girl.

OSCAR: He's crazy about her! He loves her more than himself! She is the love of his life!

TONY: When it's all over, he surfs out into the rising hurricane. Right into the eye of the storm.—Ships are wrecking!—He disappears into the darkness of the oil slick. All they find is his yellow T-shirt.

OSCAR: Jealousy. Sure.—But maybe we should show how the hero isn't so big from the start. He starts small. Like everyone. The oil slick symbolizes the depressions.

TONY: He's a little nobody. He cooks spaghetti on the central radiator in his apartment. A Polish family lives below him. It stinks of dirty underwear and sour socks. Brandy orgies. He staggers into the hallway . . .

OSCAR: Do you know my apartment? He finds this shell on the beach, the hero, that is, the tycoon. When he's still poor, in the beginning. He just knows this one will bring him fortune. He feels it somehow. It becomes an obsession with him. At night he sits up in his room and lets candle wax drip over the shell.

TONY: A bit too psychological.

OSCAR: He has to want to get rich! Rich! That's his obsession. His vision. This will make the audience rich, too!

TONY: And if he's got nothing, the dream girl won't want him.

OSCAR: The loser, the second guy, who jumps off the cliff, who gets eaten by the sharks at the end, he's an alcoholic artist, a scriptwriter in a TV studio, a man going nowhere, a creative flop.

TONY: Hey, that's me!

OSCAR: And the dream girl belongs to me. Rita has a gold chain around her hips, and when she points her toes and nails into the air, she looks like the Valley of Canaan!

(*They begin to wrestle.*)

DIRECTOR (*enters, wearing a trenchcoat and a Fellini hat, and attempts to block out the wrestling men with his script book*) This has gotten a little embarrassing. My apologies. Because we're in the midst of a set change, I can't give you the two leading ladies, Rita, whom we were just talking about, and her daughter Agnes! That would be so meaningful just now. Maybe I should just recite their lines for you?
Rita says: "Yeah, it was weird. Just that morning we'd been on the beach together. At the stopover on

the tax-free island, Roberto was taking care of the luggage. He was wearing an Armani suit and looking fabulous. I'd gained a little weight and my dress was tight under the arms. I go to the bar in the terminal for a Martini. Roberto was taking way too long. Agnes was getting real nervous. There was lots going on in the terminal. She was about to cry. I bought her a straw hat, to cheer her up. With flowers on it.—In the plane I notice that the baggage claim tags are missing from the tickets. I thought I'd die. I sat there like I'd been struck by lightning. Roberto had disappeared with the luggage, the fine gentleman! He ran off with all of our jewelry and stuff. You can imagine how I felt. And then there's Agnes, on top of that, constantly squirming in her seat. What's the matter with you? I *itch*! Yeah, and then, it was about eleven, we were in the middle of the ocean, and the plane went down.—So I don't even exist any more."

Agnes says: "Me, neither." (*he bows and exits*)

ACT THREE: IN THE SERIES

(*Paid commercials can be inserted between the individual parts.*)

(*In the dream villa at the seaside.*)

RITA (*lying on a lounge chair, just awakening*): A drink, you hear me? A drink! Quick!

AGNES (*hurrying to her*): Right away, Mama!

RITA: And straighten up that Picasso over there!

AGNES: But it *is* straight.

RITA: Oh, God, what time is it? My hair, my lips, my cheeks, my figure! I still have to get all that done.

AGNES (*brings a huge glass*): Here, Mama, this'll do you good.

RITA: What do you mean, do me good? (*drinks, tosses the glass into a corner*)

AGNES: You'll wake Papa!

RITA: My hair. My hair, my hair—and my peach fuzz! Cute. Papa is always upstairs, in his sunny studio. For months now. For years he's been up there. I have to admire him, God knows. He's writing the great epic.

AGNES: You should fix yourself up a little, shouldn't you? Aren't you expecting company?

RITA: You call that company? Mind your own business. I have my suspicions anyway. Thank God we still have money, plenty of money, from Papa. Ever since we returned from the Pacific Islands, you've been totally mixed up. Forget the honeymoon and the palm-leaf fans. I think those black men have turned your head, those niggers!

AGNES: Mama! They're such poor devils! The over-population and starvation drive them to extremes.

RITA: What *I'd* be afraid of is . . . (*points to her glass*) Bring me another one!—Wonder if he found anything? Gold earrings? Chains? A nose ring?

(*AGNES exits carrying the glass.*)

VOICE OF TONY FROM UPSTAIRS (*sounds somewhat unclear in the room where RITA is lying on her lounge*): Returning home from the Island of Phocis, Orestes, the faithful son of Agamemnon and Clytemnestra—yes, even to her, his mother, he is unwaveringly faithful!—he comes upon Aegisthus, his mother's lover, in place of his father. Aegisthus now shares his mother's bed—and not his father, who lies rotting in his blood.

RITA: Shall I put on make-up? (*she decides not to*) What's keeping her with that whisky. Probably afraid I'm too drunk. Because of the millions.

OSCAR (*enters from the patio wearing an expensive dinner jacket*): Hi there! I knew I'd find you here. Here! A rose! (*kisses RITA and pins the rose on her dress*) A red rose. How are you doing?

RITA: Did you bring the money, Oscar? I admire him like crazy, and whom the Gods love they summon home to them.

OSCAR: I've just been to see Roberto, the real estate broker. Imagine, the bastard doesn't want to cough up a single dime. Instead he started babbling something about the Japanese. They commit harakiri when they don't see another way out. So, how about today—how is it going?

RITA: He's the guy you've known since your early days as a taxi driver, isn't he?

OSCAR: We go back a long ways, to when we were kids. Well, at least the hotel is full to capacity. Running like a well-oiled machine.

RITA: Did you bring me anything? (*she pulls him down to her*)

(*The telephone rings. OSCAR tries to free himself from her embrace.*)

RITA: Let it ring.

VOICE FROM UPSTAIRS: It was Apollo who had incited him to the deed. Orestes returned home from the island Phokis. With the genitals of a bull, Aegisthus entered Orestes' mother, in her bed, the bed of

Clytemnestra. Elektra showed the way with her pointed finger.

OSCAR (*frees himself*): Where's Agnes?

(*The telephone rings again.*)

OSCAR: You're shaking!

RITA: Did you bring the money? Give me the money now! I'll pay you back right away.

OSCAR (*produces several bundles of money*): You're completely cleaned out? His last three novels were a total bust. What's the old man writing now?

RITA: Something about a family called the Atrides. He wants the Nobel prize.

OSCAR (*hands her the money*): Now, where's Agnes?

RITA: Let's go look. (*exits, followed by OSCAR*)

(*AGNES enters the empty room with the huge drink in her hand.*)

AGNES: Mama!—(*notices one of the money bundles, which has fallen on the floor*) This must be from Oscar, that gigolo. You're not going to get me! (*picks up the money*) I'll take this to *him*! (*takes the glass and drains it in one gulp*) Better than nothing.—Where are you, my love? For days now I've been sitting, waiting. I'm all alone. I know you only take the stuff to block out your loneliness. You wander through the realm of the dead every night. They call you "the Hacker"! The great Hacker of Terror! They're afraid of you! Mutant eyes open onto the icy wasteland of all knowledge, onto the slippery monopoly of power. Oh, don't get caught in the steel web of their terminals! Don't lose your way in the tangle of the information jungle! Don't let the rainbow glitter of the mother-of-pearl microchips drive you crazy! "Almovox, come in please!" Don't give your-

self the shot, the terrible, golden, final one! I'll fly to
you, in your drab, gray apartment building. Stay
tough, at your keyboard. Stay faithful—I'll fly
across the sea! (*she breaks down, falls unconscious*)

(*At this moment, a terrible scream can be heard from
above.*)

(*On the proscenium, during the set change, there is a large-
screen computer. Barely visible is the Japanese brand
name. Large yellow letters run across the screen. A GUY
with his hair styled like a Spanish nobleman or à la Cap-
tain Hook enters. He is wearing a rowing jersey, hastily eats
a couple of bites from a fast food container, and types something into the computer.*)

GUY: Wonder if they're gonna throw me out? (*he reaches
for a saxophone and plays a while*)

GUY (*shaking his head*): Do I hear angels? Or the police?
(*sits down and inspects his torn shoes and socks*) To
you, I'm just a freeloader anyway.

(*He types a while longer like a madman. Three gorgeous
women enter and hover around him. They disappear
again.*)

GUY: Hate! Hate! Hate! Should I kill myself? Am I supposed to live forever?

(*He reaches for the saxophone, plays heart-rendingly,
tosses it into a corner.*)

GUY: Utopia—will it be Atlantis? Atlantis?? Your gold
bracelets, Agnes! Your Lady Rolex!

(*He slowly begins to undress.*)

GUY: People? People?? People???

(Behind him the computer goes berserk.)

(In the office building:)

ROBERTO *(at his desk, on the telephone)* Go ahead and bump the guy off. Yeah. Leave him in the subway station—near the stairs—near the post office, beneath the blocks. We'll kill 'em all!—Don't call me Roberto! To you I'm the Boss! Actually I got my start in interior design. And they'll get into the apartment houses, later. What, no locks? No *locks* on the doors? *(laughs)* The police? They're screwing up their investigation? That gives me a fantastic idea.

MARTHA *(enters, ROBERTO doesn't even notice her)*: A gentleman from the Mayor's office is here, Boss! May I see him in? From Social Services!

ROBERTO: No, Martha! *(laughs out loud)* Tell him . . . tell him we're about to crack this nut wide open. *(holds his finger to his lips)* Shhh! Shhh! Are the keys to the bank safe here?

MARTHA: You have made enormous contributions to the revival of the inner city, Boss! You need to give yourself credit. They probably want to give you an award, a gold pin or something.

ROBERT *(thinking)*: The refugees have only . . . we have to find a solution. Without a shirt! Take everything away! For the lots. In the dust.

MARTHA: You worry too much, Boss.

(ROBERTO hustles her out the door, reaches for the telephone and begins to dial.)

MARTHA'S VOICE *through the intercom*: I have a caller for you on the line, a woman, says her name is Rita!

ROBERTO: Put her through! What's the holdup?—Rita, is that you? Yeah? Nice to hear from you. Oh, how nice. A delivery van? At eleven? With a loading ramp? Wait, I'm switching to speaker phone. (*switches*) Your voice sounds so strange.

VOICE OF RITA (*unclear*): Bullshit!

ROBERTO: I can't go on without you.

VOICE OF RITA: What?

ROBERTO: We've been living in a fortress, for the longest time. On an island of desperate people, the starving, the hungry, from overseas, from everywhere— they're attacking. There are sharks approaching from the east, smelling prey here; the Yen . . . bullying their way through to the cashier! We have to be tough! Tough! I see it, I see it right in front of me . . .

(*A plainly dressed WARRIOR carries in, piggyback, a SAMURAI in full armor, with helmet and iron visor, breastplate and chain-mail shirt. He looks around. From a distance we hear shouting and gunshots. The WARRIOR sets the SAMURAI down. The WARRIOR bows. The SAMURAI bows as well and then commits harakiri. A large pool of blood spreads out from him. The WARRIOR grabs the dead SAMURAI by the feet and carefully drags him out. The threatening noise has become louder and closer.*)

ROBERTO (*as if talking in his sleep*): I am the King! I am the King! Yes! (*he turns on the desk lamp*)

VOICE OF RITA (*unclear*): Why do you love me so much?

(*ROBERTO shrugs his shoulders.*)

MARTHA (*runs into the room*): The gentleman from Social

Services won't wait any longer. He says we're on
fire! Everything is on fire! The whole city is in
flames!

(*Windows and doors are breaking under the force of massive iron crowbars.*)

MARTHA (*discovers the pool of blood from the SAMURAI on the floor*): Boss! (*she is pushed away*)

(*The HAVE-NOTS from the suburbs, all blacks, run in and murder ROBERTO.*)

THE HAVE-NOTS: Death to Capitalism!

ROBERTO (*dying*): I haven't had a drop to drink for years! I can't believe this! This is atrocious.

ACT FOUR: EVERYDAY LIFE

(*An average apartment; the dialogue drags somewhat.*)

TONY (*dressed as a woman*): Do you believe in God?

RITA (*dressed as a man*): Leave me alone! What time does your watch say?

TONY: I know, all you care about anymore are your surfboards. And out on the street it's rush hour. I wish we had a bigger apartment!

RITA: That's the disadvantage of living on the ground floor. (*turns off the TV*) Idiotic!

TONY: In the last series, didn't they have one of those movers and shakers, those captains of industry on an island somewhere? Looking for oil?

RITA: Exciting! They were surfing like crazy!

TONY: And the one died, the one who was in love? Must

have been at the end of the line when they were handing out luck.

RITA: What if we were all dead now? In a nuclear disaster? From space radiation? Would we be better off?

TONY: Where'd you get that idea? Because you're out of work?

RITA: The kid's boyfriend, the hacker, he predicted it: that we'd all become slaves. That's what he predicted. Because we don't know anything. *Can't* know anything. The monopolies!

TONY: That's nothing but a stupid excuse! Because you haven't done any work for years! You don't make any money! (*digs around in some photos*) We were happy back then!

RITA: Where is Agnes anyway? On the Adriatic?

TONY: Your daughter is nothing but a distraction from your own misery! Since she finished school, you don't care about her one bit! You just live in your rainbow world of surfboards! Totally anti-social. Like a Neaderthal.

RITA: The ocean surrounds the old earth. The earth developed out of the sea. It's a fact!

(*Typewriter noise from upstairs.*)

TONY: Oh, shit! There *he* goes again!

RITA: Who, Rosei? A nowhere man. A mutant. (*scratches herself*) Do we have bugs now? He bangs away day and night. I don't know what women see in him. He's a bum!

TONY: Armenians? Or was it Italians? What he's writing about? Just like the guy, what was his name again, in the series?

RITA: I didn't quite get it. Did you? Do they *kill* him? In the series? I mean the writer. Or is it the other guy, the hotel owner? Rita is such a slut.

TONY: You got a problem with that? Just because she doesn't work for a living? Because she has style? Because she has a weakness for the pleasures of life?

(*All this time we have been hearing waves of street noise from outside. Occasionally loud explosions. Now two voices materialize out of the background noise.*)

VOICE OF OSCAR (*imitating a woman*): We've been standing here forever!

VOICE OF MARTHA (*imitating a man*): It's tough in the inner city.

WOMAN'S VOICE: I can't get this TV series out of my mind. (*inside the apartment, on the sofa, TONY and RITA exchange meaningful glances*) Why does the author, the scriptwriter, have the young Keats appear in the first episode? Is he a romantic? Or is he trying to portray himself, that fool? Does he think he's God?

MAN'S VOICE: Probably has something to do with love. Somehow! Everything does. I think it's inconsistent that he, if he has Thomas More walking across the beach—and the beach of course symbolizes our world—that he doesn't just go ahead and put in Marx. That would have been bigger! With *that* beard. But then maybe they wouldn't put on his play.

(*TONY and RITA look at each other quizzically.*)

WOMAN'S VOICE: But then he may as well have Freud, the professor, come on, too; you know, with glasses? The family situation is just begging for an analysis.

The Electra complex of the kid! And she's a nymphomaniac, too.

MAN'S VOICE: Why not just use Goethe, with his "Elective Affinities?" Or something from science, maybe Watson, with his double helix: "We can't put in any more information, try as we might!?" No, no.

WOMAN'S VOICE: Maybe it has to do with language? With the various languages? The language levels, as they say?

MAN'S VOICE: Language is just a piece of nature. That much is sure!

(*The voices are drowned out by the sound of traffic.*)

RITA: Shall we watch a few commercials? (*gets up*)

TONY: You don't even care if that guy Pollack grabs my butt.

RITA: But that was in private, at the summer party.

TONY: Summer party? Then our whole life would be private?

RITA: Looks that way! I'm going to go do the dishes.

(*As the lights go out, a tape of a radio commercial for dishwashing liquid is played.*)

Afterword

The five plays presented in this volume, all written between 1985 and 1992, testify to the continued prominence of the folk play (*Volksstück*) in contemporary Austrian literature. The traditional *Volksstück*, which includes the writings that belong to the old Viennese folk theater as well as peasant farces, evolved in the eighteenth and early nineteenth centuries. Usually written in local dialect, these popular plays had a simple, unified plot, drawn from the daily life of common people and intended to reinforce the idea of a just and harmonious order of the universe. From the beginning, however, these early plays also addressed social and political concerns of their times, albeit under the guise of entertainment. In the course of the nineteenth century the *Volksstück* form degenerated and became more and more associated with trivial entertainment, although it maintained its importance to a degree in the works of writers like Ludwig Anzengruber, Ludwig Thoma, and Gerhart Hauptmann. In the 1920s the enormous success of Carl Zuckmayer's *Der fröhliche Weinberg* (The Merry Vineyard) and especially the innovative works of Ödön von Horváth and Marie Luise Fleißer led to a renewed interest in the genre. Horváth's and Fleißer's plays critically depict the struggles of the petit-bourgeoisie. Because of their emphasis on socio-economic concerns, these plays contrast sharply with the traditional *Volksstück* of the nineteenth century.

In the late 1960s and early 1970s, another revival of the *Volksstück* was prompted by the rediscovery of Horváth's and Fleißer's plays. Young German authors like Franz Xaver Kroetz, Martin Sperr, Rainer Werner Fassbinder, and Austrian writers like Peter Turrini and Wolfgang Bauer turned to the genre of the *Volksstück* as the form best suited to express their artistic and political intentions. Like Horváth and Fleißer, they use formal and structural conventions of the *Volksstück* (e.g., the provincial setting, dialect, and stock figures) only to invert or subvert their traditional functions, for this was the time of the anti-provinces movement (*Anti-Heimat Bewegung*). Thus, unlike the traditional *Volksstück*, their plays do not affirm the existing social order, but rather criticize or at least question it.

The five plays presented here stand very much in the tradition of these new critical *Volksstücke*. Each of them critically explores contemporary political, social, or artistic issues. The fact that these plays are so inherently different from each other testifies to the diverse formal and thematic possibilities of this genre. In addition, Jelinek's and Unger's specific recourse to the nineteenth-century Viennese *Volksstück* and the peasant farce indicates how current these traditional conventions still are in the twentieth century and how easily they can be adapted for a critical purpose.

Heinz R. Unger's play *The Bell Tolls at Twelve* (*Zwölfeläuten*) was written in 1985 as the second play of the trilogy *Die Republik des Vergessens* (*The Republic of Forgetting*), published in 1987. This trilogy represents Unger's reaction to the controversy surrounding the campaign and election of Kurt Waldheim as president of Austria in 1986. Unger focuses not on the person of Kurt Waldheim but on the false sense of history that prevails in Austria. *Zwölfeläuten* explores the mentality and the motivation that led first to a collaboration with the National Socialists and second to a denial of any guilt in the atrocities committed by the regime. The villagers use their single act of resistance against the Nazis—a deed of questionable value—to absolve themselves of any crimes committed during the war. Opportunistically, they collaborate with the Allies just as they did with the Nazis, and the expectation of economic advantages silences even those among them who had previously suffered for their anti-Nazi sentiments.

The rural environment, the dialect, the stock figures, and the happy ending (a wedding) characterize the play as a typical peasant farce. As with many examples of this type of *Volksstück*, the danger exists that the serious topic of the play may be overshadowed by the comical elements. However, Unger effectively counteracts this danger with sharp satire and by using one of the stock figures of the peasant farce, the village idiot, to unmask the contradictory and self-serving behavior of the villagers. Thus the play provokes not a conspiratorial laughter by one of recognition.

Thomas Baum's *Cold Hands* (*Kalte Hände*, 1990) affirms the tradition of the modern critical *Volksstück* of the late 1960s and 1970s. Baum explores a highly sensitive issue: sexual abuse of children. In *Cold Hands*, a twelve-year-old girl has been suffering the incestual assaults of her father for years. The emphasis of the play is not on the shock value of the taboo-breaking topic. Rather, Baum, who conducted extensive research on incest, wants to educate and inform his audience. He focuses on the pain, fear, and isolation of the victim, and criticizes the abuse of power and authority by the father as well as the general helplessness with which society reacts toward the problem of incest. In contrast to most examples of the critical *Volksstück*, the play is not situated in a lower social milieu. The father remains "normal." In this way the audience is prevented from stigmatizing the father as a pathological pervert and from relegating the problem to a specific milieu.

Society's discomfort in dealing with incest is evident in the fact that *Cold Hands* was initially rejected by Austrian theaters. Only after its successful premiere in Bielefeld on September 29, 1990 and subsequent runs in Zürich and Magdeburg, was the play shown in Austria, premiering in Linz on February 13, 1992. Moreover, because of its topic, the play was not measured by aesthetic criteria but by its social relevance. Many theaters held discussions after the performances, and in Innsbruck the theater audience was provided with literature on incest as well as information on where to get assistance. The reactions to Baum's play suggest that while the theater may not bring about social change, it is able to focus attention on a problem and raise the awareness of audiences.

Like Thomas Baum's work, Friedrich Ch. Zauner's play *A Handful of Earth* is also an example of a critical realistic *Volksstück*. As in his novels, Zauner chronicles the past rather than the present. Clearly the most traditional of the five plays, combining as it does features of the realistic as well as of the naturalistic *Volksstück* of the late nineteenth century, the original version of *A Handful of Earth* takes place in a rural setting in Austria at the turn of the century. The translation here transfers the setting to California, where the problem is equally important and still relevant. As is typical for the *Volksstück*, the conflict in Zauner's play results from social structures as well as from the character of the protagonist. Rowena, a blend of ambition, vitality, and cunning, acts from a desire to impress the disdainful relatives of her cultured but invalid husband. Coming from a lower social class and being a mere female, she challenges the power structure of the village, resorting even to illegal means. Her ambition has become all consuming and jeopardizes the life and happiness of her children, in whose interest she claims to act.

Like the other plays of the volume, *A Handful of Earth* deals with relevant contemporary issues: class prejudices, desire to advance socially, corrupt local politics, and the crucial importance of water rights. Technical progress as well as the foreshadowing of altruistic socialism are represented by the weakest characters in the play, Rowena's wheelchair-bound husband Charles, and her gentle, idealistic son Raymond. However, Charles dies and Raymond fails in his attempt to convince the smaller farmers of the area to unite and to improve their lives by using the new irrigation system his father has designed. Ironically, the farmers' violent rejection of Raymond because they view him as a representative of his unscrupulous, power-hungry mother restores Rowena's dominance over the family at the very moment when she seems to have lost it. She is able to reunite her family behind her and regain her position as undisputed head of the family even though they do not approve of her methods. At the end, like Brecht's Mother Courage, Rowena has triumphed over her enemies and possesses the land she has long coveted but ironically at the cost of her family whom all of her efforts were intended to benefit.

Like Unger's play, Elfriede Jelinek's *President Evening Breeze. A Dramolet Freely Adapted from Nestroy* (*Präsident Abendwind. Ein Dramolet sehr frei nach Nestroy*, 1987) was written as an answer to Kurt Waldheim's election. The main character of Jelinek's play, the cannibalistic president of an island rich in culture, tradition, and beautiful landscapes shows marked parallels to the former Austrian president. Like Waldheim, Evening Breeze conveniently forgets his past in order to be elected president. In addition, the play contains many allusions to the Waldheim election and to the Austrian government in general. Jelinek satirically portrays a media-oriented election campaign which consists mainly of images and no substance, the exploitation of culture and nature for political and economical gain and a cynical attitude towards foreigners, who are either exploited as consumers or are themselves consumed.

Jelinek satirizes and parodies elements from the traditional and modern *Volksstück*. She mercilessly destroys the family idyll by having Evening Breeze attempt to devour his daughter and son-in-law. However, the cannibalism which was often employed for its shock value in the plays of the 1960s and 1970s appears in Jelinek's play more comical than provoking. It can be seen as a metaphor for capitalism (the chief cannibal Evening Breeze owns a sausage emporium), and at the same time it suggests that beneath all its culture and traditions, Austria has remained a basically barbaric country.

As its subtitle suggests, Jelinek's play is an adaptation of Nestroy or, more precisely, of the traditional Viennese *Volksstück*. Although materialism and commercialism in society are prevalent topics in Nestroy's plays, the parallels between the plays are mostly structural (interspersing of songs) and linguistic. Again, Jelinek proves her extraordinary talent in using language and delivers a precise parody of Nestroy's language, which is rich in word play and witticism. It is a language that has a primarily satirical function in Nestroy's plays. In Jelinek's play, however, this language, as a symbol of a tradition coopted for political and economical ends, satirizes itself.

It may seem surprising at first to categorize Peter Rosei's play *Blameless* (*Die Unschuldigen*, 1990) as a *Volksstück*, since it contains neither formal nor thematic elements of the genre. The play focuses on the role of television production as a new form of art as well as a vehicle for entertainment. The first scene turns out be a segment from a television series, the second scene shows the production of the first scene, the third scene presents another part of the series, while the last scene presents its reception by an audience. With its emphasis on the production and reception process and the combination of popular and high culture, Rosei's play reads more as an example of postmodern literature than a *Volksstück*.

The connection between Rosei's play and the *Volksstück* becomes clearer if one takes into account the parallels between the *Volksstück* and television series. These popular programs can be interpreted as a continuation of the type of the *Volksstück* which primarily aims at the entertainment of its audience. TV series have integrated many of the elements and strategies of the *Volksstück*: they show ordinary people as subjects of history, they underscore individuality and popularize (and often trivialize) current issues. All of these elements are present in Rosei's plays albeit with a critical intention. Rosei emphasizes the aim of television plays: they are meant for easy consumption and invite the audience to escape from its social reality. His approach is to show the manner in which serious matters are trivialized by the modern media.

The five plays of this volume testify to the continued prominence of the *Volksstück* on the contemporary literary scene. However, they are not stagnent reproductions of well-known conventions. Rather their authors use this form in new ways, thus continuously revitalizing this genre as a means of social criticism. As these five plays demonstrate, this critical potential can be used to explore questions concerning Austria's past, to criticize contemporary political developments, to raise awareness on social and cultural issues, and to challenge theatrical conventions as well as audience expectations. Clearly the flexibility of the *Volkstück* in theme and form has enabled it to prevail for the last two centuries.

—Helga Schreckenberger